Encoding Across Frontiers: Proceedings of the European Conference on Encoded Archival Description and Context (EAD and EAC), Paris, France, 7-8 October 2004

Encoding Across Frontiers: Proceedings of the European Conference on Encoded Archival Description and Context (EAD and EAC), Paris, France, 7-8 October 2004 has been co-published simultaneously as *Journal of Archival Organization*, Volume 3, Numbers 2/3 2005.

Encoding Across Frontiers: Proceedings of the European Conference on Encoded Archival Description and Context (EAD and EAC), Paris, France, 7-8 October 2004

Bill Stockting
Fabienne Queyroux
Editors

Encoding Across Frontiers: Proceedings of the European Conference on Encoded Archival Description and Context (EAD and EAC), Paris, France, 7-8 October 2004 has been co-published simultaneously as *Journal of Archival Organization*, Volume 3, Numbers 2/3 2005.

Routledge
Taylor & Francis Group
NEW YORK AND LONDON

First published by
The Haworth Information Press®, 10 Alice Street, Binghamton, NY 13904-1580 USA
This edition published 2012 by Routledge
711 Third Avenue, New York, NY 10017
2 Park Square, Milton Park, Abingdon, Oxon OX14 4RN

Encoding Across Frontiers: Proceedings of the European Conference on Encoded Archival Description and Context (EAD and EAC), Paris, France, 7-8 October 2004 has been co-published simultaneously as *Journal of Archival Organization*, Volume 3, Numbers 2/3 2005.

Cover design by Lora Wiggins.

Library of Congress Cataloging-in-Publication Data

European Conference on Encoded Archival Description and Context (EAD and EAC) (2004 : Paris, France) Encoding across frontiers : proceedings of the European Conference on Encoded Archival Description and Context (EAD and EAC), Paris, France, 7-8 October, 2004 / Bill Stockting, Fabienne Queyroux, editors.

p. cm.

"Co-published simultaneously as Journal of archival organization, volume 3, numbers 2/3, 2005."

Includes bibliographical references and index.
ISBN-13: 978-0-7890-3026-9 (alk. paper)
ISBN-10: 0-7890-3026-8 (alk. paper)
ISBN-13: 978-0-7890-3027-6 (pbk. : alk. paper)
ISBN-10: 0-7890-3027-6 (pbk. : alk. paper)

1. Encoded Archival Description (Document type definition)–Congresses. 2. Cataloging of archival material–Europe–Data processing–Congresses. 3. Archives–Technological innovations–Europe–Congresses. I. Stockting, Bill. II. Queyroux, Fabienne. III. Journal of archival organization. IV. Title.

Z695.2.E88 2004
025.3'414–dc22 2005030754

Encoding Across Frontiers: Proceedings of the European Conference on Encoded Archival Description and Context (EAD and EAC), Paris, France, 7-8 October 2004

CONTENTS

ABOUT THE EDITORS

Bill Stockting has degrees in History and Politics from The University of Kent at Canterbury and Medieval Studies from the University of York. He graduated with a Master of Archive Administration from the University of Liverpool in 1988. After working at the then Greater London Record Office and Nottinghamshire Archives, he joined the Public Record Office, now National Archives of the UK (TNA), in 1993. In his time at TNA, Bill has specialised in the theory and practice of archival description in electronic environments. He was a senior member of teams preparing data about the TNA's own holdings for inclusion in the Online Catalogue and co-wrote the first cataloguing standards for the system. Since 2000, Bill has been the Senior Editor for Access to Archives (A2A), with responsibility for standards conformance and the contract management for the retroconversion of about one million pages of paper archival finding aids from holders of archives all over England.

As part of this work Bill started to use EAD in 1997 and has become an established expert in the standard in the UK and internationally. At home, he was the first Training Officer for the EAD/Data Exchange Group of the Society of Archivists, becoming Chair of the group in 2003. Internationally, Bill sits on RLG's EAD Advisory Group, which published the current award winning EAD Best Practice Guidelines. Since 2002, he has also represented the UK and Ireland on the EAD Working Group.

Bill has lectured fellow professionals in archival description standards, EAD and related matters across Europe, and has spoken at national and international conferences, most recently at the International Council on Archives' Congress in Vienna in 2004. He has also published many papers and articles in professional journals, including the International Yearbook of Library and Information Management 2003.

Fabienne Queyroux graduated from the Ecole des Chartes in 1990, with the degree of "archivist-paleographer." She has specialized in seventeenth century intellectual history, working on Gabriel Naudé and other figures of the libertine movement.

Between 1990 and 1994, she worked in two university libraries in Paris, first as system librarian, then as head of periodicals. Since 1995, she has held the position of Curator of Manuscript Collections at the Bibliothèque de l'Institut de France. She is responsible for the arrangement and description of collections, as well as reference work.

She became interested in EAD in 1999, when she won a Fulbright grant that allowed her to visit the United States and learn about how American colleagues have computerized their cataloging and publish their finding aids.

In 2000, she was one of the founding members of the French EAD working group, which published the French translation of the EAD Tag library and is now elaborating national application guidelines. As a member of that group, Fabienne is involved in various EAD-related activities, doing presentations on EAD, teaching workshops, and participating to the national project of conversion of the Catalogue Général des Manuscrits des Bibliothèques Publiques de France.

INTRODUCTION

Encoding Across Frontiers: An Introduction

BACKGROUND

In the summer of 2003 four European archivists[1] attended the meeting of the Encoded Archival Description (EAD) Working Group, held as part of the Society of American Archivists Annual Meeting in Los Angeles. Coming at the same time as the publication of the revised version, EAD 2002, this represented the greatest international representation on the group to date and set the seal on the internationalization of the standard itself. Given this, the European representatives thought that it would be a good idea to have a European conference on EAD. The Direction des Archives de France was receptive to the idea and provided funding for the event, which was organized almost single-handedly by Claire Sibille. The conference took place on October 7-8, 2004, in Paris, France, at the Musée des Arts et Traditions Populaires.

This was not the first European conference on EAD, as there had been such an event at the then Public Record Office (PRO), in Kew, London in 1999. The differences between the two events, however, speak clearly of the changed context that European archivists are now working in. The first conference had EAD as its only subject, while the sec-

[Haworth co-indexing entry note]: "Encoding Across Frontiers: An Introduction." Stockting, Bill and Fabienne Queyroux. Co-published simultaneously in *Journal of Archival Organization* (The Haworth Information Press, an imprint of The Haworth Press, Inc.) Vol. 3, No. 2/3, 2005, pp. 1-8; and: *Encoding Across Frontiers: Proceedings of the European Conference on Encoded Archival Description and Context (EAD and EAC), Paris, France, 7-8 October 2004* (ed: Bill Stockting, and Fabienne Queyroux) The Haworth Information Press, an imprint of The Haworth Press, Inc., 2005, pp. 1-8. Single or multiple copies of this article are available for a fee from The Haworth Document Delivery Service [1-800-HAWORTH, 9:00 a.m. - 5:00 p.m. (EST). E-mail address: docdelivery@haworthpress.com].

Available online at http://www.haworthpress.com/web/JAO

doi:10.1300/J201v03n02_01

ond also discussed Encoded Archival Context (EAC) and Encoded Archival Guide (EAG). The Paris conference also gathered its speakers and audience from a much greater range of countries. There were contributors from France, Germany, Italy, Netherlands, Poland, Portugal, Spain, Sweden, Switzerland, the United Kingdom as well as the United States, and a packed auditorium with nearly 300 people from Greece and Iceland as well as the above named countries. In addition to practicing archivists, librarians and museum professionals, technologists and the commercial sector were also represented. Beside the formal papers reproduced here, there were also demonstrations of various projects and products.

Between the two conferences, a lot of EAD related activity has taken place in Europe, reflecting the desire by archivists to make information about their holdings visible to users on the Internet and the realization that descriptive practice needed standardization in order to achieve this. In this context EAD was the right tool at the right time. There have been, therefore, a number of national conferences on EAD, the official documentation has been translated into a number of languages, and archive professionals have been trained in EAD, XML and related matters. A great deal of work has been done on relating EAD, as a data structure standard, to diverse national traditions and developing international archival descriptive standards, especially the International Council on Archives' (ICA) *General International Standard Archival Description, ISAD(G)*. Many projects of varying scope and intent have been launched, application guidelines written, and online services offered that reach out to new users of archives. Thought has also begun on the wider descriptive world for archives with the revision of the ICA's *International Standard Archival Authority Record for Corporate Bodies, Persons, and Families (ISAAR(CPF))* and the development of its data structure standard in EAC, as well as the development of a proto-standard for archive repositories in EAG. Given all this, it seemed an opportune time to hold a conference, to reflect on where we had been and where we were going. It is hoped that there will not be such a long wait for the next conference and that current plans for Germany in 2006 are successful.

CONFERENCE THEMES

It is entirely appropriate, of course, that our introductory essay is provided by Daniel Pitti, who has contributed so much to the development of both EAD and EAC. He sets the scene by explaining how archivists have made use of the two Document Type Definitions (DTD) within the wider context of the use of technologies allowing them to "free [archival description] from the limits of the print media" and bring information about the material we hold to wider audiences online. In doing so, he develops major themes that are picked up time and again in the detailed studies that follow. He discusses the tensions between "data-centric" (relational databases) and "document-centric" (markup technologies), and the principles of archival description. He argues that our experience of markup technologies gained with EAD lays a good foundation for going further than the basic description of records, to describing the context of creation, the functions producing the records, and the last piece in the puzzle, describing the relationships between all these separate entities. Only in this way will we give our users the whole picture represented by the archives and in doing so both types of technology, which are moving closer together, will have a role.

Encoded Archival Guide (EAG)

An important contextual relationship users need to be aware of is, of course, that between the archives themselves and the institutions that house, preserve, and allow access to them. In her article, Blanca Desantes argues that, while many countries present information about archive repositories online, there are no internationally agreed standards for this data. To answer this need she puts forward the Encoded Archival Guide (EAG) DTD developed as part of the Electronic Guide to Spanish and Iberian American Archives (*Censo Guía de Archivos de España e Iberoamérica*) project. The EAG DTD is explained in detail and an appendix gives an overview of the structure of EAG documents for the first time in English.

Encoded Archival Description (EAD)

We then move on to look at the EAD sessions that took up a day and a half of the two-day conference. The program broke down the sessions into the major stages of the workflow process, from the initial implementation of EAD, working with it to create finding aids and, finally, their presentation to users online. The European case studies in these sections come from Germany, Poland, Switzerland, and the United Kingdom as well as France. They show clearly that the issues facing the archivist in this area are truly international in scope and will be readily recognized by readers in North America.

European archivists, then, have been asking themselves questions such as:

- How do we make use of the tools of ICT and the Internet?
- How do we create electronic finding aids?
- What effects do new technologies have on descriptive practices?
- How do we publish electronic finding aids online?
- What do our users want from online archival finding aids and services?

Implementing EAD

The two papers that follow look at the issues of implementing EAD and in particular the process of retrospective conversion of descriptive metadata in projects representing different types of archival organization: a public archives office in France (Archives Départementales des Pyrénées-Atlantiques) and an academic library based manuscripts department (Department of Special Collections and Western Manuscripts at the Bodleian Library, University of Oxford) in the UK. Despite the differences, the same issues in converting legacy data held on paper to electronic form are noted. These include the need to standardize the content and archival hierarchies found in paper finding aids in accordance with local traditions and international descriptive standards such as *ISAD(G)*, as well as the need to deal with practice from the paper world, such as footnotes and indexes. It is suggested by both, to quote Mike Webb of the Bodleian, that "the impact on current cataloguing practice was immense."

The final paper is an abridgement of a panel session, chaired by Michael Fox, which reported on the status of training for archivists in the use of EAD across Europe as well as in the U.S. The relationship of EAD training to that of archival description on the one hand and new technologies on the other was also considered.

Using EAD

A group of five papers present case studies of the development and use of EAD from national bodies in Germany and Poland (the Bundesarchiv, and the Central Archives of Historical Records in Warsaw), to a local project dealing with public records relating to building regulation from a city record office (Archives de Paris, France) and a partnership between the city archives and the manuscript department of the local university in Geneva, Switzerland. The case studies mainly deal with the development of technical solutions involving the use of EAD for the creation and dissemination of finding aids. The importance for those taking their first steps with EAD of the help and support provided by EAD practitioners and organizations such as RLG (Research Libraries Group) is underlined. Again the issue of the relationship of descriptive practice to particular technological solutions presents itself. This is seen most clearly perhaps in the experience of German Federal Archives of XML tool development. On the one hand they have developed such a tool to create, edit, exchange and publish finding aids (MidosaXML), while on the other XML tools are also used to augment and publish online data from large datasets held in relational databases whose origins go back to the 1970s. While it is argued by Angelika Menne-Haritz that XML better represents archival descriptive data structured according to the principles of provenance to the user, we can see here perhaps Pitti's drawing together of document and data centric technologies in practice.

Publishing EAD

The final section on EAD presents a number of case studies from France and the UK relating to the presentation of finding aids for searching and navigation online. While EAD is again seen to be a key technology, its precise role differs with the nature and scope of the particular projects and programs discussed. While EAD as XML is a common theme, other technologies are also being used. For example, Perl is commonly used in the UK for data manipulation. Many different software tools are also in use. Some, such as PLEADE from France, are based on open-source components while others are customized commercial systems. Also discussed are the issues for archivists of working with IT professionals, whether ITC departments within organizations or commercial consultants and suppliers. Alongside technical considerations are those relating to the metadata itself. The federated nature of UK projects allowing users to search finding aids relating to material held in a number of repositories raises interesting questions about who creates and manages the metadata and the relative roles of local contributing repositories and central online services. The need to take user interests fully into account when designing such systems is underlined and questions are raised about the nature of the impact here on descriptive practice. User desire to gain access to digital representations is unquestioned and seen with the development of the Navimages tool in France and the linking to such representations by the UK online services. There are, finally, glimpses into the future of the re-use of data and interoperability outside purely archival contexts with the French experiments in mapping EAD data to the Dublin Core element set and the exposure of the result by means of the Open Archives Initiative Protocol of Metadata Harvesting (OAI-PMH).

The EAD part of this volume fittingly concludes with a survey of the standard's development and success by Kris Kiesling, the Chair of the EAD Working Group. She argues that EAD has helped archivists create partnerships and get funds, develop an online presence and become involved in the development of software and related tools such as EAC and EAG. She concludes that perhaps the greatest effect of EAD has been to make us question our descriptive practice and the need for standards, most recently evidenced by the publication of *Describing Archives a Content Standard* (*DACS*) in the United States.

Encoded Archival Context (EAC)

In contrast to the detailed case studies of EAD, the papers presented in the EAC sessions are perhaps more theoretical in tone and expand on Pitti's arguments. In his background paper Richard Szary argues, with others here, that contextual information is a major access route for users to archival information. To make this possible, archivists need to define and structure contextual information about the people, families and organizations that create, and are the subject of, archival material. Users will then be able to run precise searches via the authority-controlled names of these entities. With *ISAAR(CPF)* and EAC, the tools to enable us to do this do now exist and examples of this "expanded view" of archival context are given with illustrations of the resulting architecture for descriptive systems such as that of the Florence State Archives.

It is argued strongly, however, that this work cannot be carried out by institutions working in isolation and examples of national efforts in this area, such as the National Register of Archives in the United Kingdom, are discussed by Per-Gunnar Ottosson. It is stressed that the description of these entities is not restricted to archives: people, families and organizations of course create many other types of cultural heritage artifact. The pan-European Linking and Exchanging Authority Files (LEAF) prototype project to provide shared access to authority information, therefore, had partners representing archives, libraries and museums. In her article discussing the French standards framework in this area and the translation of EAC, Françoise Bourdon analyses the different perspectives of archivists and librarians to authority control, and concludes that this is an area where we can fruitfully work together.

Finally, given the cross-institutional, cross-sectoral, and international nature of this work, some difficult questions about funding are also raised. There is a need for resources to maintain the development of standards such as EAC. It is also not clear where the resources to undertake the huge task of describing all these entities will come from, although the involvement of users as suggested for the LEAF project will surely help. It is also noted that the development of national and international gateways can only take place with funding models that will maintain and run services as well as develop them. Only when these issues have been resolved will we be able to offer users full access to all the contexts of archival material.

CONCLUSION

The articles, which are generally in the same order as they were presented, give then a snapshot of the efforts of the European archive profession to make use of the quick changing online world to provide access to the material they hold. Certain heterogeneity in the content and style of the contributions will be noticed, which simply reflects the variety of topics, projects, institutions and nations involved.

We hope that our work in translating and editing these papers will be of interest to a wide professional readership. Included in particular will be the North American reader, already familiar with EAD and its application, but less familiar with the European archival context, and wanting to learn about the internationalization of EAD insofar as it might influence the evolution of the standard; and the European archivist, perhaps less familiar with EAD, in the quest for more information about EAD and especially European applications of it. Both will also hopefully want to get more information about EAC and EAG. Finally, we hope all readers share a desire to discover more about the broader European archival landscape, and perhaps to gain inspiration from it.

Bill Stockting
Fabienne Queyroux

AUTHOR NOTE

Bill Stockting became the Senior Editor for the Access to Archives (A2A) Programme in 2000. He has presented papers and trained fellow professionals in archival description standards and EAD in the United States and across Europe. Bill is a member of the EAD Working Group and RLG's EAD Advisory Group as well as Chair of the EAD/Data Exchange Group of the UK Society of Archivists. He can be reached at: The National Archives, Kew, Richmond, Surrey, TW9 4DU UK (E-mail: william.stocking@nationalarchives.gov.uk).

Fabienne Queyroux has held the position of Curator of Manuscript collections at the Bibliothèque de l'Institut de France since 1995. In 2000, she was one of the founding members of the French EAD working group, which published the French translation of the EAD Tag Library and is now elaborating national application guidelines. As a member of that group, Fabienne Queyroux is involved in various EAD-related activities, doing presentations on EAD, teaching workshops and participating to the national project of conversion of the *Catalogue Général des Manuscrits des Bibliothèques Publiques de France*. She can be reached at: Bibliothèque de l'Institut de France, 23, quai de Conti, 75006 Paris, France (E-mail: fabienne.queyroux@bif.univ-paris5.fr).

Claire Sibille, Direction des Archives de France, has also contributed to this introduction.

NOTE

1. These European attendees were Angelika Menne-Haritz, Fabienne Queyroux, Bill Stockting, and Henny Van Schie. A full list can be found at http://www.loc.gov/ead/eadwg.html.

Technology and the Transformation of Archival Description

Daniel V. Pitti

SUMMARY. The emergence of computer and network technologies has presented the archival profession with daunting challenges as well as inspiring opportunities. Archivists have been actively imagining and realizing the application of advanced technologies to their professional functions and activities. Using advanced technologies, archivists have been transforming archival description, freeing it from the limits of traditional media. Markup and database technologies are the two most prevalent methods for representing textual information. Each best represents and exploits textual data with different though complementary characteristics. Researchers and developers are increasingly working to integrate the two technologies. The integration of the two technologies will enable archivists to collaboratively further the ongoing transformation of archival description. *[Article copies available for a fee from The Haworth Document Delivery Service: 1-800-HAWORTH. E-mail address: <docdelivery@haworthpress.com> Website: <http://www.HaworthPress.com> © 2005 by The Haworth Press, Inc. All rights reserved.]*

Daniel V. Pitti is Associate Director, Institute for Advanced Technology in the Humanities, University of Virginia. He has extensive experience designing humanities research projects using markup and database technologies. Since the inception of EAD in 1993, he has been its chief technical architect, and since 1999, the chief technical architect of EAC.

[Haworth co-indexing entry note]: "Technology and the Transformation of Archival Description." Pitti, Daniel V. Co-published simultaneously in *Journal of Archival Organization* (The Haworth Information Press, an imprint of The Haworth Press, Inc.) Vol. 3, No. 2/3, 2005, pp. 9-22; and: *Encoding Across Frontiers: Proceedings of the European Conference on Encoded Archival Description and Context (EAD and EAC), Paris, France, 7-8 October 2004* (ed: Bill Stockting, and Fabienne Queyroux) The Haworth Information Press, an imprint of The Haworth Press, Inc., 2005, pp. 9-22. Single or multiple copies of this article are available for a fee from The Haworth Document Delivery Service [1-800-HAWORTH, 9:00 a.m. - 5:00 p.m. (EST). E-mail address: docdelivery@haworthpress.com].

Available online at http://www.haworthpress.com/web/JAO

doi:10.1300/J201v03n02_02

KEYWORDS. Archival description, authority control, communication standards, database technologies, EAC, EAD, Encoded Archival Context, Encoded Archival Description, function description, markup technologies

INTRODUCTION

Over the course of the last thirty years, the emergence of computer and network technologies has presented the archival profession with daunting challenges as well as inspiring opportunities. The now pervasive use of computers in conducting both public and private business has led to perhaps the most difficult challenge: electronic records. At the same time, archivists themselves have been actively imagining and realizing the application of advanced technologies to their own professional functions and activities. Perhaps most inspiring is the opportunity to transform archival description, to free it from the limits that traditional media–print in particular–have imposed on it.

Standard Generalized Markup Language (SGML), a markup technology, was released in 1986 by the International Standards Organization (ISO). Using markup technologies to create machine-readable archival description was first conceived in 1993. The effort to develop a method for representing archival description using markup technologies resulted five years later in the release of Encoded Archival Description (EAD).[1] The effort focused on developing a method for representing printed archival finding aids, an apparatus that focuses on the description of archival records. Because of the complex hierarchical nature of archival record description, the developers decided to use SGML, a technology well suited to the representation of complex, hierarchical documents.

The decision to focus on developing a method for representing traditional finding aids was based on complementary intellectual and political factors. The developers felt that the archival community, including themselves, did not understand the technology sufficiently well to reinvent archival description. It was better to explore the unfamiliar while firmly grounded in the familiar. At the same time, an attempt to transform archival description was likely to be met with suspicion by the archival community. Over the course of the five-year development of EAD, the technological environment changed significantly. In 1998, the year EAD version 1.0 was released, Extensible Markup Language (XML), a derivative of SGML that is more compatible with formal computer grammars, was released by the World Wide Web Consortium (W3C). Version 1.0 of EAD was designed for use as either an SGML or XML encoding schema or system.

Since 1998, XML has been widely embraced by the government, business, and academic communities. Though XML emerged from communities interested in the representation of text documents, since its release it has been adopted for many other uses, including as a syntax for machine-to-machine and machine-to-human communication of information that is maintained via an alternative method of representation, Structured Query Language (SQL). SQL is the standard underlying most but not all databases. Though XML and SQL have some common or similar characteristics, each optimally represents and processes different forms of textual information. Deciding which technology is best for representing a given set of information is often very difficult, since information often mixes together data best represented in one with data best represented in the other. Archival description is one such mixed data set. Fortunately, the differences between markup and database technologies are becoming less distinct. Increasingly there are efforts to blend the strengths of each in representational systems. These efforts are still in the early stages, but, in conjunction with ongoing efforts to develop related standards, they permit us to envision archival descriptive systems that integrate markup and database technologies.

ADVANCED TECHNOLOGIES– DOCUMENT-CENTRIC versus DATA-CENTRIC

Though database and markup technologies differ significantly, they share several essential characteristics and features. Both exist in widely supported standard forms. Open, community-based and widely embraced standards offer reasonable assurance that the represented information will be durable and portable. Database and markup technologies are either based on or will accept standard character encodings (ASCII or, increasingly, Unicode). Both technologies enable an explicit separation of the logical components of information from the operations that are applied to them. This separation is effected by means of two essential features. First, each requires user-assigned names for designating and delimiting the logical components of textual objects. While there are some constraints, given the available character repertoire, the number of possible names is unlimited. Second, each supports the logical interrelating and structuring of the data components.

Though both of these technologies involve naming and structurally interrelating textual entities and components, each does so using distinctly different methods, and each exploits the data in different ways. Deciding which technology to use requires analyzing the nature of the information to be represented and identifying those operations which are to be performed on it. With both technologies, the naming and structuring requires anticipating the operations. Each of these technologies is optimized to perform a set of well-defined operations. Though there is some overlap in functionality, the two technologies are best described as complementary rather than competitive. Information best represented in databases is characterized as "data-centric," and information best represented in markup technologies is characterized as "document-centric."[2]

Information collected on many kinds of forms is data-centric. Job applications are a familiar example. Name, birth date, street address, city, country or state, postal codes, education, skills, previous employment, date application completed, name or description of a position sought, references, and so on, are easily mapped into a database and easily retrieved in a variety of ways. Medical records, student records, and census data are other common examples of data-centric information. These familiar examples of data-centric information have the following characteristics in common:

- Regular number of components or fields in each discrete information unit.
- Order of the components or fields is generally not significant.
- Each information component is restricted to data. That is, it has no embedded delimiters, other than the formal constraints of data typing (for example, a date may be constrained to a sequence of eight Arabic numbers, in the order year-month-day).
- Highly regularized structure, possibly with a fixed but shallow hierarchy.
- Relations between discrete information units have a fixed number of types (though the number of occurrences of each type may or may not be constrained).
- Processing of data-centric information (such as accurate recall and relevance retrieval, sorting, value comparison, and mathematical computation) is highly dependent on controlled values and thus highly dependent on machine-enforced data typing, authority files, and a high degree of formality, accuracy, and consistency in data creation and maintenance.

Common types of databases are hierarchical, network, relational, and object-oriented. Today, relational databases are by far the most prevalent. SQL, an ISO standard first codified in 1986 and substantially revised in 1992 and again in 1999, is the major standard for relational databases. While compliance with the standard is somewhat irregular, most relational databases comply sufficiently to assure the portability and durability of data across applications. There are only a few viable implementations of object-oriented databases, though the technology contributed conceptual and functional models that influenced the 1999 revision of SQL. SQL is both a Data Definition Language (DDL) and a Data Manipulation Language (DML). As a DDL, it allows users to define and name tables of data, and to interrelate the tables. Such definitions are frequently called database schemas. Tables have rows and columns. Within the context of databases, rows are commonly called records and columns are called fields. Each column or field is assigned a name, typically a descriptive term that indicates the type of data to be contained in it. The DML facilitates updating and maintaining the data, as well as sophisticated querying and manipulating data and data relations.

Textbooks, novels, poems, collections of poetry, newspapers, journals, and journal articles are all examples of document-centric data. These familiar objects have in common the following characteristics:

- An irregular number of parts or pieces. Documents, even documents of a particular type, do not all have the same number of textual divisions (parts, chapters, sections), paragraphs, tables, lists, and so on.
- Serial order is significant. It matters whether this chapter follows that chapter, and whether this paragraph follows that paragraph. If the order is not maintained, intelligibility and sense break down.
- Semi-regular structure and unbounded hierarchy.
- Arbitrary intermixing of text and markup, or what is technically called mixed content.
- Arbitrary number of interrelations (or references) within and among documents and other information types, and generally the types of relations are unconstrained or only loosely constrained.

XML, first codified in 1998 by the World Wide Web Consortium (W3C), is the predominant markup technologies standard. XML is a direct descendent of SGML. While the relation of XML to SGML is quite complex, XML may be viewed as "normalized" SGML. It retains

SGML's essential functionality while eliminating those features that were problematic for computer programmers.

XML is a descriptive or declarative approach to encoding textual information in computers. It does not provide an off-the-shelf set of tags that one can simply take home and apply to a letter, novel, article, or poem. Instead it is a standard grammar for expressing a set of rules according to which a class of documents will be marked up. XML provides conventions for naming the logical components of documents, and a syntax and meta-language for defining and expressing the logical structure and relations among the components. Using these conventions, individuals or members of a community with shared objectives with respect to a particular document type can work together to encode those documents.

Sets of rules for specifying the names of components and their logical relations are called schemas. The most prevalent schema grammar is called a Document Type Definition or DTD. Recently two alternative methods for writing schemas have emerged, W3C Schema and Relax NG. While DTDs continue to be an important method of representing XML schemas, W3C and Relax NG schemas increasingly are the preferred method.

There are currently many communities that are collaboratively developing XML schemas for shared document types. A consortium of software developers and producers developed a schema for computer manuals and documentation called DocBook. The Text Encoding Initiative (TEI) Consortium developed a complex suite of schemas for the representation of literary and linguistic materials. A large number of government, education and research, business, industry, and other institutions and professions are currently developing schemas for their own shared document types. Schemas shared and followed by a community can themselves become standards. The DocBook and TEI schemas are examples of standard XML schemas.

The standard schemas listed above have two common features. First, they are developed and promulgated by broad communities. For example, TEI was developed by humanists representing a wide variety of disciplines and interests. The development process (which is ongoing) requires negotiation and consensus building. Second, each schema is authoritatively documented, with semantics and structure defined and described in detail. Such documentation helps make the language public rather than private, open rather than closed, standard rather than proprietary, and thereby promotes communication. These two features–consensus and documentation–are essential characteristics of standards, but they are not sufficient in and of themselves to make standards successful (that is, make them widely understood and applied within an acceptable range of uniformity).

In addition to text representation, XML is increasingly used to realize other functional objectives. Since the advent of XML in 1998, many database developers have embraced XML syntax as a data-transport syntax, that is, for machine-to-machine and machine-to-human communication. XML is also increasingly being used to develop standards for declarative processing of information. Rendering and querying are probably the two primary operations performed on XML-encoded textual documents. We want to be able to transform encoded documents into human readable form, on computer screens as well as on paper. We also want to be able to query individual documents and collections of documents. There are currently several related standards for rendering and querying XML documents that have been approved or are under development: Extensible Stylesheet Language-Transformation (XSLT), Extensible Stylesheet Language-Formatting Objects (XSL-FO), and XQUERY. These declarative standards are significant because they offer reasonable assurance of not only the durability of encoded texts, but also the durability of the experienced presentation.

The distinction between document-centric and data-centric information, while useful, is also problematic. It is a useful distinction because it highlights the strengths of markup languages and databases, but it does not reflect reality. Frequently, a given instance of information is not purely one or the other, but a mixture of both. Predominately data-centric information may have some components or features that are document-centric, and vice-versa. The distinction is of more than theoretical interest, since each information type is best represented with a different technology, and each technology is optimized to perform a specific set of defined functions and either does not perform other functions or performs them less than optimally. When deciding the best method, it is unfortunately still necessary to weigh what is more and less important in the information and to make trade-offs.

In a paper delivered at a 1995 conference devoted to discussing the encoding of archival finding aids, Steve DeRose, an internationally respected expert on markup technologies, observed that traditional archival description employs both document-centric and data-centric components, though he used the terms "document" and "form" to distinguish the two information types.[3] The document-centric and data-centric components are both essential to the objectives of archival description. Neither can be subordinated to the other without loss of potentially essential functionality and economies. As a "mixed form," archival description presents a very difficult representational challenge.

Along with many other communities, archivists would greatly benefit from a representational system that integrates the functional strengths of both markup and database technologies. As XML has become increasingly accepted, efforts to integrate the two technologies have increased, and the distinctions between them are beginning to blur. The attempts so far at integration have typically emphasized one at the expense of the other. Nevertheless, it is an opportune time for archivists to begin envisioning archival description that exploits the strengths of both technologies and to continue the process of transcending the limits of traditional print media.

ARCHIVAL DESCRIPTION AND ADVANCED TECHNOLOGIES

Provenance, or *respect des fonds*, has traditionally served as the primary principle of archival description. The principle states that the integrity of all records of a single creating entity and the original order of the records are to be preserved. The corpus of all records with a common creator is frequently referred to as a fonds. When using print as the primary medium of description, archivists have generally employed a single "records-centered" apparatus, the finding aid, to describe all of the records with a common creator or source. Within an individual finding aid, description of the creator, functions performed by the creator, and the records generated as a product or by-product of the performance of the functions are combined to describe the fonds. Finding aids begin with a description of the fonds as a whole and proceed progressively from the whole to components of the whole, components of the components, and so on. While the description may terminate with a description of items, it commonly does not: the archivist may judge that such detail is economically not feasible, that the significance of individual items does not merit the effort, or that the descriptive detail will obscure rather than reveal the records.

Applying the principle of provenance within a single print apparatus has been challenging. While it is possible to establish the provenance of most records, it is common for records to be of mixed provenance, or for records of the same provenance to be dispersed. Relations between creators, records, and the functions documented in the records also present problems. Within a fonds, there are commonly groups of records that document or reflect the same function or activity. But functions and activities are *not fixed* in one person or corporate body, which is to say, in one fonds. They frequently are shared by two or more creators, or transferred from one creator to another. In a descriptive print system based on provenance, transferring functions leads to the descriptive separation of records documenting the same function. Records documenting the same function may be described in two or more finding aids. Such separation presents a serious access challenge for records of corporate bodies, where access by function (for example, the registering of births or marriages) is arguably far more important to many users than access by provenance. Separating records that reflect the same or similar activities of families or persons is also an access challenge, especially when the user is more interested in the functions and activities as such, rather than the families or persons performing them.

Relations between records, creators, and functions are thus dynamic and complex, and not fixed and simple. Creators are related to other creators. Records are related to other records. Functions and activities are related to other functions and activities. And each of these is interrelated with the others. With the emergence of markup and database technologies, it is now possible to not only envision but also to begin developing and realizing an archival descriptive system with dedicated apparatus for the description and interrelating of the principle components of archival description: description of creators, description of functions, and description of records. By developing dedicated semantics and structures for describing creators, functions, and records and their complex interrelations in space and time, we can develop flexible, dynamic, and sustainable descriptive systems that are far more useful than traditional print-based finding aids.[4]

Record Description

Development of an XML-based schema for archival record description began in 1993 and culminated in the 1998 release of EAD, since revised in 2002. EAD is intended to represent traditional print finding aids in machine-readable form. Because EAD is intended to represent traditional finding aids, it has descriptive elements for creators and functions, as well as an array of elements for describing the records themselves. EAD thus enables combining record, creator, and function description in a single document to describe an individual fonds. EAD essentially reflects the "records-centered" nature of the finding aids it is designed to represent.

EAD adheres closely to the structure and logic of traditional finding aids, but its detailed semantics and structure and advances in representational technologies since its conception now make it possible to consider separating the description of creators and the description of the functions carried out by them. Through the use of dedicated schemas we can describe records, creators, and functions independently of each other. By interrelating the independent descriptions using machine-readable techniques, we can combine them at the time of use to form a complete archival description.

Context Description

EAD has several elements for the description of persons, families, and corporate bodies associated with records. The Origination (<origination>) element and the elements Personal Name (<persname>), Corporate Name (<corpname>), and Family Name (<famname>) contained within it provide the means to associate one or more creators with the records being described. The Biography or History (<bioghist>) element may be used to provide biographical detail for persons and families, and historical description of corporate bodies. The EAD Controlled Access (<controlaccess>) element and elements within it enable associating other persons, families, and corporate bodies with records, and specifying the nature of the association.

When records of the same provenance are dispersed across administrative units or across repositories, each administrative unit or repository typically describes only those records held by it. One creator is thus described more than once. When records are dispersed, each administrative unit or repository essentially duplicates the work of each of the others. Embedding creator description in the description of records also makes it exceedingly difficult to consistently identify and describe and efficiently link them with related creators and with the functions and activities carried out by them. An additional advantage of separating creator description from record description is demonstrated by the Australian series description system. It enables describing individual series separately, rather than in a single fonds-level description, without the loss of the provenance of the records. Arguably the series system is far easier to maintain and thus more economical when describing the records of large, complex corporate bodies.

Wendy Duff (University of Toronto) and Richard Szary (Yale University) first proposed an effort to develop an encoding standard for context description in 1998.[5] With the assistance of the author, and with funding from the Digital Library Federation in the United States, they organized a meeting held at Yale University in 1999. In 2000, with the encouragement and assistance of Anne Van Camp of the Research Libraries Group (RLG), funding was secured from the Gladys Krieble Delmas Foundation. Two meetings were organized and convened in 2001, at the University of Toronto and the University of Virginia. At the Toronto meeting, the prototype encoding standard was named Encoded Archival Context (EAC).

The development of EAC has taken place within the context of related initiatives within the international archival community. In 1996, the International Council on Archives (ICA) published *International Standard Archival Authority Record for Corporate Bodies, Persons and Families (ISAAR(CPF)).*[6] Under the auspices of ICA's Ad Hoc Commission on Descriptive Standards, work on this structural standard was initiated in 1993. The development of EAC has roughly coincided with the review and revision of *ISAAR*. EAC development and ISAAR review influenced one another, with several individuals involved in both efforts. EAC beta was released in August 2004, and the second edition of ISAAR in October 2004.

EAC is an XML-based apparatus for describing persons, families, and corporate bodies. EAC facilitates identifying record creating entities; recording the names or designations used by and for them; describing their essential functions, activities, and characteristics; and the dates and places they were active. EAC delineates three major areas of description for creating entities: identity or authority control; biographical or historical information, as well as descriptions of important characteristics of the entity; and finally, mechanisms for relating each creating entity to other creating entities record descriptions and function and activity descriptions.[7]

Function Description

The EAD element for describing and associating functions and activities with record description is <function>. Functions and activities, as noted above, are not fixed in one person, family, or corporate body. A particular government agency, for example, may be responsible for monitoring water quality. In the course of a reorganization, the responsibility may be assigned to a different agency. Using a single provenance-based descriptive apparatus, the description of the records documenting monitoring of water quality will be separated. Embedding function description in the description of records makes it difficult to consistently describe them, and to efficiently link them with related functions and with the creators that perform them.

There is currently no active, organized international effort underway to develop an encoding standard for describing functions. Participants at the Toronto EAC meeting discussed the need for such a standard, to follow the development of EAC. Work in Australia and New Zealand in support of the series description system has begun to explore the challenges presented by function description, as has a project confined to the higher education sector in Scotland.[8] Within an international context, linguistic, legal, and other cultural differences will undoubtedly present serious challenges to developing a schema for function description. Nevertheless, there is abundant experience in the library and museum communities in developing thesauri upon which the archival community can draw in approaching the challenges, and the recent emergence of topic maps and ontologies as subjects of intensive research suggests the possibility of new techniques.

Relations

Once creator, function, and record descriptions are separated, relations between these descriptions must also be described. Each category of description in itself is a component of archival description. It is only when related components are combined that you have a complete archival description. In order to combine them, the relations must be described and represented in an accurate, sustainable machine-readable form. The description and representation of relations presents a major technological challenge.

Both EAC and EAD provide elements for describing related creators, functions, and records. Presumably, an encoding standard for function description will follow this pattern. The rationale for providing these elements in EAC and EAD is based on the need to communicate information about related creators, functions, and records to users. The need to support communicating information about related entities does not require embedding the information in each description. Indeed, embedding relations information makes the accurate description of relations economically unfeasible. Maintenance of embedded relations information requires editing each description involved in a relation at the time of establishing the relation and subsequently when any correction or change is needed. Relations exist *between* descriptions, not within them.

Given that relations exist between and not within descriptive entities, relations are themselves entities. Relations must be described. When context entities, records, and functions are related, it is essential to establish the relation itself. It is also necessary to describe other characteristics of the relation. For example, a corporate body associated with records may be the creator of the records, but may also be the subject of or have custodial responsibility for them. It is thus important to describe the role of the relation. It is also necessary to specify the time and frequently the place of the relation. For example, a corporate body may perform a function for a given period of time and in a particular place. Later, responsibility for this function may be transferred to another corporate body. It is thus essential to describe the characteristics of relations in order to facilitate combining record, function, and context descriptions into full archival descriptions.

CONCLUSION

The emergence of computer and network technologies has presented the archival profession with the opportunity to transform archival description, to free it from the limits of the print media upon which it has been based. As personal computers, network, word processing, and database technologies have become available, many archivists have enthusiastically employed them in one fashion or another to pursue their professional objectives more efficiently and effectively than had previously been possible. Archival theorists also have and continue to explore the potential of advanced technologies to transform archival description. It is only with the emergence of markup technologies and the increasing integration of markup and database technologies, however, that *both* the intellectual and technological future of archival description are beginning to form.

Traditional archival description has employed a single records-oriented apparatus. EAD reflects this traditional archival description, but its underlying technology and semantics and structure, and the archival community's experience in applying them provide a strong base for transforming archival description. Realizing the future of archival description will require continuing development of promising though still emerging technologies outside the archival community. It will also require, within the archival community, ongoing theorizing, experimentation, and dialogue as we struggle together to apply the technologies to be faithful to our professional principle, the *respect des fonds*.

NOTES

1. For a description of the history of EAD development and an overview of its semantics and structure, see Janice Ruth, "The Development and Structure of Encoded Archival Description (EAD) Document Type Definition," *Encoded Archival Description on the Internet* (New York: The Haworth Press, Inc., 2001), 27-59.

2. Ronald Bourret. *XML and Databases* (http://www.rpbourret.com/xml/XMLAndDatabases.htm). 1999-2004. The terms "document-centric" and "data-centric" were used as early as 1997 on the xml-dev list.

3. Steve DeRose, "Navigation, Access, and Control Using Structured Information," in *The American Archivist* 60, no. 3 (Summer 1997), 298-309.

4. David Bearman and Richard Lytle, "The Power of the Principle of Provenance," Archivaria, no. 21 (1985), 14-27. Bearman and Lytle recognized early the potential for advanced technologies to transform the effectiveness and efficiency of archival description and the need for dedicated apparatus for describing and dynamically interrelating creators, functions, and records.

5. The term "context" is used rather than "creator" because not all persons, families, and corporate bodies associated with records are responsible for creating them.

6. EAC beta is available online at http://www.iath.virginia.edu/eac/ and *ISAAR(CPF)*, second edition at http://www.ica.org/biblio/ISAAR2EN.pdf.

7. For a fuller description of the development and structure of EAC, see Daniel Pitti, "Creator Description: Encoded Archival Context," *Cataloging and Classification Quarterly*, 38, nos. 3/4 (2004), 201-226.

8. Chris Hurley, "What, if anything, is a function?" *Archives and Manuscripts* 21, no. 2 (1993), 218. For further information on the *Developing Archival Context Standards for Functions in the Higher Education Sector* project, which is based at Glasgow University Archive Services, see contacts at http://www.gashe.ac.uk.

The Encoded Archival Guide (EAG) DTD and the *Censo-Guía de los Archivos de España e Iberoamérica* Project: An Electronic Guide to Spanish and Iberian American Archives

Blanca Desantes

SUMMARY. This paper argues that there is a need for specific standards for the description of archive repositories. With this objective in mind a DTD has been created, called Encoded Archival Guide (EAG) that provides an electronic format for the storage, publication and exchange of information related to archive repositories. The different elements and attributes that make up the EAG DTD are described, as well

Blanca Desantes is Professional Archivist in Medieval History, Complutense University, Madrid, Spain (E-mail: blanca.desantes@dglab.mcu.es).

[Haworth co-indexing entry note]: "The Encoded Archival Guide (EAG) DTD and the *Censo-Guía de los Archivos de España e Iberoamérica* Project: An Electronic Guide to Spanish and Iberian American Archives." Desantes, Blanca. Co-published simultaneously in *Journal of Archival Organization* (The Haworth Information Press, an imprint of The Haworth Press, Inc.) Vol. 3, No. 2/3, 2005, pp. 23-38; and: *Encoding Across Frontiers: Proceedings of the European Conference on Encoded Archival Description and Context (EAD and EAC), Paris, France, 7-8 October 2004* (ed: Bill Stockting, and Fabienne Queyroux) The Haworth Information Press, an imprint of The Haworth Press, Inc., 2005, pp. 23-38. Single or multiple copies of this article are available for a fee from The Haworth Document Delivery Service [1-800-HAWORTH, 9:00 a.m. - 5:00 p.m. (EST). E-mail address: docdelivery@haworthpress.com].

Available online at http://www.haworthpress.com/web/JAO

doi:10.1300/J201v03n02_03

as their application to the Electronic Guide to Spanish and Iberian American Archives that includes information about more than 42,000 institutions.

KEYWORDS. Archive repositories, EAG, Encoded Archival Guide, Electronic Guide to Spanish and Iberian American Archives, Extensible Markup Language, XML

INTRODUCTION

The *Censo Guía de Archivos*, the home page of which is shown in Figure 1, is an electronic guide[1] to Spanish and Iberian American archives that provides information on the Internet related to:

- Repositories responsible for the custody and management of archives and related documentation. From this point of view, the *Censo Guía* is a directory of archive repositories.
- The archives that each centre has custody of at the level of fonds and collection.
- General information about the archive repositories and the services they offer citizens.

The fundamental objective of the project, therefore, is to provide online the information that has traditionally been collected in the finding aids called 'Guides.'

The project has an international scope and is the fruit of mutual cooperation. Although at first, in 1979, the project was focused on Spanish archives alone, its scope was expanded to include repositories in Iberian American countries, including Colombia, Argentina, Bolivia, Costa Rica, Chile, El Salvador, Guatemala, Nicaragua, Paraguay, Venezuela, Brazil, Puerto Rico, Peru, Cuba, and Mexico. This has been achieved through collaboration agreements and currently over 42,000 Spanish and Iberian American archive repositories are registered.

The guide is an instrument for the online dissemination and promotion of cultural content as found in archives. It is also a framework and information portal that brings together information about archive repositories and their archival holdings. It offers, therefore, a global vision of Hispanic archival heritage, thereby facilitating more detailed queries

FIGURE 1. Home Page of the Electronic Guide to Spanish and Iberian American Archives

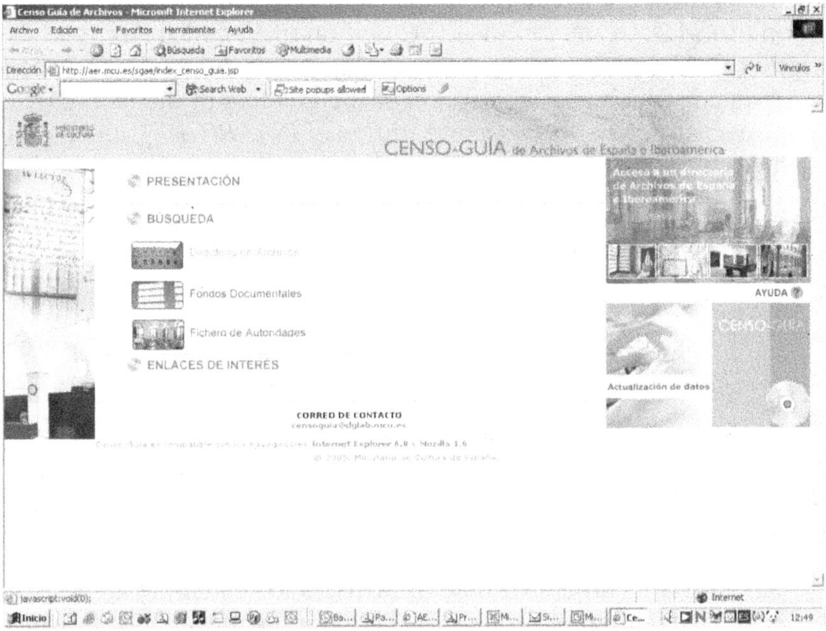

from users. The guide also incorporates links to other relevant resources available on the Internet, such as Web pages, e-mails, and videos related to the archives, and finding aids for electronic objects.

The project has also the central goal of standardization. The *Censo Guía de Archivos* is contributing to the standardization of archival descriptions and to the consolidation of the international standards used by archivists. Standardization is of particular importance in a context where archival descriptions come from many diverse archive repositories from a large number of different countries.

INFORMATION MODEL AND DATA STRUCTURE

The descriptions of the archive repositories have been formatted in a data structure designed by the Subdirección General de Archivos of the

Ministerio de Cultura in Spain:[2] an XML DTD called Encoded Archive Guide (EAG). The descriptions of the fonds and collections managed in these archives are formatted in a data structure adapted to the second edition of *ISAD(G)*[3] and to the 2002 edition of Encoded Archival Description (EAD). A further important related data component has been incorporated, which is a description of the creators of the records. For this the data structure of the second edition of *ISAAR(CPF)*[4] and the Encoded Archival Context (EAC) DTD have been used. The authorities file is shared with the Spanish Archives on the Web project (*Archivos Españoles en Red–AER*).[5]

SYSTEM FEATURES

The *Censo Guía de Archivos* is divided into three clearly separated access zones:

- Internet: This zone is accessible by any user and allows searches to be made for archive repositories and their fonds and/or collections. Searches can be either simple or advanced and interactive maps have been incorporated that allow users to search the archival resources by different geographical areas in Spain and Iberian America, as illustrated in Figures 2 and 3. Likewise, pop-up windows have been used to provide the user with assisted searches. Combination searches can also be carried out that incorporate different classification criteria for the archive repositories, allowing them to be identified from diverse points of view. The queries can be viewed in different formats such as HTML and XML.
- Extranet: This is a zone of access restricted to archive systems, archive repositories and accredited staff for the maintenance of the information associated with the archive repository. It allows information to be added or modified if it has become obsolete or could be enriched with the new description data. This involves the integration, via document management, with the workflow of the *Subdirección General de Archivos Estatales* (SGAE) of Spain. Standardized templates have been designed for entering the data.
- Intranet: This zone is for the exclusive access of the SGAE staff that coordinate the management of the *Censo Guía de Archivos*. The application allows expert searches that can be configured by

the user; management of the temporary repository of information that allows the data supplied by the archive repositories to be verified through the extranet; management of Web access statistics (monthly number of accesses and access by countries, etc.); creation of reports; management of lookup tables (including countries, municipalities and types of archives); and data exchange via the import and export of data in different formats (XML, Microsoft Access, etc.).

In 2003 the ability to update information online was introduced, which involved a quantitative and qualitative leap in the process of updating information. This functionality has been consolidated through the development of two pilot projects in the Autonomous Community of Murcia in Spain and in Mexico, respectively, in order to verify the proper functioning of the communication channels and to allow its extension to the rest of the Spanish and Iberian American archives.

FIGURE 2. Geographic Search Screen for Spain

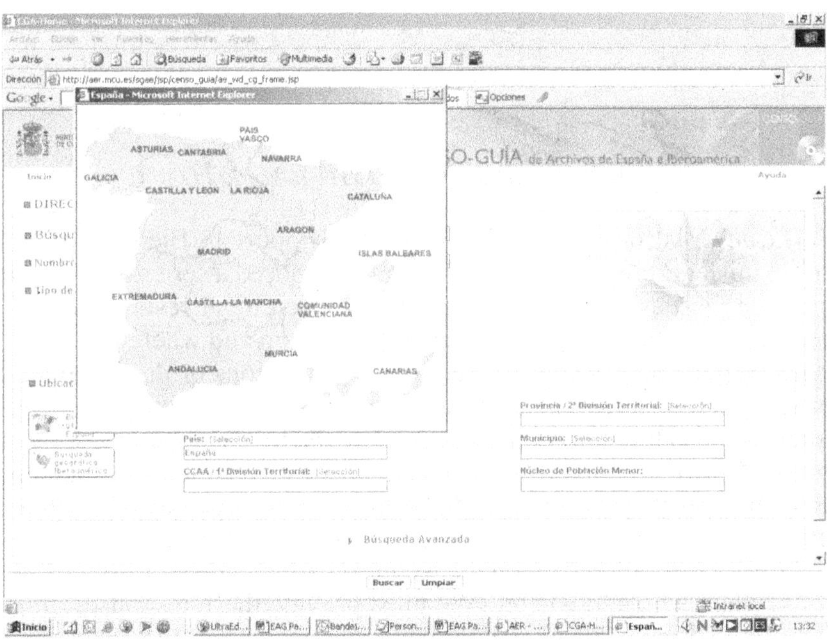

FIGURE 3. Geographic Search Screen for Latin America

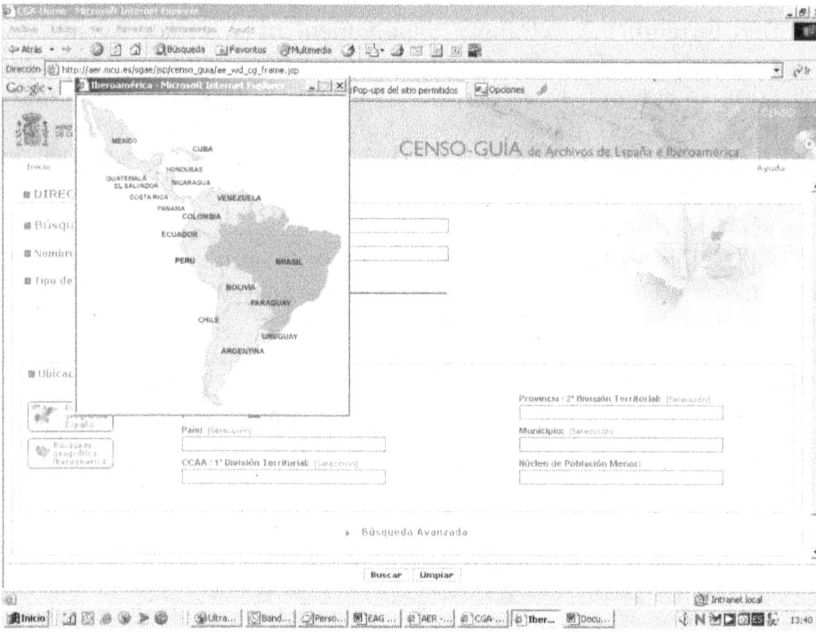

THE PURPOSE OF THE EAG DTD

The new platform that was developed to support the Electronic Guide for Spanish and Iberian American Archives posed a series of structural and basic issues. The citizen that accesses archival resources on the Internet needs to know who has custody of them and where they are located. When users search for the fonds, collections or documents that exist about a specific topic, they also need to know who created the documentation so that they can contextualize the historic source they want to use. They undoubtedly also need to know where the material comes from and how they can contact the archive that has custody of it, what its opening hours are and what technical services it offers.

As information professionals, we must provide answers to the questions ‘what, who and where.’ We must provide these responses, moreover, in a structured and standardized manner so that the exchange of information between persons and countries can become a reality. From the point of view of the archivist, we have instruments for standardization that allow us to respond to the question of 'what' documentary resources we have custody of in the multilevel rules of *ISAD(G)* and with EAD as the format for electronic data exchange. Again, from the point of view of the archivist, we can answer the question 'who' is the corporate body, person or family responsible for the creation of this documentation by providing the contextual information that is fundamental to our discipline and also necessary for the user, by applying the rules of *ISAAR(CPF)*, with EAC as the format for electronic exchange of this data. We find ourselves, however, in a regulatory vacuum when it comes to the provision of practical information related to 'where' to find existing archival resources, as we do not have adequate rules for describing archive repositories.

One possible option is to use *ISAAR(CPF)* to describe archive repositories, analysing them as if they were a corporate body, but this solution has its disadvantages:

- An authority record is an intellectual creation that gives contextual information. It does not offer the citizen the practical information that they need for their research such as opening and closing hours and the services that a repository offers (photocopies, microfilm, digital reproductions, access for disabled users, computing services, etc.).
- Usage of *ISAAR(CPF)* in this way would be a distortion, as an archive repository is not a creator of archives but an institution that has custody of them.
- Including information related to archive repositories in an authority file would probably not provide citizens with the practical information they need rapidly, clearly and in a pertinent way.

We must bear in mind that the process of creating standards should progress in accordance with descriptive needs and with the needs of information users. *ISAD(G)* provided some contextual information, but it was not in itself sufficient. *ISAAR(CPF)* has covered and complemented the descriptive needs for contextual information in archives. *ISAAR(CPF)* provides information that may be of use in describing archive repositories as if they were corporate bodies. It also provides information regarding the functions of a specific corporate body, but it does not cover the descriptive needs and needs of users in this respect. We consider it essential, therefore, that standards or guidelines should be prepared to describe archive repositories and their functions, which usually continue when the creators of the archives change. Consequently, the process of standardisation must adapt to new needs and establish mappings with existing standards, as there are common elements and interconnections between them. Furthermore, the inclusion of 42,000 archive repositories and the need to update the information about them online within the platform of the Electronic Guide makes an XML exchange format necessary, in order that information included in the project can be easily exported from the computer platform to the archive repositories that are updating, modifying or adding new information. Such an exhaustive directory of Spanish and Iberian American archives needs a solid, yet extremely flexible structure for data exchange. The *Censo Guía de Archivos*, moreover, includes a lot of information that can be used for the creation of reports and statistics (such as linear metres of shelves, storage capacity, number of seats in the research rooms and weekly opening hours for example) that would be very difficult to recover from an information structure such as the *ISAAR(CPF)*, let alone intellectually focus it to offer information related to the context of records creation and control of the information access point.

All of these factors led us to come up with the idea of a simple DTD in XML, called EAG, that pragmatically solved this issue of the exchange of information related to the archive repositories. In the description of EAG below, the following important points should be borne in mind:

- The EAG DTD is not supported by any internationally agreed standard similar to *ISAD(G)* or *ISAAR(CPF)*. It has been presented at the Committee on Descriptive Standards of the International Council on Archives (ICA/CDS), which has included the creation of a description standard for archive repositories as a possible piece of work in the coming years. In this sense, the EAG DTD could be used as a working document and a good starting point.
- Although we feel that *ISAAR(CPF)* does not meet all the descriptive needs of an archive repository, some equivalencies and similarities of elements have been established with *ISAAR(CPF)* in EAG. This means we are not "reinventing the wheel" but rather using structures in standards that have been previously agreed on and are useful for our objectives.
- The creation of a standard for the description of archive repositories and its EAG exchange format can be an interdisciplinary meeting point with museums and libraries as holders of cultural in-

formation resources that also need to give an answer to the question of where resources may be found by users in a way very similar to archives.

- The EAG format is actually being used for the exchange of information about archive repositories between Spain and Iberian America–successfully and without difficulties.

DESCRIPTION OF THE EAG DTD

EAG is a simple XML DTD, currently in the version Alpha 0.2, which standardizes data about archive repositories, and provides an electronic format for the storage, publication and exchange of this information by their staff. The DTD is designed to operate only as XML and is a 'valid' document that respects the basic rules of XML syntax and complies with the restrictions expressed in the file. As well as the DTD itself a tag library has also been prepared.[6] There follows a description of the major elements and attributes of the DTD.

Encoded Archival Guide (<eag>)

Encoded Archival Guide (<eag>) is the "wrapper" tag for an electronic description of an archive repository in accordance with the EAG DTD. It is a digital reference instrument that contains the elements and attributes necessary to provide information about the repository, its history and formation, opening hours and user services, etc. It is a mandatory element and is unrepeatable. It can include an "audience" attribute that notes whether the general public can consult the document or has restricted access. The <eag> element is the root element of the DTD and is made up of two fundamental elements EAG Header (<eagheader>) and Archival Guide (<archiguide>).

EAG Header (<eagheader>)

This element contains all the information related to the creation of the description of the archive repository. It includes elements and attributes for the unique identification of the description, as well as its maintenance history, including:

- Information about the different "events" performed on the description (creation, modification or deletion);

- The date of each "event," standardized according to ISO-8601;
- The name of the person responsible for the creation or modification of the description (name, surnames, position or function and source used);
- A language declaration and the script employed in the description (standardized according to ISO 15924 and ISO 639-b).

Archival Guide (<archguide>)

This element contains all data related to the archive repository that is being described, both identification data that makes it unique with respect to the other archive repositories and descriptive information about the archive itself. It is mandatory and unrepeatable. The Archival Guide element is made up of two principal elements: Identity Area (<identity>) and Description Area (<desc>).

Identity Area (<identity>)

This element groups all descriptive data related to the identification of the archive repository, or in other words, the information that allows us to unequivocally identify a particular repository. It includes information related to the repository identifier (country code in ISO 3166-1 format and repository code); information about the authorized form of the repository name, including parallel forms in case of multiple languages and excluded forms of the name. The similarity of these elements with *ISAAR(CPF)* should be noted.

Description Area (<desc>)

This element includes descriptive information about the archive repository being registered including:

- Geographical or location details of the archive repository (<geogarea>). This is one of the key elements for searching in the *Censo Guía de Archivos de España e Iberoamérica*;
- Contact details of the archive repository, including address, Web page, telephone, fax, and e-mail. The data here may be used for correspondence;
- Details about access to the archive repository, including opening hours, holidays, and free or restricted access (<timetable> and <access>). This data could also be included in reports or statistics;

- Information about the director or person responsible for the archive, including surname, name, role or function and naming date (<resprepositor>). Again the data here may be used for correspondence;
- Elements that relate to the institutional history of the archive, its creation date, its administrative structure and guides published (<respositorhist>, etc.). It is again possible to observe similarities here with the structure of information included in *ISAAR(CPF)*;
- Information about the archive building including its general characteristics, area and storage capacity, capacity of research room and facilities for handicapped persons, etc. (<buildinginfo> and <extent>). This data provides important details that can be used in statistics;
- Details of the technical services offered by the archive repository, such as restoration, reproduction (photocopies, microforms, photographs and digital reproductions), auxiliary library, automation (user management, description and document languages) (<techservices>). Data of interest here is usable in reports and statistics;
- A Classification table of the fonds and collections of the repository (<organization>). For each fond or collection the ID code, level, title, date and volume or extension of the documentation is included. There are similarities between the elements used here with *ISAD(G)* and EAD;
- Elements that include access points constituted by terms from controlled vocabularies that can also link to authority files with material, geographical and function descriptors, etc. (<controlaccess>). This area also contains information about the ownership of the archive repository and the life cycle of the documents stored. The elements included here are central to search strategies in the *Censo Guía de Archivos de España e Iberoamérica* platform;
- Finally, there is a notes area (<note>).

CONCLUSION

The creation of the EAG DTD enables the consistent codification in XML of all the elements necessary to describe an archive repository and to provide the public with clear information on the Internet about where to find archives and how to access them. The EAG format is being used successfully and without difficulty for the exchange of information between Spain and Iberian America referring to archive repositories registered in the *Censo Guía de Archivos de España e Iberoamérica* platform. Other similar projects developed in Europe and at an international level,[7] make regulatory considerations necessary and appropriate, as well as the development of an electronic format for the exchange, storage and publication that meets the descriptive needs of the data related to archive repositories.

AUTHOR NOTE

Blanca Desantes has been a Professional Archivist since graduating in Medieval History from the Complutense University of Madrid in 1986. Her professional career has focused on the Spanish Civil War Archive, the National History Archive and the Sub-department of State Archives of Spain. Her activities have centered on the description of documentation, especially photographs. A member of ICA/CDS, she is the coordinator of the Spanish State Working Group for Archival Description Standards. She is responsible for the Web site of the Subdirección General de Archivos Estatales (SGAE) and the Electronic Guide to Spanish and Iberian American Archives (*Censo Guía de Archivos de España e Iberoámerica)* project. She is also a collaborator on the Spanish Archives on the Web (*Archivos Españoles en Red*-AER) project. She sits as an expert on several working groups of the European Union and has published numerous finding aids about the collections in the custody of State Archives and collaborated, through specialised articles, to diverse publications and technical journals.

NOTES

1. The *Censo Guía de los Archivos de España e Iberoamérica* can be consulted at http://aer.mcu.es/sgae/index_censo_guia.jsp. For further information about the projects and activities of the Spanish State Archives see http://www.mcu.es/archivos/index.html.

2. The working group included the following archivists: Abelardo Santamaría, Francisco Javier Fito and Blanca Desantes. Abelardo Santamaría has been in charge of the XML encoding of the results of the group's work. The DTD created was verified by the development team of the *Censo Guía de los Archivos de España e Iberoamérica* project.

3. International Council on Archives, *ISAD(G): General International Standard Archival Description*, 2nd edition (Ottawa, 2000) is available at http://www.ica.org/biblio/isad_g_2e.pdf.

4. International Council on Archives, *ISAAR(CPF): International Standard Archival Authority Record for Corporate Bodies, Persons and Families* (2004) is available at http://www.ica.org/biblio.php?pdocid=144.

5. The AER project can be consulted at http://www.aer.es. It has been presented in several publications such as E. C. De Santos Canalejo, and B. Desantes Fernández, "The AER Project (Spanish Archives on the Net)," *Digicult Info* 7 (April 2004), 24-28.

Both the *Censo Guía de Archivos de España e Iberoámerica* project and the AER project have been the object of studies: for example B. Desantes Fernández and F. J. Fito Manteca, "*Internet y Archivos, el proyecto AER (Archivos Españoles en Red) y la Guía Electrónica de Archivos de España e Iberoamérica,*" *Archives and Computer* 2 (2004).

6. See Appendix A for a view of the elements and attributes and of the DTD. The DTD and Tag Library are available at http://aer.mcu.es/sgae/jsp/censo_guia/seg_nivel/set_presenta.html.

7. In Europe, similar projects have been developed, which are designed to offer information about archives and/or documentary collections of different administrations. For the European Archival Network (EAN) initiated in 1998, organized by the European Committee of the ICA and maintained by the Swiss Federal Archive, see http://www.european-archival.net/. In the UK, the ARCHON Directory, found at http://www.archon.nationalarchives.gov.uk/archon/, provides information about UK archives held in the UK or other parts of the world that are registered with the National Register of Archives (NRA) at http://www.nra.nationalarchives.gov.uk/nra/. In Germany, some of the Länder have developed computer systems of archives, like that of Rhenania of North Westphalia, for which see http://www.archive.nrw.de/. In the Czech Republic, a database offering information about the documentary fonds kept at the Czech archives that can be consulted in Czech, English, German and French is available at http://www.mvcr.cz/archivy/peva/. A directory of Czech archives is also available at http://www.cesarch.cz/adresar.aspx. In Italy, the *Guida Generale degli Archivi di Stato Italiani*, found at http://www.maas.ccr.it/cgi-win/h3.exe/aguida/findex, started in 1998 as a project to convert the General Guide of Italian State Archives.

APPENDIX A

View of Elements and Attributes of the Complete EAG DTD

```
<eag audience="">
      <eagheader>
            < eagid/>
            <mainhist>
                  <mainevent maintype="">
                        <date normal="">
                        <respevent>
                              <surnames></surnames>
                              <name></name>
                        </respevent>
                        <charge></charge>
                        <source></source>
             </mainevent>
         </mainhist>
            <languagedecl langcode="" scriptcode=""/>
   </eagheaeder>
      <archguide>
            <identity>
                  <respositorid countrycode="" repositorycode="" />
              <autform></autform>
                   <parform></parform>
                   <nonpreform></nonpreform>
            </identity>
            <desc>
                  <geogarea></geogarea>
                  <country></country>
                  <firstdem></firstdem>
                  <secondem></secondem>
                  <municipality></municipality>
                  <localentity></ localentity>
                  <street></street>
                  <postalcode></postalcode>
                  <telephone></telephone>
                  <fax></fax>
                  <email href=""></email>
                  <webpage href=""></webpage>
                  <timetable>
                        <opening></opening>
                        <weekopen>
                              <num unit="hour"></num>
```

```
                    </weekopen>
                    <closing></closing>
                </timetable>
    <access question=""">
            <restaccess></restaccess>
</access>
  <resprepositor>
            <date normal=""">
            <surnames></surnames>
            <name></name>
            <charge></charge>
  </resprepositor>
  <repositorhist></repositorhist>
  <repositorfound>
            <date normal=""">
            <rule></rule>
  </repositorfound>
  <repositorsup>
            <date normal=""">
            <rule></rule>
  </repositorsup>
  <repositorguides>
            <repositorguides></ repositorguide>
  </repositorguides>
  <adminhierarchy>
            <adminunit></adminunit>
  </adminhierarchy>
  <buildinginfo>
            <building></building>
            <repositorarea>
                    <num unit=”squaremeter”></num>
            </repositorarea>
            <lengthshelf>
                    <num unit=”linearmetre”></num>
            </lengthshelf>
            <searchroom>
                    <num unit=”site”></num>
            </searchroom>
            <handicapped question="""></handicapped>
  </buildinginfo>
  <extent>
            <num unit=”linearmetre”></num>
  </extent>
  <organization>
```

APPENDIX A (continued)

```
                    <descunit level=”” classcode=”” fathercode=””>
                              <unitid href=””></unitid>
                              <unittitle></ unittitle>
                              <date normal=””>
          <extent>
                    <num unit=”linearmetre”></num>
          </extent>
     </descunit>
</organization>

<techservices>
     <restorationlab question=”” />
   <reproductionser question=””>
          <photocopyser question=”” />
          <microformser question=”” />
          <photographser question=”” />
          <digitalser question=”” />
   </reproductionser>
   <library question=”” >
          <monographicpub>
                    <num unit=”monographicpub”></num>
          </monographicpub>
          <serialpub>
                    <num unit=”serialpub”></num>
          </serialpub>
     </library>
</techservices>
<automation>
     <autusermanag question=”” />
     <autdescription question=”” />
     <indexvoc question=”” />
     <odautomation>
     </odautomation>
     </automation>
     <controlaccess>
          <controlaccess>
                    <head></head>
                    <subject></subject>
          </controlaccess>
     </controlaccess>
     <notes></notes>
   </desc>
  </archguide>
</eag>
```

EAD: IMPLEMENTATION OF EAD IN EUROPE: ISSUES AND CASE STUDIES

Giving Structure to Legacy Finding Aids Before Conversion to EAD: The Case of the Archives Départementales des Pyrénées-Atlantiques, France

Anne Goulet
Nicolas Maftei

SUMMARY. At the Archives Départementales des Pyrénées-Atlantiques, the encoding of more than forty legacy finding aids written between 1863 and 2000 is part of a program of digitization of the collections. Because of the size of the project, an external consultant, ArchProteus, has

Anne Goulet is Head of Archives, Départementales des Pyrénées-Atlantiques, France.

Nicolas Maftei is Computer Scientist, with his own consulting company, ArchProteus, Vancouver, BC, Canada. He also teaches at the School of Library, Archival and Information Studies, University of British Columbia.

[Haworth co-indexing entry note]: "Giving Structure to Legacy Finding Aids Before Conversion to EAD: The Case of the Archives Départementales des Pyrénées-Atlantiques, France." Goulet, Anne, and Nicolas Maftei. Co-published simultaneously in *Journal of Archival Organization* (The Haworth Information Press, an imprint of The Haworth Press, Inc.) Vol. 3, No. 2/3, 2005, pp. 39-53; and: *Encoding Across Frontiers: Proceedings of the European Conference on Encoded Archival Description and Context (EAD and EAC), Paris, France, 7-8 October 2004* (ed: Bill Stockting, and Fabienne Queyroux) The Haworth Information Press, an imprint of The Haworth Press, Inc., 2005, pp. 39-53. Single or multiple copies of this article are available for a fee from The Haworth Document Delivery Service [1-800-HAWORTH, 9:00 a.m. - 5:00 p.m. (EST). E-mail address: docdelivery@haworthpress.com].

Available online at http://www.haworthpress.com/web/JAO

doi:10.1300/J201v03n02_04

been brought in and specific management procedures have been put in place within the institution. The conversion has allowed the testing and verification of the flexibility of the EAD DTD, despite the various hurdles negotiated throughout the project, such as the necessity of reengineering finding aids, and standardizing index terms, etc. It becomes clear that a conversion project–in this case, a retrospective conversion–will lead the archivist to rethink the production of finding aids and the relationship with users and patrons.

KEYWORDS. Archival description, Archives Départementales des Pyrénées-Atlantiques, Encoded Archival Description, EAD, finding aids, indexing, retrospective conversion, standardization

THE PROJECT

As part of a five-year program (2003-2007), the Conseil Général des Pyrénées-Atlantiques has undertaken the digitization of 850 linear meters of archives kept at the Archives Départementales, materials concerning the Basque Country (i.e., the Western part of the Département), in order to facilitate their diffusion via Intranet or Internet.[1] With such a goal in mind, it was decided, as a preliminary step, to digitize and encode the finding aids relating to that material in Encoded Archival Description (EAD). If selection of finding aids for encoding was based on that sole criterion, it was nonetheless decided, for consistency's sake, to encode these finding aids in their totality, and not just to encode the parts relative to the Basque Country, even if all the documents of a fonds or a series described in the finding aids will not be digitized in the near future.

Given the size of the conversion project, the Conseil Général chose to outsource, and selected as a contractor the company ArchProteus, based in Vancouver, Canada, mainly because of its experience in EAD. The contract stipulated that the work would be completed in one year, from the fall of 2003 to the fall of 2004. ArchProteus was to scan the finding aids, use Optical Character Recognition (OCR) to produce a digital version, and finally encode them, on the basis of detailed specifications elaborated by the Archives Départementales.

Forty-three finding aids were selected amounting to 8,500 pages. They describe the following series:[2]

- Old Regime series, prior to the French Revolution (series B, C, IIC, E, G, H)
- Series for the Revolutionary period, 1790-1800 (series L)
- Modern series, 1800-1940 (series U, V, Y, Z)
- Notarial archives (series IIIE)
- Town and city archives from the Basque Country, deposited at the Archives Départementales (forty-three fonds)
- Hospital archives from the Basque Country (three fonds deposited)
- Private fonds (subseries 1J and eleven fonds)
- Series of the microfilms of the birth, marriage, and death records.

This corpus is challenging in several ways:

- It covers series of different types: closed or open, composed of both public and private fonds, and holding materials of various types and physical forms.
- The finding aids were written between 1863 and 2000, during which time the principles of archival description have changed. The corpus consists, therefore, of summary inventories, with their indexes (constituted 100 years later and not standardized) and registers.
- Finally, a major hurdle is the physical layout of the nineteenth-century finding aids. Several of them do not exist in a clean copy or have a clear typeface, thus making the use of OCR impossible and they have to be rekeyed as a result.

These few issues show the amount of work required by the project; even with the help of a contractor, it was a real challenge for our institution. However, such difficulties should not outweigh the great opportunity presented by the project. Retrospective conversion gave us the chance to update finding aids that were in some cases obsolete, and sometimes even to reengineer them completely. Finally, it gave us the opportunity to present all of them to users in a more consistent and friendlier form.

METHODOLOGY

Encoding such a large number of finding aids in just one year required a great deal of involvement by a significant portion of the regular staff, as well as the permanent exchange of information, both with the contractor as well as within the institution. Regarding communication with the vendor, geographical distance was never a problem, but rather a benefit, since by efficiently using the communication infrastructure we were able to take advantage of the nine hours time difference separating France from the western coast of Canada.

Constitution of the Team

Five senior staff members were involved in the project. They all had formal training in archival science, and/or long and significant experience of arrangement and description. Even though they were very familiar with the principles for the structuring of fonds and collections, they had almost no knowledge of the *General International Standard of Archival Description* (*ISAD(G)*)[3] and EAD. The first task, therefore, was to give them basic training, in-house, which was happily completed with intensive practice and lively discussions.

This team divided up the finding aids amongst themselves, in order to prepare the specifications. The appointment of a project manager and the arrangement of regular meetings, especially at the onset of the work, have enabled us to maintain a certain consistency and to compensate for problems generated by the division of the work.

Two issues here deserve more discussion: the training of the team, and the standardization of the content of the level attribute in EAD.

Training of the Staff

The team was first trained in *ISAD(G)*, and only then in EAD. It must be remembered that *ISAD(G)* is the actual archival description standard, i.e., the standard that gives structure to descriptions, whereas EAD is mainly an encoding technique, which permits rendering the structure of a finding aid via markup. EAD follows *ISAD(G)* quite closely. These two standards have different roles and complement each other; ideally, they should be reconciled.

A Prerequisite: Standardization of the Level Attribute

The EAD DTD gives a closed list of values for the optional level attribute: fonds, series, etc. The value "otherlevel" allows the introduction of a new value, by means of another attribute, otherlevel (for example, <c level = "otherlevel" otherlevel = "sub-sub-fonds">).

We decided, even if it is not required by the DTD, to systematically give a value to the Otherlevel attribute. From the various cases we met in the finding aids, we established a list (shown in Table 1), in order to make sure that we would all use the same terms.

Physical Preparation of the Finding Aids for Conversion

Is a finding aid ever completed? The answer is probably no, if one looks at the number of annotations that archivists, in the course of the years, add to printed or typewritten finding aids when they discover, for instance while arranging other fonds, materials to be returned to their proper place. Unfortunately, these handwritten annotations (such as added shelfmarks with "bis," "ter," "quater" in total contradiction with numbering rules, or supplementary scope and content information) are unlikely to be present on all existing copies of a given finding aid.

It is therefore absolutely necessary, before encoding, to compare and correct all the copies, in order to obtain the most complete copy of a finding aid. In the case of outsourcing, it is much preferable for the vendor and the institution to have identical copies. Such work is time-consuming and tedious, but it avoids many an unpleasant surprise later. Finally, it is good to keep in mind that, contrary to conventional wisdom, the copy available for users in the reading room is not always the most accurate.

TABLE 1. Archives des Pyrénées-Atlantiques: Levels of Description

Values of the «level» attribute	Levels in the «otherlevel» attribute
	Group of-fonds
Fonds	
Sub-fonds	
	Sub-sub-fonds
	Sub-sub-sub-fonds
Series	
Sub-series	
	Sub-sub-series
	Sub-sub-sub-series
	Sub-sub-sub-sub-series
File	

Intellectual Preparation of the Finding Aids and Control of the Encoding

For each inventory or register, individual encoding specifications were elaborated and sent to ArchProteus. They dealt with:

- The structuring of the inventory and assigning attributes for each descriptive level.
- Defining the appropriate EAD tags to be used for the various parts of the introduction, the appendices, and the footnotes.

More details on the problems met with are given below.

Such preparatory work requires an in-depth study of each finding aid–and it goes without saying that giving structure to and marking up a nineteenth-century inventory, for instance, according to current international standards is not exactly an easy task. However, it greatly facilitated the quality control of the encoding undertaken by the team as soon as ArchProteus sent back the encoded files. Such quality control too can take an extremely long time for large finding aids, if only because of the time needed for proofreading. In such cases the specifications proved particularly helpful. We will come back below to the thorny question of the control of the indexes.

In terms of workflow, there is yet another factor to consider. The nineteenth-century published finding aids have been completely rekeyed by ArchProteus in Microsoft Word format, and our team had to proofread the files before their encoding. Reading several thousands of pages of word-processed text and comparing them to the original amounts to whole days of full-time work for several members of staff. This time must be taken into account when figuring out the time needed for quality control.

THE DIFFICULTIES OF RETROSPECTIVE CONVERSION

One of the first difficulties of retrospective conversion resides in freeing oneself from the paper finding aid, as a material object, in order to conceive of a totally renewed access tool, sometimes even a transformed one, and to accomplish this without any alteration of the entries themselves. Here the stumbling block does not spring from the EAD DTD itself, nor from the quality of the paper finding aid, but rather from the necessary mutation of the archivist's mindset, or, more exactly, from his or her ability to envision a different approach to archival description. Retrospective conversion provides the opportunity to give back full archival value to the series and the fonds they contain, even if the encoding is necessarily based on paper finding aids. These finding aids become only partial documents that must be left behind, as they stop being the definitive reference tool they used to be. Several concrete examples will illustrate this idea.

Decisions on Structure

It was decided not to encode each finding aid separately, but to choose the series (as defined in the official filing plan) as the highest level. Each series was considered to be a "group of fonds." A consequence of this decision was that we sometimes encoded as one digital finding aid all the finding aids that referred to the same series, as illustrated in Table 2.

Giving Structure to the Finding Aids Relative to the Same Series . . .

Choosing the official series as the highest level of encoding is not a problem in itself. However, it means that it is necessary in some cases to

TABLE 2. Archives des Pyrénées-Atlantiques: Examples of Encoding from the Highest Level

Series as defined in the official filing plan	Levels of description
Series J (private fonds)	«group of fonds»
Sub-series 1J (single items and small fonds)	«records group»
Sub-series 2J (fonds Batcave) Sub-series 83J (fonds of the Fédération française de pelote basque) Etc.	«fonds» «fonds»
Series E deposit (town and city archives deposited)	«group of fonds»
Archives of a town	«fonds»
Series U (judiciary archives from 1800 to 1940)	«group of fonds»
1U1-1U35 Fonds of the Préfecture	«fonds»
2U1-2U1899 Fonds of the Court of Appeal and of the Criminal Court	«fonds»
2U1-251 General prosecution	«sub-fonds»
2U252-511 Chamber of accusation Etc.	«sub-fonds»

merge several finding aids relating to the same series. One particular example may be examined, the series IIIE (fonds of the notarial archives).

In Pyrénées-Atlantiques, all notarial records dating back more than a hundred years are kept at the Archives Départementales. They were collected over several decades, and as a result there are three paper finding aids, respectively dated 1944, 1950 and 2000. Consequently, records from the same city, the same notary office, or even the same notary, might be found in all three finding aids. In the current situation users obviously need to exert ingenuity and the conversion can create, therefore, great added value. In order to prepare the work for ArchProteus, it was necessary to provide them with a structured list of notaries, arranged by city, and then by office. We had to use caution as it is not always possible to establish a certain link between a notary and an office in Old Regime records, and we did not have enough time to research in detail the genealogy of the offices.

An example of structure for the notaries from Anglet, whose records are described in the inventories of 1950 and 2000, as shown by the differences in shelfmarks is shown in Table 3.

. . . to the Presentation of the Fonds . . .

Series B (courts and jurisdictions of the Old Regime) offered different challenges. The three paper finding aids that describe it were written

TABLE 3. Archives des Pyrénées-Atlantiques: Structure of the Fonds of the Anglet Notaries

Official series	Levels of description
Série IIIE Fonds of notaries	«group of fonds«
Notaries of Pyrénées-Atlantiques	«fonds«
IIIE4722-4756, IIIE18278-18324 Notaries of Anglet	«sub-fonds«
IIIE4722-4756, IIIE18278-18324 Etude I Study I or office I?	«sub-sub-fonds«
IIIE4722-4726 Notaire Dhiriart (Pierre)	«sub-sub-sub-fonds«
IIIE4727-4737, IIIE18278 Notaire Darancette (?)	«sub-sub-sub-fonds«
IIIE4738-4756, IIIE18279-18289 Notaire Dhiriart (Pierre-Florentin) Etc.	«sub-sub-sub-fonds«
Notaries of other départements	«fonds«

in 1863, 1876 and 1980. The most recent one describes materials "discovered" in the twentieth century, which sometimes complete collections previously described. The main difficulty in this case, however, was not the fusion of the finding aids. We were mostly pondering whether we should revise the work of our predecessors and opt for a completely different organization of the information.

The nineteenth-century archivist had included with the fonds of the Parliament of Navarre other fonds, and subsequently the whole was wrongly designed as the fonds of the Parliament of Navarre. But is this structure, though familiar to historians and users, valid from an archival point of view? We decided, even if it would force a change of habits for regular users, to modify the structure of the finding aid, and to render unto Caesar that which is Caesar's. We reduced the fonds of the Parliament of Navarre to its real content and gave back to the various fonds that had been attached to it by the nineteenth-century finding aids their own archival existence. They were presented as fonds, and no longer as sub-fonds of the Parliament of Navarre.

. . . and Sometimes to the Shelfmarks

We met with another problem, especially in the series B and E (family titles in the Old Regime). Within the fonds, the nineteenth-century archivist had sometimes described materials, and assigned them shelfmarks, almost in the order he found them, without any attempt to organize them according to their type. We had to reconstruct the series by type, even if the shelfmarks were not in consecutive order. For instance, in series E:

- E13-E236: Titles of the Albret family
- E13-E16, E100, E236: inventory of archives and titles
- E17-57, E59, E61-99, E101-235: titles of the Albret family
- E58, E60: inventories of furniture

Other Problems, Besides the Structure of the Finding Aids

Introductions

In theory, every introduction to a finding aid should follow *ISAD(G)*'s rules. In practice, we did not revise the introductions, except for series B, because it would have required too much work. We will consider doing it later, but it is questionable whether introductions as complete–and as complex–as required by *ISAD(G)* are really relevant for an online publication directed to a large audience. We will come back to this question below.

Footnotes

Even if footnotes have meaning only on paper, the information they contain is far from worthless. In an encoded version they need to be included in a new context, i.e., to be marked up as appropriate elements of the EAD DTD, by avoiding as much as possible turning them systematically into <note> tags. This decision led us to sometimes dismember a footnote into two or three tags. Here is one example of many, chosen from the series of notary records. One can read in a footnote:

> Master Tisset transferred his office to Biarritz in May 1870. The Anglet office was closed. Registers kept under shelfmarks 8U28-39.

The first two sentences were tagged as Biography or History (<bioghist>) and the third one as Separated Material (<separatedmaterial>).

It is not always possible to split notes in this way, especially for footnotes within introductions. ArchProteus suggested simple solutions, such as:

- bringing the footnotes back inside the text and inserting them where they are called for, so that their order and their intelligibility are preserved
- gathering them at the end of the text, with hyperlinks
- displaying them in a balloon that opens when the cursor passes on the reference point.

Indexes

Last, but not least, the indexes presented the most complex problems, which may even perhaps be impossible to solve within our time limits.

The main reason for this is a change of role. In traditional finding aids, indexes are more than simple alphabetical lists: they present the users with a different approach to the documentary corpus available for them. This is why index entries often come with additional information, such as dates, qualifications, secondary entries, “see” and “see also” cross-references, etc. However, in the EAD DTD, the main job of indexes is to provide search engines with the means of building their own internal indexes. In this context the additional information so plentiful in paper indexes becomes superfluous, even unhelpful.

In fact EAD gives the option of encoding indexes either on their own as a whole, like in the paper version (with hyperlinks pointing towards the relevant descriptive units), or by distributing the entries in Controlled Access Headings (<controlaccess>) within the appropriate Components (<c>). In the latter case, a further option is to use a stylesheet to prevent the display of the Controlled Access Headings.

Whichever option is chosen, encoding is relatively simple if the paper index is sufficiently standardized. In Pyrénées-Atlantiques, we opted for distribution, at least insofar as that was possible. In the context of retrospective conversion, many difficulties arise. Let us take, for example, the subseries 1J (discrete items and small fonds of private records). There are four finding aids for this subseries. Their indexes contain many "see" cross-references to other entries, such as: "Shooting, *see* Sports associations"; one must then refer to the entry "Sports associations," which offers about ten secondary entries, in order to determine which descriptive unit should be indexed under "Shooting," and then establish a link between that unit and the entry "Shooting" in the digital index. Repeating that operation for an index of 300 or 400 pages obviously makes for a particularly tedious and excessively time-consuming task, impossible to achieve within our time-limits.

We have also given up on the encoding of the indexes of series B and E that had been established in the 1950s and amount to almost 2,500 typewritten pages. For series E alone, ArchProteus counted in the three volumes of indexes 65,500 entries, without any typographical distinction that would enable distinguishing between subjects, geographical names, and personal names, and without any standardization. For instance, the word "chevalier" (knight) appears 276 times. ArchProteus has tried to standardize all the entries, but the repository staff would have to check them all and make them compliant with the *International Standard Archival Authority Record for Corporate Bodies, Persons and Families* (*ISAAR(CPF)*)[4] and Encoded Archival Context (EAC). We just can't engage in such work at this point; for the time being, we will rely on hypertext searching, even if we are aware that it is not the most satisfying option for our users.

At least we can console ourselves by noting that one especially thorny problem was spared to Pyrénées-Atlantiques and that is paper indexes that refer to page numbers instead of shelfmarks.

The unresolved indexes problem, however, should not darken the picture. In general we have experienced the flexibility of the EAD DTD, and its capability of adjusting to all existing types of finding aids. All the information contained in the finding aids was restructured and encoded in appropriate EAD tags. But that does not mean that the work is finished: deciding to encode, whether it is a retrospective conversion or not, leads to the consideration of questions that go far beyond markup techniques.

QUESTIONS FOR THE FUTURE

The few questions that follow are not an exhaustive list. They can be gathered under three headings, for the short, middle and long terms.

Publishing the Encoded Finding Aids

Encoding is but the first step towards making finding aids available online for users; though fundamental, it remains purely technical. We are currently assessing the various technical approaches that would allow us to publish our corpus of finding aids, now that they are renovated in form as well as in content. But while we are trying to decide which software, open-source or not, we will use for publication, we also need to think about specific questions, such as the presentation of the encoded finding aids, and particularly the standardization of their indexes. Our thinking takes place in the larger context of the automation of our institution and the diffusion of digital images of archival materials, since the goal of the Conseil Général of Pyrénées-Atlantiques is to give public access to a corpus of digital facsimiles, through Internet, Extranet or Intranet.

Producing New Finding Aids

We need to find out how we will move from retrospective conversion of old finding aids to in-house production of new encoded finding aids, ready to be published online. The senior staff of our institution have acquired valuable experience that needs to be transmitted to all the staff members involved in arrangement and description.

But what exactly should be transmitted? Should it not be first of all the knowledge of *ISAD(G)* and its principles of structure, rather than knowledge of the EAD DTD? In the future, should every staff member produce EAD encoded finding aids, and, therefore, have on his or her computer specific editing software, like XMetaL? In the case of Archives départementales, is it really necessary, when several of the commercially available archives management systems in France offer an option for database export to EAD? The main issue would then be to verify that the said databases are structured in compliance with *ISAD(G)* and that the export in EAD works well.

Therefore, is it not enough to simply introduce the staff to EAD, as part of their general culture in archival science, and to focus the training on one or two staff members who could provide an expert resource, and edit all finding aids prior to their publication online?

The Archives Départementales of Pyrénées-Atlantiques will move to automation in the near future. As a consequence the work procedures will change, notably the mode of production of finding aids. At this point, the questions regarding production of encoded finding aids and the related workflow are crucial.

Establishing a New Relationship with the Users?

Encoding finding aids leads us to reconsider, in a larger perspective, the way we publish information for our regular users. Is it still necessary to publish in a printed format finding aids that are available online? True, all users are not yet connected to the Internet from their homes. But shouldn't we try to convert to EAD Word files, when they exist, rather than bringing them to the print shop? From a financial point of view, and regarding our relationship with our supervising body, i.e., the *Conseil Général*, such an alternative is not neutral and deserves consideration.

In the coming years, we will probably witness a complete change in our relationship with the public, through the online publication of structured and indexed finding aids. For a long time, archivists wrote finding aids in order to, first, achieve intellectual and physical control of the fonds and collections they managed, and second, to fulfill the needs of other information and research specialists. During recent decades, the growing taste for genealogy has already brought us to adjust our relationship with users, since we needed to facilitate access to collections for new, "uninformed" users. Online publication of finding aids will open another new era, which will have a double effect. First, our audience will become larger and include "non-specialists" who until then did not even suspect the existence of archival repositories and of archival resources. Second, archivists will no longer be able to help lost users to focus their search as they currently do in the reading room. Our audience will be wider, but also more distant, and it might very well be baffled by the sheer mass of available information.

This double effect must initiate reflection on the form, and perhaps also the content, of finding aids, so that we can make them intelligible to a totally novice audience, for whom the notions of fonds and series mean absolutely nothing. This is not about giving up arrangement and presentation of fonds according to official filing plans, especially since their indexing will improve access. But that presentation works in a way as an expert search mode and certainly not something to be dismissed, since an archivist's primary mission remains to arrange and inventory the collections he or she is responsible for. However, shouldn't we also think about a simplified search mode that would give the neophyte Internet user in archives the desire to go deeper? Such a mode remains to be imagined. Is it enough to create value-enhancing products by putting together bodies of digital facsimiles? Or is it necessary to elaborate specific tools to help online searching, based on finding aids? May we even imagine virtual workshops for introducing users to research, inspired by the real workshops that are conducted in several archival repositories?

Online publication of EAD encoded finding aids allows us to attract new users, and to introduce them to the civic and cultural dimensions of archives. But to achieve this we must learn, for transparency's sake, to modify our technical language and the ways we distribute information, in order to transmit our knowledge to the great majority of people.

AUTHORS' NOTES

Anne Goulet is Conservateur du Patrimoine. She was Head of Archives Départementales des Deux-Sèvres from 1989 to 1994, before taking charge of the archives of the Paris Chamber of commerce and industry (1994-1998) and afterwards holding the position of Counselor for Archives, Direction régionale des Affaires culturelles d'Ile-de-France (1998-2003). She is now Head of Archives Départementales des Pyrénées-Atlantiques.

Nicolas Maftei is a Computer Scientist, who in 1992, after a long career with IBM in France and Canada, founded his own consulting company, ArchProteus, specializing in products and services for archives. As an expert in the conception of archives management systems compliant with established descriptive standards and in automatic encoding in XML-EAD, he teaches a course in automation at the School of Library, Archival and Information Studies at the University of British Columbia (UBC).

NOTES

1. In France, a "*département*" is an administrative subdivision; there are ninety-five of them. Each "*département*" is run by an elected council, the "*Conseil Général*." All public archives of a "*département*" find their way to an archival repository, the Archives départementales, directly funded by the *Conseil Général* but placed under the scientific control of the Direction des Archives de France.

2. The official filing plan of all Archives Départementales in France gathers the fonds, groups of fonds and subdivisions of fonds within a system of "series" named by letters of the alphabet.

3. International Council on Archives, *ISAD(G): General International Standard Archival Description*, 2nd edition (Ottawa, 2000) is available at http://www.ica.org/biblio/isad_g_2e.pdf.

4. International Council on Archives, *ISAAR(CPF): International Standard Archival Authority Record for Corporate Bodies, Persons and Families* (2004) is available at http://www.ica.org/biblio.php?pdocid=144.

EAD in the Department of Special Collections and Western Manuscripts at the Bodleian Library, United Kingdom

Mike Webb

SUMMARY. The strategy for conversion to electronic cataloguing of western manuscripts in the Bodleian Library has been to a large extent determined by circumstances–the size and variety of the manuscript collections, the existence of detailed published catalogues for the earlier collections, the availability of funds for specific purposes, and, above all, by the increasing demand of scholars worldwide for online catalogues. From 1996, we began to investigate options for the conversion of our catalogues to electronic form. We were advised to look at EAD by the New Media Librarian in the Bodleian. It soon became apparent that EAD provided the flexibility needed to handle the great variety of manuscripts in the Library's collections. It also seemed to be sustainable and relatively cheap to implement, and excellent documentation was available from the United States. The adoption of EAD as the cataloguing system in Western Manuscripts was largely driven by the funds made available for retrospective conversion through the Research Libraries Group. This diverted our main efforts away from current cataloguing initially. However, the need to analyze our existing catalogues to provide instructions for data converters has had an enormous impact on cur-

---

Mike Webb is Assistant Librarian, Department of Special Collections and Western Manuscripts, Bodleian Library, Oxford, UK (E-mail: mnw@bodley.ox.ac.uk).

[Haworth co-indexing entry note]: "EAD in the Department of Special Collections and Western Manuscripts at the Bodleian Library, United Kingdom." Webb, Mike. Co-published simultaneously in *Journal of Archival Organization* (The Haworth Information Press, an imprint of The Haworth Press, Inc.) Vol. 3, No. 2/3, 2005, pp. 55-69; and: *Encoding Across Frontiers: Proceedings of the European Conference on Encoded Archival Description and Context (EAD and EAC), Paris, France, 7-8 October 2004* (ed: Bill Stockting, and Fabienne Queyroux) The Haworth Information Press, an imprint of The Haworth Press, Inc., 2005, pp. 55-69. Single or multiple copies of this article are available for a fee from The Haworth Document Delivery Service [1-800-HAWORTH, 9:00 a.m. - 5:00 p.m. (EST). E-mail address: docdelivery@haworthpress.com].

Available online at http://www.haworthpress.com/web/JAO

doi:10.1300/J201v03n02_05

rent cataloguing practice in our department. Our choice of EAD for our electronic catalogues has been vindicated by its increasing use worldwide, and the numerous opportunities that have arisen for cooperative ventures founded on the use of EAD. Contributing to the Archives Hub in the United Kingdom has enabled us to create the first ever overview of the Bodleian's western manuscript collections. We are now also contributing our first detailed EAD catalogue to the Access to Archives (A2A) database. The adoption of EAD for cataloguing medieval manuscripts was unusual, but has created the essential building block for the extension of these descriptions using other XML schema now being adopted by cataloguers of medieval manuscripts.

KEYWORDS. Bodleian Library: University of Oxford, EAD, Encoded Archival Description, finding aids, retrospective conversion, standardization

BACKGROUND

The Bodleian Library has accumulated manuscripts for over 400 years, ranging in date from the fourth century BC to the present day. Our manuscript collection is a hybrid, consisting of large numbers of older individual manuscripts, mostly in codex form, together with a growing number of collections of modern papers, each of which might be defined as an archive in its own right.

Traditionally, catalogues of Bodleian manuscripts have been published and made available worldwide in printed form. The nineteenth century quarto catalogues, many in Latin, are in daily use. The most recent catalogue, published in 1991, provided summary descriptions and detailed indexes of post-medieval manuscripts acquired between 1916 and 1975. However, this method of making catalogues available is slow and expensive. The published catalogues conform to an in-house Bodleian standard for description and indexing, not compatible with national and international standards. Catalogues of manuscripts acquired after 1975 remain in typescript form and it might have been many years before they were published.

The lack of resources, the increasing demands of readers for online access to descriptions, and developments in the archival community emphasizing automation, collaboration and interoperability (and the availability of public funds to carry out such projects) led to the decision in 1996 to investigate the possibilities of converting to electronic cataloguing. Having investigated several database options, it became clear that Encoded Archival Description (EAD) offered an excellent solution to the needs of our manuscript collections: it offered independence of proprietary software (one or two commercial packages in use in the British archival community had hit difficulties at this time); it had the flexibility needed to deal with the great range of collections held in the Bodleian; it seemed to be taking hold in the United States as an effective means of implementing cataloguing rules and standards; the Bodleian had in-house expertise in markup languages (in particular, Richard Gartner, our New Media Librarian, had investigated EAD); excellent documentation was available from the United States in the form of the EAD Tag Library and the Research Libraries Group's Best Practice Guidelines; and the necessary software for implementation was relatively cheap.

THE IMPACT OF EAD

The decision to adopt EAD was really made for us in the end, because funds were made available to convert unpublished catalogues to EAD by the Gladys Krieble Foundation, under the auspices of the Research Libraries Group (RLG). This has also meant the concentration of our initial efforts on retrospective conversion rather than current cataloguing. Although our inclination had been to concentrate on current cataloguing, the importance of the inherited collections and the demand from scholars for remote access to the printed and typescript catalogues, combined with the need to demonstrate results to funding bodies (and to our colleagues in Oxford) forced us to focus our effort on the conversion of existing catalogues into electronic format.

However, the impact on current cataloguing practice was immense. We were immediately confronted with the need for recognised standards of description for the purposes of interoperability, since the resulting EAD catalogues were going to be made available through two very different systems: the RLG's portal, 'Archival Resources,' and our own Web site.

Unpublished typescript catalogues were sent to APEX, a data conversion company in the United States recommended by RLG. The pilot was not a great success because, rather naïvely, we sent two catalogues with no instructions as to the function of the layout and structure of the text. The result was unusable, but we learned two very important things. Firstly, that the structure and layout of a finding aid has an implicit meaning which we needed to make explicit for conversion to be successful. The function of text, the level of description, the relationship of components in a hierarchy were all implied simply by means of font sizes and indentation in the printed catalogues, as seen in the example of the *Summary Catalogue* description of the Carte MSS in Figure 1.[1]

Secondly, we could see that the efforts of the data conversion company were very good indeed considering the lack of instruction. When we sent a further batch of catalogues to APEX we provided much more detailed instructions about the function of the text and its relationship to an EAD schema. The experience did not, however, merely allow us to formulate better instructions for the data converters; it led to a review of cataloguing practice, from which new cataloguing rules were drawn up

FIGURE 1. *Summary Catalogue* description of the Carte MSS

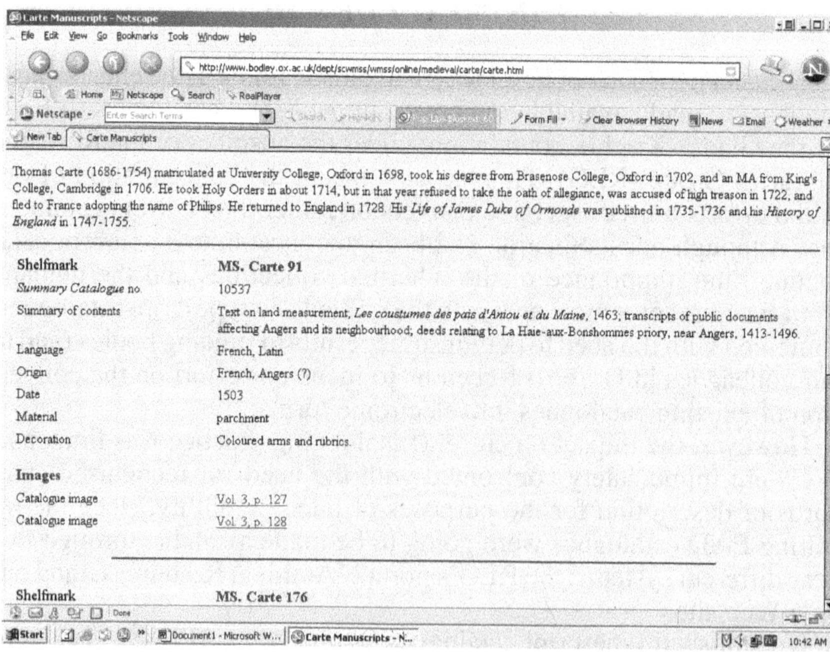

for Western MSS., with much more awareness of the way information can be presented and understood in an electronic environment. In the past the Bodleian had perhaps relied on the richness of its collections and its status as a premier university library and had done things its own way, but the world has changed immensely, and the expectations of our users, academics and others, have changed with it.

One example of the kind of change implemented was the abandonment of the back-of-the-book index, very much a publishing convention. EAD allowed the markup of names, for example, anywhere in the text, so now it made no sense to put all index terms at the end of the finding aid when they could be included as part of the description of components. In effect, this meant the abandonment of summary cataloguing, where most of the detail was in the index. This can be seen from a comparison of an early conversion, the catalogue of the Kimberley papers,[2] with a catalogue using current practice, the catalogue of the Giles papers (see Figures 2 and 3).[3]

FIGURE 2. Catalogue of the Kimberley Papers

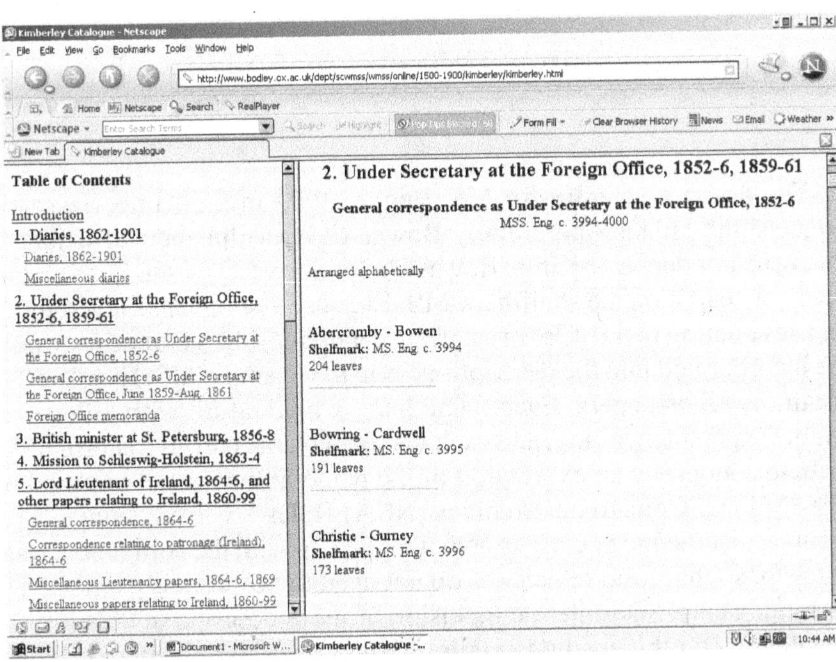

FIGURE 3. Catalogue of the Giles Papers

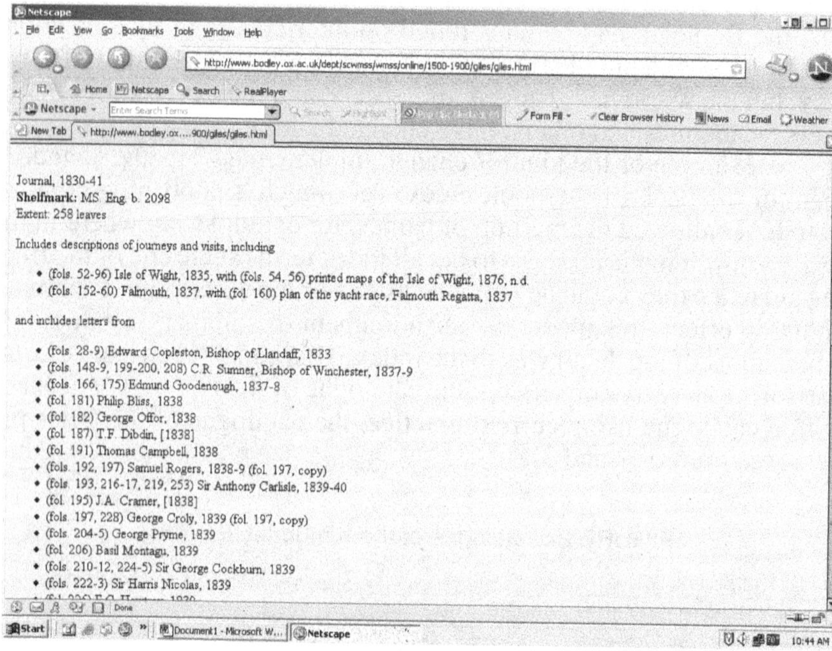

Journal, 1830-41
Shelfmark: MS. Eng. b. 2098
Extent: 258 leaves

Includes descriptions of journeys and visits, including

- (fols. 52-96) Isle of Wight, 1835, with (fols. 54, 56) printed maps of the Isle of Wight, 1876, n.d.
- (fols. 152-60) Falmouth, 1837, with (fol. 160) plan of the yacht race, Falmouth Regatta, 1837

and includes letters from

- (fols. 28-9) Edward Copleston, Bishop of Llandaff, 1833
- (fols. 148-9, 199-200, 208) C.R. Sumner, Bishop of Winchester, 1837-9
- (fols. 166, 175) Edmund Goodenough, 1837-8
- (fol. 181) Philip Bliss, 1838
- (fol. 182) George Offor, 1838
- (fol. 187) T.F. Dibdin, [1838]
- (fol. 191) Thomas Campbell, 1838
- (fols. 192, 197) Samuel Rogers, 1838-9 (fol. 197, copy)
- (fols. 193, 216-17, 219, 253) Sir Anthony Carlisle, 1839-40
- (fol. 195) J.A. Cramer, [1838]
- (fols. 197, 228) George Croly, 1839 (fol. 197, copy)
- (fols. 204-5) George Pryme, 1839
- (fol. 206) Basil Montagu, 1839
- (fols. 210-12, 224-5) Sir George Cockburn, 1839
- (fols. 222-3) Sir Harris Nicolas, 1839

The descriptive entry for MS. Eng. c. 3994 in the Kimberley catalogue simply reads Abercromby-Bowen (it is an alphabetical sequence of correspondence of Kimberley as Under Secretary at the Foreign Office). A search on the shelfmark MS. Eng. c. 3994 reveals eleven index entries relating to this file. In a current catalogue, all those entries would be incorporated into the description, as in the example MS. Eng. b. 2098 from the Giles papers. Each name here is marked-up with a Personal Name (<persname>) tag, and each Personal Name carries a 'normal' attribute containing an expression of the name in the format required by the National Council on Archives (NCA) Rules.[4] The advantage is, of course, that the index entry is now wrapped up with the component it relates to, so that folio references do not need to be explicitly attached to the index entry. Despite the inclusion of more descriptive detail in the catalogue that this method entails, it has proven to be a more efficient way of indexing than creating separate index references. If a name occurs several times in a catalogue, it can simply be copied and pasted, together with its 'normal' attribute, into the relevant component.

Other 'summary catalogue' conventions were also abandoned. The need to compress descriptions in a published catalogue led to combined descriptions, and information packed into difficult to read paragraphs. The example of the summary catalogue description of MSS. Carte 87-8 shows the point. In a compressed description such as this, even the essential reference MS. Carte 88 is nowhere stated in full.[5]

All this could be unbundled in an electronic catalogue, and each item given its own electronic identity. We carefully analysed the data structure of our catalogues, and using RLG Best Practice Guidelines as a basis, created an EAD schema to handle the descriptive elements. We have now written in-house rules for cataloguing archival collections in EAD, and for cataloguing single items (see Figure 4).[6] These may seem rather basic concepts, but to an institution with decades of history in

FIGURE 4. Single Item Catalogue Using an EAD Schema

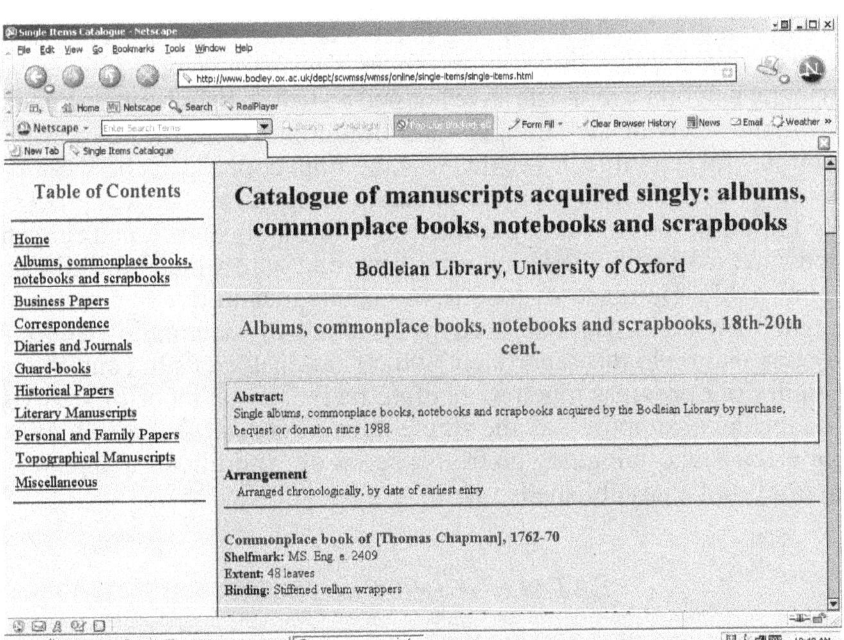

publishing catalogues to precise specifications, these were radical measures.

Before I say a little more about the projects being undertaken in the Western Manuscripts section, I need to emphasize another aspect of our work, which has been crucial in establishing our electronic cataloguing program. This is the allocation of a member of staff, Lawrence Mielniczuk, from SERS (Systems and Electronic Resources Service) to work almost exclusively with Western Manuscripts in the development of a strategy for presenting and maintaining our EAD catalogues. In the past, technical support would be called in when it was deemed to be necessary. The archivist, with little understanding of technical requirements, would all too often ask the wrong questions and have unrealistic expectations. As the systems people had little idea about the needs and conventions of archivists, unworkable solutions were suggested. The employment of dedicated systems support has had an impact well beyond our expectations. Initially, I am sure, we thought that all we needed was someone who had the technical know-how to transform our EAD to HTML for presentation on the World Wide Web and who would be able to design a search interface for our catalogues. In order to achieve this, he or she was going to have to learn about archives, cataloguing conventions, indexing and so on. This has indeed happened, but in many ways the archivists have learned a great deal more about technical matters, about the strengths and limitations of technology. Much more useful than this, however, was the impact of a detached, critical observer on our whole approach to cataloguing. Lawrence was processing large amounts of catalogue data, and constantly questioned conventions that may have made sense in print, and with which we had been comfortable. He made us look at our catalogues in a way a new user might view them. He also brought a culture of systematic electronic documentation to the department, which has enabled us to control, and monitor our progress much more effectively. This alliance of archivist and technical support was the single most important factor in moving our electronic cataloguing on from a series of experiments to a planned strategy and an established system.

CATALOGUING PROJECTS

Our choice of EAD for our electronic catalogues has been vindicated by its increasing use worldwide, and the numerous opportunities that have arisen for national co-operative ventures founded on the use of EAD. Contributing to the Archives Hub[7] in the United Kingdom has enabled us to create the first ever overview of the Bodleian's Western Manuscript collections, and is also the first step towards creating a similar overview of manuscript collections throughout the Oxford University Library Service. We are now also contributing our first detailed EAD catalogue to the Access to Archives (A2A) database,[8] enabling us, in collaboration with the History of Parliament Trust, to convert to EAD a calendar of very important seventeenth-century state papers hitherto only available in manuscript form in the library. The adoption of EAD for cataloguing medieval manuscripts was unusual, but has created the essential building block for the extension of these descriptions using other XML schema now being adopted by cataloguers of medieval manuscripts.

In using EAD for medieval manuscript descriptions, the Bodleian Library was, and perhaps still is, alone. With the help of a grant from the Getty Foundation in Los Angeles, the Quarto and Summary catalogues, compiled and published in the nineteenth and twentieth centuries, which contain descriptions of the vast majority of our medieval and early modern manuscripts, have been digitally scanned, so that images of the 'official' published descriptions can be presented on the Web, together with new skeletal EAD records. These minimal records contain information on shelfmark, textual contents, date, language, material, origin and illumination. To these records have been added images of the *Summary Catalogue* entries for each manuscript; selected digital images of the manuscripts themselves, scanned from our large stock of 35mm colour slides and filmstrips; and lists of bibliographical references to each manuscript, converted from a card index and from electronic files maintained in the department.

We are now in a position to begin the enhancement of this skeletal EAD catalogue. For the near future this will mean inputting more up-to-date information about the manuscripts into the catalogue, and the availability of funding has already allowed for a project to enhance the descriptions of Italian and English illuminated manuscripts. There is also a small-scale project to provide more full descriptions of German language manuscripts. This has been made possible by the generous help of the Professor of German Medieval Studies in Oxford University who has located external expertise to carry out the work.

In the long term it may be that our EAD descriptions of medieval manuscripts will be converted to another markup format more appropriate for extended descriptions. The Master Project at De Montfort University and the TEI Medieval Manuscripts Description Work Group (TEI MMSS) have been working on TEI schema for some years, and we expect an agreed TEI schema to emerge in the course of the next few months.[9] While we were always aware of this work going on, the need to produce relatively quick results led to the decision to adopt EAD for medieval manuscript descriptions at a time when a public version of the EAD DTD was already available. We were very much aware that by adopting a markup formula any necessary conversion or migration of records would be made simpler. We may indeed choose to preserve the skeletal EAD records and link them to extended TEI descriptions, and work on METS (Metadata Encoding and Transmission Standard) in Oxford may well provide the architecture for such a strategy. METS is a newly emergent standard designed to encode metadata for electronic texts, still images, digitized video, sound files and other digital materials.[10] Written in XML schema, METS offers an overall structure for encoding all relevant types of metadata used to describe digital library objects. In the medieval manuscripts context, this might mean the EAD and TEI catalogues, and digital images of the manuscripts themselves.

I have already referred to the complexity and variety of the existing catalogues of western manuscripts. It has always been very difficult for new readers to gain an overview of the kind of collections we have. The establishment of the Archives Hub, a national gateway to descriptions of archives in UK universities and colleges, has given us an excellent opportunity to create collection-level descriptions of all our holdings. As the data is created using EAD, the records can be reused on our own Web site, and it is our intention to make the collection-level records the first port of call on the online catalogues page, linking to extended descriptions as and when these become available. At present we have more than 1,500 such descriptions available on the Hub.

We took a very pragmatic approach, initially designating collections as anything comprising four separate items. There was little science behind this decision, but as is so often the case, the time and money allocated to the project by the JISC (Joint Information Systems Committee) dictated the timescale and scope of the project. A subsequent round of funding has enabled us to redefine a collection as anything comprising more than one item, and so thanks to the Archives Hub we will, by the end of the year, have a collection-level record for almost all manuscripts in published and unpublished catalogues, other than single items, acquired since our foundation in 1598. The funding for this year has also allowed us to include collection-level descriptions of manuscripts in other Bodleian sections such as Maps, Music and Oriental manuscripts;

and in other specialist Oxford University libraries such as the Plant Sciences, and English Faculty libraries.

A very important aspect of the creation of descriptions for the Hub is the inclusion of collection-level index terms according to national and international standards. Before the advent of electronic cataloguing, we used in-house indexing standards. The style can be seen in the online catalogues with back-of-the-book indexes. The Hub requires collection-level index entries to be compiled according to the UNESCO Thesaurus,[11] the NCA or the Library of Congress Subject Headings. We had already made the decision to use NCA Rules for personal, place and corporate names in our current catalogues in order to comply with national archival standards; and, in line with Oxford University printed book cataloguing, to use Library of Congress Subject Headings (LCSH) for subject indexing. The work of compiling collection-level index terms for the Archives Hub has allowed us to incorporate these index entries retrospectively into our earlier catalogues as they go online, as for example in the catalogue of the papers of Sir Edmund Monson, British representative in Paris at the time of the *Entente Cordiale*, whose hundredth anniversary we are celebrating this year (see Figure 5).[12]

Outside factors have driven our first contribution to the A2A database. This time we were approached by the History of Parliament Trust who wanted to create an electronic version of a calendar of seventeenth-century state papers (the Carte Papers) available only in the Bodleian Library in the form of seventy-five manuscript volumes written in the nineteenth century. They needed the data for their own publication programme, and we wished to create a catalogue compatible with our electronic cataloguing strategy. It soon became apparent that if we were able to submit an EAD version of the calendar to A2A, we might secure funding from the Heritage Lottery Fund (HLF), which has supported other A2A projects, knowing this to be a tried and trusted method of delivering vast ranges of information about archives to new audiences. The HLF is very keen to encourage new users in all areas of British cultural life, and for an institution with an academic raison d'être such as ours, the application for a grant was a challenging experience, making us think of the ways in which our collections might be used other than by academics. The Carte papers mainly relate to seventeenth-century Ireland, and we made a strong case for providing access for the Irish diaspora in Britain to perhaps the most significant collection of papers relating to Stuart Ireland, a crucial period in the formation of that country. In particular, the numerous petitions to the Lord Lieu-

FIGURE 5. Collection-Level Index Terms in the Catalogue of the Sir Edmund Monson Papers

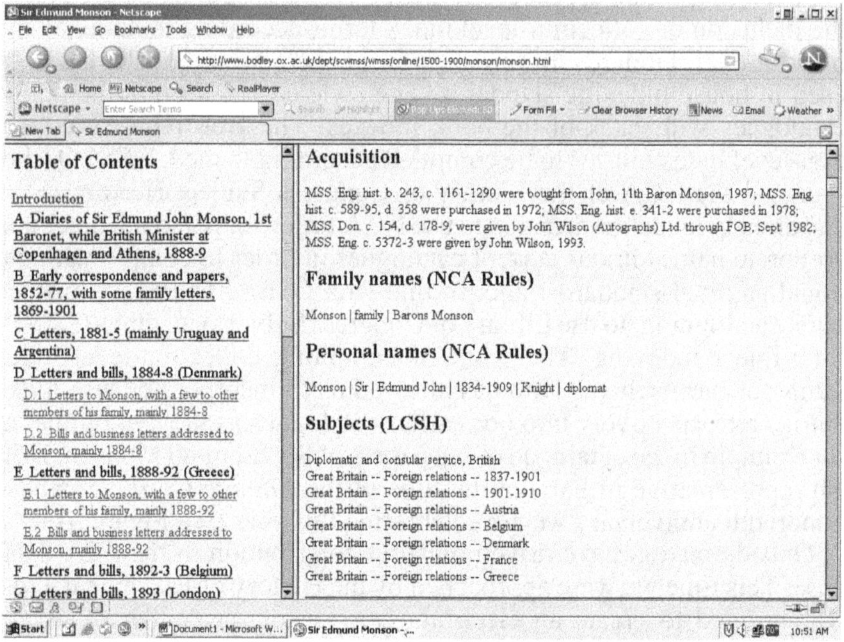

tenant, the Duke of Ormonde, form a very rich source for social and family history.

So now we are pushing EAD in another new direction, using a template based on the requirements of the A2A database to encode detailed descriptions and abstracts of each document in the Carte collection for the period 1660 to 1688, some 17,000 pages (see Figure 6). It is intended to submit this to A2A by the spring of 2005.[13]

CONCLUSION

I would like to emphasise that the route we have taken in the Bodleian has been to a large extent determined by circumstances–the size and variety of the manuscript collections, the existence of detailed published catalogues for the earlier collections, the availability of funds for specific purposes, and, above all, by the increasing demand of scholars

FIGURE 6. Description of Documents in the Carte Collection, 1660 to 1688

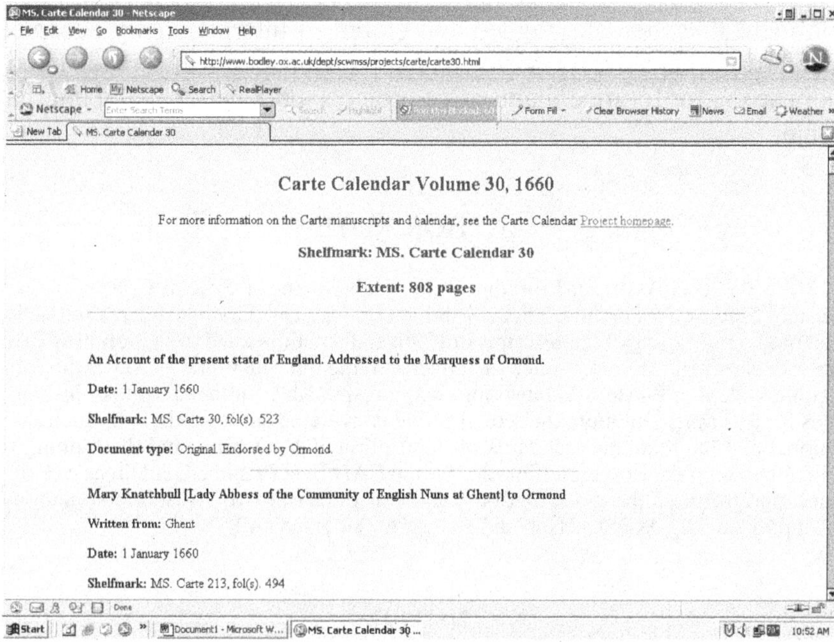

worldwide for online catalogues. Progress has been slow, partly because for several years we have had to rely on the efforts of existing curatorial staff, who have been able to devote only a part of their time to cataloguing development. We have been greatly assisted by grants from a number of funding councils and foundations. Reliance on outside grants has necessarily influenced the direction we have taken, but with EAD as the keystone of our cataloguing strategy we have been able to keep a unified structure for a variety of projects. As well as using EAD for the cataloguing of archival collections and single items, we have applied it to create skeletal records of medieval manuscripts; collection-level descriptions; and extended descriptions of individual papers. Where we are still behind is in the delivery of these materials, for although our electronic catalogues are available over the Internet, at present we can only offer basic searches of the HTML pages, and we are currently investigating the possibilities offered by document management systems. In the context of library integration in Oxford, this may well be something that has to be considered across the Oxford University Libraries Service rather than by individual departments, but we are confident that the data, tagged and stored to internationally accepted standards, is capable of revision and expansion, and will provide maximum scope for future collaborative projects–both national and international.

AUTHOR NOTE

Mike Webb is Assistant Librarian in the Department of Special Collections and Western Manuscripts in the Bodleian Library. He was asked to investigate options for electronic cataloguing of manuscripts in 1996, and recommended the adoption of EAD in the department. Mike has since then overseen the introduction of EAD as the cataloguing system in Western Manuscripts, being responsible for the drafting of in-house rules for its implementation, the retrospective conversion strategy, the introduction of national and international standards of description and indexing, and the training of staff. He was on the Research Libraries Group EAD Best Practice Guidelines working party, and oversees the work of Bodleian contributors to two collaborative national EAD projects, the Archives Hub and Access to Archives (A2A).

NOTES

1. Images of the published catalogue entries for the medieval manuscripts in the Carte collection can be viewed at http://www.bodley.ox.ac.uk/dept/scwmss/wmss/online/medieval/carte/carte.html.

2. The Kimberley papers can be seen at http://www.bodley.ox.ac.uk/dept/scwmss/wmss/online/1500-1900/kimberley/kimberley.html.

3. The Giles papers can be seen at http://www.bodley.ox.ac.uk/dept/scwmss/wmss/online/1500-1900/giles/giles.html.

4. National Council on Archives (NCA), *Rules for the Construction of Personal, Place and Corporate Names (1997)*, which can be found online at http://www.ncaonline.org.uk/materials/rulesfortheconstructionofpersonalplaceandcorporatenames.pdf.

5. See the link to p. 127 of volume 3 of the *Summary Catalogue* in the online catalogue entry for MS. Carte 91 at http://www.bodley.ox.ac.uk/dept/scwmss/wmss/online/medieval/carte/carte.html.

6. The online catalogue of single items is available at http://www.bodley.ox.ac.uk/dept/scwmss/wmss/online/single-items/single-items.html.

7. For further information about the Archives Hub see http://www.archiveshub.ac.uk/.

8. For further information about the Access to Archives (A2A) see http://www.nationalarchives.gov.uk/a2a.

9. Information about the MASTER project and the TEI Medieval Manuscripts description Work group is available at http://xml.coverpages.org/master.html.

10. More information about METS can be found on the Library of Congress Web site at http://www.loc.gov/standards/mets/.

11. UNESCO, *UNESCO Thesaurus: a Structured List of the Descriptors for Indexing and Retrieving Literature in the Fields of Education, Science, Social and Human Science, Culture, Communication and Information* (Paris, 1995).

12. The papers of Sir Edmund Monson can be seen at http://www.bodley.ox.ac.uk/dept/scwmss/wmss/online/1500-1900/monson/monson.html.

13. The results of the Carte A2A project so far can be viewed on the Western Manuscripts projects page at http://www.bodley.ox.ac.uk/dept/scwmss/projects/carte/carte.html.

Professional Training for Encoded Archival Description in Europe

Michael Fox

SUMMARY. This paper represents an abridgement of a panel session that reported on the status of training for archivists in the use of Encoded Archival Description (EAD) in seven countries (France, Germany, Netherlands, Portugal, Switzerland, United Kingdom, and United States). It touched on related archival descriptive standards and practices and associated technological issues. *[Article copies available for a fee from The Haworth Document Delivery Service: 1-800-HAWORTH. E-mail address: <docdelivery@haworthpress.com> Website: <http://www.HaworthPress.com> © 2005 by The Haworth Press, Inc. All rights reserved.]*

KEYWORDS. Archival description, archival instruction, EAD, Encoded Archival Description, professional training, standardization

---

Michael Fox is Director, Library, Publications and Collections Division, Minnesota Historical Society, 345 Kellogg Boulevard West, St. Paul, MN 55102 (E-mail: michael.fox@mnhs.org). A member of the EAD Development Team and the EAD Working Group, he has taught more than sixty EAD sessions in the United States and internationally. He has also been involved in the development of other archival standards including *ISAD(G)*, *ISAAR(CPF)* and *Describing Archives: A Content Standard (DACS)*.

The author, who chaired the panel, prepared this summary paper with considerable assistance from the joint editors.

[Haworth co-indexing entry note]: "Professional Training for Encoded Archival Description in Europe." Fox, Michael. Co-published simultaneously in *Journal of Archival Organization* (The Haworth Information Press, an imprint of The Haworth Press, Inc.) Vol. 3, No. 2/3, 2005, pp. 71-82; and: *Encoding Across Frontiers: Proceedings of the European Conference on Encoded Archival Description and Context (EAD and EAC), Paris, France, 7-8 October 2004* (ed: Bill Stockting, and Fabienne Queyroux) The Haworth Information Press, an imprint of The Haworth Press, Inc., 2005, pp. 71-82. Single or multiple copies of this article are available for a fee from The Haworth Document Delivery Service [1-800-HAWORTH, 9:00 a.m. - 5:00 p.m. (EST). E-mail address: docdelivery@haworthpress.com].

Available online at http://www.haworthpress.com/web/JAO

doi:10.1300/J201v03n02_06

The panel consisted of seven participants: Pierre-Yves Duchemin (France), Frank Bischoff (Germany), Henny Van Schie (Netherlands), José Mariz (Portugal), Jean-Daniel Zeller (Switzerland), Geoffrey Yeo (United Kingdom), and Michael Fox (United States). Though not a member of the panel, conference organizer Claire Sibille (France) graciously submitted additional information after the session on Encoded Archival Description (EAD) training in France. The following text represents an abridgement of the speakers' remarks rather than a verbatim transcription or translation.

PRESENTATIONS FROM THE PANELISTS

The session began with opening statements in which each of the panelists described the nature of training in EAD in their particular national context and their own personal experiences in this regard.

Michael Fox, Minnesota Historical Society, USA

Training in EAD in the United States has expanded and matured considerably since Michael Fox and his colleague Kris Kiesling presented the first EAD workshop in 1996 under the auspices of the Research Libraries Group. They have presented more than sixty workshops on EAD in the U.S. and internationally. In more recent years, an introduction to Extensible Stylesheet Language (XSLT) was added to the curriculum and sponsorship of both offerings has become part of the ongoing educational program of the Society of American Archivists. The audience for these two-day workshops continues to include individuals working both in public archives and with modern manuscript collections. This training focuses on the needs of practicing professionals as they prepare for EAD implementation projects, wish to expand their professional knowledge as part of continuing professional development, or seek to add to their list of professional credentials a skill that is increasingly a prerequisite for archival employment in the United States. A similar set of workshops has been taught for several years through the Rare Book School of the University of Virginia and several EAD implementation projects have carried out training for participants.

The training of new archivists in the U.S., however, occurs principally within the archival education programs in graduate schools of library and information science. While the decentralized nature of archival education in the U.S. means that there is no common curriculum among such programs, the teaching of EAD is widespread and is presented either in the context of archival description, as part of courses that deal with general technology issues, or, and sometimes additionally, in the context of advanced, specialized courses that investigate a variety of more specific topics such as data encoding and communication formats like Text Encoding Initiative (TEI), MARC and Dublin Core.

Henny Van Schie, National Archives, Netherlands

In the Netherlands, EAD is not specifically part of the curriculum of the archival education program of the National Archives school where Henny Van Schie taught from 1974 to 2002. Though the consensus in the Netherlands is that EAD will be the worldwide standard for the exchange of archival descriptive information and its presentation on the Web, EAD itself is seen as a technical tool like database software and is not the subject itself of concentrated training. Rather, Dutch archival education emphasizes the knowledge of and ability to apply standards like the *General International Standard for Archival Description* (*ISAD(G)*) and the *International Archival Authority Record for Corporate Bodies, Persons, and Families* (*ISAAR(CPF)*) as the basis for archival description. Such knowledge is fundamental and separate from its application in formats like Extensible Markup Language (XML) and databases. Conversion of legacy finding aids into EAD is being done by outside technical firms and as a result the average archivist does not feel a need to know the details of EAD.

José Mariz, Institute of the National Archives, Portugal

The implementation of the EAD is just beginning and its use is not widespread in Portugal where José Mariz directs the Departmental Archives of Lisbon, which is directly associated with the National Archives. To date, there has only been one workshop on EAD, organized by the Association of the Librarians, Archivists, and Documentalists, which was held three years ago and taught by Bill Stockting of the (then) Public Record Office. In 2003, the University of Lisbon asked José Mariz to establish a course on EAD within the archives option of the masters program in documentary sciences. This experiment will be extended into 2004/2005 with the participation of new archivists. The leadership of the Institute of the National Archives has also recognized the need to promote awareness of EAD and Encoded Archival Context

(EAC) and included an orientation on EAD in its training program for archivists from the National Archives in November 2004. The Departmental Archives of Lisbon has undertaken a training program for its senior staff with the object of getting descriptions of all fonds online before the end of 2004. In 2005, there will be a workshop for municipal archivists as well, with the aim of creating a consolidated collection guide using EAD.

In Portugal, the diffusion of EAD is occurring in two ways, both of which are essential. On one hand, there is continuing education for those archivists who have graduated, are already on the job, and can apply EAD immediately in their archives. The second approach is to provide additional training for young students of documentary sciences, by integrating EAD and EAC into their training in archival description using *ISAD(G)*.

In both instances, there is an urgent need to have stylesheets that more closely reflect European archival tradition. Archivists also need data-processing tools (flexible, simple to use, and available as free-ware) for the encoding of archival finding aids and for the storage, indexing, and querying of encoded documents, especially in small institutions that do not have many resources. The diffusion of the EAD in Portugal is significant for a number of reasons. The departmental archives form a network that is organically dependent on the national archives which facilitates their work, and they in turn must provide technical support to municipal archives. In addition, Portugal, as a former colonizing country, needs a method for bringing together resources relating to its cultural heritage in African countries where the official language is Portuguese, as well as with Brazil, all countries with which Portugal shares a common history. One can envisage the benefits of being able to consolidate information about the entire cultural patrimony of the Portuguese-speaking world.

Geoffrey Yeo, University College, London, United Kingdom

University College, London, where Geoffrey Yeo directs the masters program in archives and records management, is one of five universities in the United Kingdom that offer advanced degrees in archival science, the entry level qualification for archivists in that country. Approximately thirty students are enrolled each year in this program, both from the U.K. and as part of the school's international program. The curriculum includes seven required modules, one of which covers archival description including EAD in a limited way. For their eighth module, students are allowed to select from among six or seven options for advanced studies in a particular topic, one of which covers EAD. Called "Markup: EAD and TEI," this course covers XML, EAD, and the Text Encoding Initiative (TEI) specification. It is also available as a standalone class for practicing archivists who wish to take it as continuing professional development. Training in EAD is also usually included within the description module of other U.K. university courses in archives. Training in EAD for those already qualified as archivists was originally supplied by the Public Record Office and is now given by the EAD/Data Exchange Group of the Society of Archivists.[1]

Pierre-Yves Duchemin, National School of Library and Information Sciences (ENSSIB), France

The National School of Library and Information Sciences (ENSSIB), where Pierre-Yves Duchemin teaches, provides initial training for librarians and library curators as well as continuing education of library personnel, but does not train archivists. For approximately two years, lectures were presented at the school on several DTDs including EAD and TEI, but this was only on a theoretical level. Similarly, a training course has been offered for four years as part of the continuing education program that introduced XML and metadata, along with presentations on several DTDs again including EAD and TEI.

A new approach was instituted in 2004 that involves both theoretical teaching about and practical application in the use of EAD and TEI. There is interest by librarians in this area because the majority of public libraries and a certain number of university libraries hold archival fonds. Moreover, the national project to convert the General Catalogue of Manuscripts involves many libraries in France. As a result, students need this training. The continuing education program begins with a theoretical course in June on XML, metadata, and the DTDs. In November, there is a practicum that is followed by distance teaching for one month when the trainees are able to work on their own finding aids or ones provided by the trainers. In addition, the ENSSIB is introducing two new masters programs that will include training in EAD and TEI.

Claire Sibille, Direction of the Archives of France, Paris[2]

Since 2002, the management of the Archives of France has organized two training sessions on EAD each year, containing both theoretical presentations and practical encoding exercises. Several other archives across the country have also sponsored such training sessions and for two years the Association of French Archivists has also supported EAD training. Within the academic community, half-day presentations on EAD are currently offered at three universities and this curriculum will be expanded in the near future. After four years of offering training through cultural institutions, it is now clear that it will be necessary to create standardized teacher training and a larger cadre of teachers to continue this work nationwide. This instruction is being developed within the framework of a larger standardization process that is occurring within AFNOR, the French national standards organization. The first two sessions for archivists and librarians will occur in March and June 2005. It is expected that a series of standardized tools for teaching EAD developed for these workshops will be available subsequently as a sort of teaching case, a toolbox, which will be available for all who will want to use it.

Jean-Daniel Zeller, Cantonal Hospital of Geneva, Switzerland

Archival education in Switzerland in general is quite distributed, according to Jean-Daniel Zeller, Principal Archivist of the Cantonal Hospital of Geneva and an instructor in the Documentary Information Department of the High School of Management (HEG) in Geneva. Lacking a single university that offered a complete course of instruction in archivistics, Swiss archivists in the past have held degrees in other areas such as history and law and learned about archives on the job and through an introductory training course and training days sponsored by the Swiss Association of Archivists (AAS). This situation has changed in recent years with the introduction of courses at the HEG, at other specialized institutes, and through a postgraduate certificate jointly offered by the universities of Lausanne, Bern and Geneva beginning in 2002. The federal nature of Switzerland and the lack of a central school for archival education have resulted in a considerable variety of archival practice and this in turn has affected the adoption of EAD.

Following experiments with EAD in 1999 by the HEG and a meeting in Paris in 2002 with French archivists engaged with EAD, the AAS organized in the spring of 2003 a course in two parts consisting of a symposium supplemented by two applied workshops of two days each. Following two presentations by Daniel Pitti that autumn and a training day the following spring, the Commission on Training of the AAS received a mandate to develop further courses. Currently only the HEG offers formal courses on the implementation of EAD. However, such training must follow initial instruction that focuses first on description rather than the presentation of descriptions.

Frank M. Bischoff, Archives School, Marburg, Germany

The Archives School in Marburg focuses on the practical needs of archivists in various types of archives at the state, regional and local levels. The place of EAD in the school's curriculum reflects the state of archival description and descriptive systems within Germany. The existence of a centralized school for archival education has resulted in relatively standardized descriptive practices across German archives. These standards are implemented generally in the context of database software, of which a variety of commercially produced applications are available in a range of prices that make one or another possible for most institutions. The convenience and familiarity of such tools means that few if any archivists in Germany would find the manual tagging of XML files in XML editing software desirable.

Unfortunately, the proliferation of database software has resulted in systems that have structured descriptive information differently. This makes the interchange of data among archives difficult if not impossible. Most of these systems lack export mechanisms or other recognized interfaces necessary to bring together data from different institutions for consolidated presentation through national or regional access portals. An exception to this situation is the software program MidosaXML, created by the Archives School, which offers an example as to how this might be achieved as it can easily export data in a form suitable for Web presentation or as EAD instances. Various initiatives are currently underway to develop a common XML-based interchange format that will facilitate data exchange and delivery through a common portal. One option has been developed by the state archives of North Rhein-Westphalia, while other archivists are considering the use of EAD in this context. Given this environment, the Archives School requires students to study and compare the functionality of six or seven database systems currently in use for their conformance to national descriptive conventions and suitability both for retrospective conversion and presentation of new finding aids. Such comparison affords an opportunity for reflection on the nature of records and descriptive standards.

QUESTIONS FOR THE PANEL

Following the initial overviews of EAD training provided by the panelists, the chair posed a series of questions to the members. Their responses are summarized here.

Question: Where does the teaching of EAD best fit into archival education programs–with technology (technical standards and informatics) or with archival description and descriptive systems?

Geoffrey Yeo

The teaching of EAD fits closely into instruction in archival description and descriptive standards. The point of entry level education is not to teach about technology but to convey to the students what they will need as archivists. At University College, students are expected to have mastered the core curriculum before moving on to more specialized topics like EAD.

Henny Van Schie

EAD is an instance of the application of standards like *ISAD(G)* and is not necessary for all archivists. Training needs depend on the job to be performed. Perhaps the Archives School should organize specific instruction for the specialists who will have to implement EAD.

Jean-Daniel Zeller

At the HEG-Geneva, data processing and archivistics are taught as separate modules and EAD represents the convergence of the two. The drafting of descriptions must be approached from the point of view of archival standardization while the retroconversion of existing finding aids should be considered from the technical point of view.

José Mariz

In Portugal, training in EAD is of the continuous type and one naturally highlights the technological aspects. But in the future, EAD will very quickly become a part of the general culture of archivists.

Frank Bischoff

The teaching of EAD belongs with the teaching of description though EAD itself is a technology. However, since description is no longer done apart from technology, archivists in the future also must receive technical training.

Pierre-Yves Duchemin

In the ENSSIB, the teaching of EAD is part of a module on the retrieval and use of information. Technology is only a support; EAD deals with content.

Question: What preexisting skills and knowledge are required for the learning of EAD or similar technologies?

Geoffrey Yeo

Effective learning of EAD requires some level of technical experience. But the very basic knowledge of computers that most new students already possess is sufficient for this purpose. On the other hand, it is far more difficult to teach EAD to anyone who does not have a basic understanding of the principles of archival description, the teaching of which must precede that of EAD.

Frank Bischoff

It is necessary to have a basic knowledge of markup languages including an understanding of EAD. Archivists also have other tasks for which a technical training is necessary, for example, the management of electronic records. Therefore, it will be necessary to offer a technical base to future archivists.

Pierre-Yves Duchemin

For the librarians, the problem is different. They have a very long tradition of standardization. This is clearly seen in continuing education where a librarian who is well trained with the ISBD is readily able to define elements and structure them. As a result, it is then not very difficult for them to replace "245$a" with <unittitle>.

Henny Van Schie

It is necessary to consider the task of the archivist. If it is to markup existing finding aids, then one must know much more about markup languages than if one is only producing new finding aids where the computer insulates the user from the requirement of understanding the underlying encoding conventions.

Geoffrey Yeo

While agreeing with the previous remarks, a knowledge of XML itself as a separate topic may be useful for reasons beyond archival description and EAD. At University College, XML is taught as a fundamental tool in electronic records management and digital preservation.

Question: What other tools, documents, or methods would be of assistance to you in your teaching of EAD?

Geoffrey Yeo

Prompt publication of the *EAD Tag Library* and the *EAD Application Guidelines* shortly after the distribution of a new edition of EAD would be helpful.

Michael Fox

The *EAD 2002 Tag Library* was distributed both in print and electronically virtually simultaneously with the release of the DTD. The production of the new *Application Guidelines* will be a volunteer activity and the logistics associated with the publication of an update under those circumstances have delayed its preparation. However, a task force has been formed within the EAD Working Group to carry that work forward.

Henny Van Schie

More elaborated examples in various descriptive traditions and other languages would be useful.

Frank Bischoff

There needs to be working groups at the national level that can translate documentation and provide examples adapted to the traditions of the various nations.

Geoffrey Yeo

Students spend a lot of time studying various Web sites where EAD has been implemented. Some of these have information about the underlying EAD project, encoding protocols, what went on behind the scenes. More such information would be helpful.

José Mariz

It is necessary to have more data-processing tools, especially for small institutions. For example, the National Archives of Portugal uses the software application CALM, also used in England, which has an automatic export function. One needs to know only the basics of EAD. But this kind of software is too expensive for small institutions. The publication of finding aids on the Web gets us only half of the way towards a system that is really "user friendly." Current style sheets only produce finding aids that are the online equivalents of printed finding aids. It is not yet possible to conduct research in a database in native XML, a system that would be much more powerful.

Question from the audience: Please describe the use of and training in EAD by librarians.

José Mariz

In Portugal, the National Library has taken part in the MALVINE project but this is the only involvement of libraries with EAD.

Jean-Daniel Zeller

In Switzerland, at the bachelor's level, there is a common training for all I&D specialists, and an introduction on EAD (though no actual practice using it) is a part of this. In the professional community, librarians involved with manuscripts or similar collections are also interested with EAD, and some of them are now developing projects using it.

Michael Fox

In the United States, graduate archival education occurs in schools of library and information science where training in EAD is available to those who will pursue careers in librarianship as well as to those who will become archivists.

Frank Bischoff

In Germany, the training of the librarians is different from that of archivists. While certain librarians use EAD, the source of their training in its use is unclear.

Geoffrey Yeo

The experience in the United Kingdom is exactly the opposite of that in the United States. Though archival and library education may occur within the same university program, all archivists will be exposed to EAD in their education and virtually none of the librarians.

CONCLUSION

In considering the various ways in which EAD is being taught and implemented in the countries represented on this panel, it would be fair to conclude that the venues for and level of detail of such training largely reflect variations in broader national issues. These include the nature, content, history, and practice of archival description in a given country, the centralization or decentralization of archival education as a whole, the extent to which EAD implementations have already been realized, and the nature of the systems that are being employed to deliver archival information to the public. Given the diversity in these matters as presented by the panelists, it is not surprising that the training of archivists in the use of EAD will continue to reflect a rich mix of traditions.

On the other hand, there was a strongly expressed consensus among the panelists that training in and an understanding of archival descriptive principles is fundamental. No matter how important various technologies are becoming in applied archival work, training in their use must be firmly grounded in and proceed from education in descriptive theory and standards.

NOTES

1. Information about the EAD/Data Exchange Group of the Society of Archivists can be found at http://www.archives.org.uk/groups/eaddataexchangegroup.html.

2. Claire Sibille provided the following additional information after the conference to elaborate on other efforts to train French archivists in the use of EAD.

USING EAD

Enhancing the Effectiveness of Description with Innovative Tools– The Example of MidosaXML, Germany

Angelika Menne-Haritz

SUMMARY. Online description using new Internet technologies, especially XML, is an interesting way to enhance the effectiveness and productivity of archival processing. Users and archivists benefit from the developments, making the achievement of their aims easier. The provenance-based structured presentation of finding aids can be supported with many new helpful functionalities and thus deliver information more directly and with fewer irrelevant results. Using internationally

Angelika Menne-Haritz is Director of the Foundation Archives of Parties and Mass Organizations of the GDR in the Federal Archives, Berlin and Professor for Administrative Sciences at the German University for Administrative Sciences, Speyer. She was formerly the director of the Archives School Marburg, where she has taught and researched in archival sciences and business processes in public administration.

[Haworth co-indexing entry note]: "Enhancing the Effectiveness of Description with Innovative Tools–The Example of MidosaXML, Germany." Menne-Haritz, Angelika. Co-published simultaneously in *Journal of Archival Organization* (The Haworth Information Press, an imprint of The Haworth Press, Inc.) Vol. 3, No. 2/3, 2005, pp. 83-95; and: *Encoding Across Frontiers: Proceedings of the European Conference on Encoded Archival Description and Context (EAD and EAC), Paris, France, 7-8 October 2004* (ed: Bill Stockting, and Fabienne Queyroux) The Haworth Information Press, an imprint of The Haworth Press, Inc., 2005, pp. 83-95. Single or multiple copies of this article are available for a fee from The Haworth Document Delivery Service [1-800-HAWORTH, 9:00 a.m. - 5:00 p.m. (EST). E-mail address: docdelivery@haworthpress.com].

Available online at http://www.haworthpress.com/web/JAO

doi:10.1300/J201v03n02_07

accepted structures, especially EAD and EAC, enhances the ease of research at any place and at any time. On the other hand, archival description work has new tools that facilitate the capturing of data about the archives together with documentation about their processing, including appraisal. This contribution describes how the new functionalities have been tried out with MidosaXML as a pilot application and a productive tool, within a long tradition of being small yet highly sophisticated.

KEYWORDS. Archival description, Bundsarchiv, Encoded Archival Description, EAD, Extensible Stylesheet Language, online finding aids, MidosaXML, XML

NEW TECHNOLOGIES AND OLD PROFESSIONAL KNOWLEDGE

MidosaXML, like its predecessors, is an example of a highly sophisticated yet low-budget new technology for archivists to experience. It was developed with funding from the DFG (German Science Foundation) by a consortium bringing together three different kinds of professional experience: the archives school at Marburg with its teaching knowledge about the need for practical tools demonstrating how description is done, the archives directorate of Baden-Württemberg with its experience of a dispersed network of seven state archives in one region, and the Federal Archives as the most important German repository with huge and rather recent holdings. Two central aspects characterized the philosophy of Midosa from the beginning:

1. Reusability–The aim was to deliver a model of an online finding aid with all necessary functionalities and at the same time a tool that could be used for the repeated production of finding aids. Centralized access via finding aids was more important from the beginning than centralized data.
2. Instrumentality for the archivist's workbench–The tool should not prescribe how to work, but should be used by professionals in different technical contexts, in one-person archives with low budgets as well as in network installations in large institutions. It should

offer a broad range of possibilities to be adaptable to changing situations. It should open up new ways to do what archivists want to do: give as much information about their holdings as needed in the most self-explanatory and unobtrusive way.

MidosaXML is the latest member of the Midosa family and has been distributed since 2002. It is an example of a combination of sound professional archival methods with highly developed technology. Based on XML, MidosaXML is strongly influenced by Encoded Archival Description (EAD) and can be used to produce EAD finding aids.

MIDOSA AND THE ARCHIVISTS' EXPERIENCES WITH TECHNOLOGY

MidosaXML had its origins in an archival database application developed nearly twenty years ago, known simply as MIDOSA. In 1994 under the name of MIDOSA 95 it was transformed into a dBase tool and was distributed at a low price to a number of smaller archives by the archives school in Marburg. In 1997 the archives school received funding of 160,000 DM (80,000 US$) from the DFG (German Science Foundation) for the development of a generator that transformed the data from the relational database into an HTML presentation for the Internet. During this project, with support by the GMD (Society for Mathematics and Data Processing, Darmstadt), the concept of the presentation format with four interrelated frames was developed. That format is still used today.

In 2000 and 2001 the DFG again funded a project, this time bringing together a working group of American and German archivists to discuss the applicability of the American standard EAD in Germany. At the same time the archives school started to draft a DTD for German finding aids closely based on EAD. A mapping table was established as part of the manual for the new XML-based software developed on these foundations, now called MidosaXML. Previously the data had been converted to HTML. Now the whole software tool was based on XML both as the working format and for the presentation via transformation to HTML. Besides allowing a closer relationship to EAD, the XML format offered the possibility of circumventing the use of a word processor for editing data from large databases for publication.

Several clearly stated intentions concerning practical experience in daily archival work were closely linked to the development. The main point was to give archivists back the possibility of working with texts when they do description work and create finding aids. Before the introduction of IT, archivists had described every single unit on filing cards and after arranging the cards in the structural order of the fonds they were typed with a typewriter by a secretary. This list was the main part of a manuscript, which could be supplemented with a title page, an introduction and a list of index terms in case it was to be prepared for printing and publishing. In the 1970s, German archivists began to work with relational databases to capture and manage the metadata for single descriptive units in the form of data records instead of cards. This was accompanied by several articles in the archival literature of the time with reflections on a new trend in archive studies, which might be called the "post-finding aids approach." It was suggested that with constantly growing record groups in a time of relatively stable administrations on the one hand, and the increasing use of information technologies on the other, finding aids on paper were outdated and should be replaced by card files or directly by databases. It was thought that the ability to search large relational databases would provide the main possibility of modernisation for the archival profession and to adapt it to the use of IT. An interesting parallel can be observed in the theoretical rejection of the continued validity of the principle of provenance, especially in the context of appraisal, as pronounced by Hans Booms in 1972.[1] The principle of provenance and with it the structured form of finding aids was openly regarded as belonging to the nineteenth century together with its authoritarian state, which had, therefore, been surpassed by modern society.

However, in spite of the theoretical and public debate in practice, a mixture of both approaches, with traditional structured finding aids as well as the use of databases for the management of descriptions was applied in a rather pragmatic way in different archival IT-systems. The databases served to rearrange records groups after new accruals and to insert new descriptions with the sorting function of the database software. To do this a new field was added to the categories on the traditional cards ready for capturing an indication of the place inside the arrangement scheme with the decimal notation of the corresponding group. After re-sorting the database, the whole record group was printed out and a new version of the finding aid was ready after adding the introduction, the title page and a list of index terms.

In the nineteenth century the principle of provenance was introduced for practical reasons, as it allowed the easiest way to arrange and present records in their original order and was, therefore, easily understandable. The most practical way of handling records also needed a representation of the inherent structures, even if the descriptions were managed with a database. Archivists, however, had a hard time explaining to computer specialists in the big computer centres of the public administration of the time that they only needed databases in order to print out the data on paper in the end.

These experiences show the weight of traditions that cannot be deliberately wiped away. When the Internet came within the reach of archivists, a burst of productivity was possible with just the same approach as before. A structured digital presentation was possible with the new IT that was no longer linked to the old-fashioned use of paper. Now the database report generator producing paper copies could be replaced by an HTML generator that allowed greater flexibility and ease of production and use of the final product. The data could be updated when needed, the presentation could be redone instantly and further information could be added to the descriptive information. This story tells us the importance of taking seriously the hidden aims of working methods, in this case the structured description of archives, which might be covered by technical restrictions, but is unveiled when new technical developments allow their re-recognition.

MidosaXML emerged then as the concept of a tool for taking advantage of the new possibilities of the Internet. There is a straight line from the report generator of dBase for paper printouts to the HTML presentation of the data, and finally to the use of XML as a structured text format, allowing the integration of both techniques, database and text, into one flexible format. From its beginnings, efforts with Midosa were oriented towards the production of texts. With the technology of the Internet, especially XML, the system now has the best means for achieving these goals in the context of the new digital world. Its first predecessor Midosa used the relational database for the final establishment of a structured text, the finding aid. More important than the search of single terms was the structure of the finding aid. With XML both approaches can now be brought together, the choice of which is the most important depending on the user and his research needs. From the beginning Midosa was a tool for the production of finding aids, even if initially parts of the text had to be managed and added outside the description software.

THE AIMS OF ARCHIVAL DESCRIPTION

The German term for description, *Erschließung*, means something like to unclose or unlock the holdings and to open them like a window or a door that allows one to enter new, unknown, or even undiscovered spaces. It conceptualises more than just capturing metadata about the records. The term alludes to the function of the activity, in making the holdings open, transparent and accessible. It includes the capturing of the descriptive data about the individual records as well as the ordering and arranging of the whole record group according to its inherent structure, formed by the interrelations of the communications, that made them emerge from daily administrative work.

Description in this more philosophical sense is, with appraisal and preservation, a major part of archival methodologies that serve a common professional aim, that is the provision of access to former realities that might become important for unanticipated reasons. It is much more than just the capturing of data about single files. It is a professional method for opening access and providing paths to the unknown past. It is helping people to generate knowledge which cannot be found elsewhere, and which is not yet written down. Finding aids are like maps helping one to navigate through an unknown territory.

The products of description are accessible holdings. Finding aids are part of these products. The exploitation of archives is hard work for users, because the most interesting findings are not in the texts, but in the relations between the texts. The use of archives means a lot of interpretation, of questioning and of deciding whether a hypothesis, suggested by what one can see, can be regarded as proven or not. The German historian Koselleck once said that the main importance of archives is their power to veto.[2] A negative answer is as valuable as a positive one and in many cases the exclusion of a certain presumption is even more important. The work of users of archives consists to a large extent in understanding what they see, drawing their conclusions from it and verifying their assumptions by comparing them to what can be interpreted in other sources. The results are products of active cognitive work and not just picked up information.

Raul Hilberg noted in his résumé of his studies on the Holocaust many observations that illustrate well the way users generate knowledge from archival holdings. On the quality of information available in records, he wrote, "Finally one must keep in mind that the internal correspondence was more than an aggregate of pages. Each piece of paper was once an action. It became a concrete step with real consequences in the ongoing process of destruction. . . . A report, which at first glance is just a record of events, fulfilled two purposes. It confirmed to the leadership the continual functioning of the administrative machine, and it provided an overview that was a tool for shaping future decisions."[3] Two aspects are addressed here. First, records are traces of the organisation of actions, not only of actions themselves, and they are written down with the intention to make something happen. So they might reveal intentions and their consequences, not in form of a narrative, but hidden behind the papers themselves. Second, the narrative texts in the records are always influenced by communication intentions and structures. Records are tools for communication, but what they want to convey may not be what the texts say. A certain message is intended by the writer anticipating a certain understanding by his addressee, who again understands in the text what is needed for planning further steps in fulfilling his duties or plans. Archive users are confronted with this very complex network of communications and actions that only left traces of their material part, excluding all oral communication or other ways of transmitting and gaining information by all the different actors. But all this is not in the records. Users gain experience and learn to read between the lines. When they have finished their studies they are experts in reading archival material. Like archivists they see a lot of unarticulated things, hidden to inexperienced users, and often both are not aware that they are not simply reading records but interpreting traces. The underlying intention of description is to make users experts before they start their research. It follows that many further developments are necessary, however, including digital representations of records and e-learning tools. The structured presentation of the finding aids and their continuous supplementation with further information opens new ways for supporting future users with the preparation for their research work.

Records emerge as steps in communication processes. Difficulties in using archives arise with the amount of unarticulated episodes in the chain of communication. These might be oral exchanges as well as formalized procedures assuming a certain amount of self-understanding by the members of a group but opaque or cryptic to outsiders. The first especially happens in administrations that are based to a large extent on board meetings. Minutes of such meetings capture some of the oral communication, but only those parts that might be relevant for later reference, depending on the power of the board, the need for continuity and other factors. The second occurs in rather stable organisations where communication structures have had time to mature. They create a large amount of tacit knowledge about rules and habits underlying each communication. Organisations that are strongly oriented towards action like the German administration in the Prussian tradition, long before the time that Raul Hilberg studied in depth, may develop a sort of grammar for action-oriented communication using nonverbal signs for organizing marks and notes and for the planning of internal cooperation in single cases.[4] The effects of all these forms of communication organized outside the actual records but forming a sort of communicative layer underneath must be understood and respected when using archives in order to understand what they have to tell. Often the most important information is outside the records but can be found and identified only with their help. To understand records it is necessary to reconstruct what was behind them, even though they were generated for a quite different purpose.

Finding aids are much more than just lists of items. They convey the unarticulated, the nonverbal and, if they are really good, they help people to understand the underlying level of communication on which the visible traces in the records are based. The structure of finding aids with its navigable hierarchy of series helps to identify in a rather straightforward process the relevant record groups for certain research questions. Seen from the methodological perspective such structures are very effective search tools because they allow the exclusion of large parts as irrelevant, rather than the need to choose the relevant among a huge number of irrelevant hits. The items of a series inside a structure are interrelated and may explain each other. That is valuable for the groups at the other levels of the hierarchy too. Unlike a classification system, which gathers similar objects with the same characteristics into one group, for instance trees with leaves in contrast to trees with needles, and leaving some like the ginkgo tree that have neither, as miscellaneous, the structure of a finding aid is a subdivision of a whole starting at the top. Therefore all group nominations are at the same time negative designations of the others, and included in the comprehensive description of the superior group. A government's policies can be subdivided into the spheres of economics, culture, education, health, but there are no miscellaneous activities left over. What is not dealt with by the health ministry falls into the jurisdiction of one of the others. Every organisation has it aims and they focus the perspectives of the common effort. There are no miscellaneous functions, either for businesses or for administrations. The structure of the finding aid is based on the structure of the activities of the originating organisation. This structure in itself conveys information by simply representing, not verbally describing, the structures of the communications of which the records are the traces.

So the structure is the main means that helps one to understand archives. The search for certain terms, however, may also help a lot. A search by name and locality aims at finding more information about that person or place. A prerequisite for such a search is to know the name. It might be that the name is found during the navigation of a finding aid and than it serves to find out what else this person did. Or the name is known, but not the occupation of the person and after finding it being mentioned in the finding aid the responsibilities can be identified more fully, while for their understanding it is necessary to navigate further and read other files. It also may be the case that a person has played a really important role without his or her name being mentioned. Perhaps it was mentioned at the beginning of an affair and then everybody knew who was meant and it was not necessary to repeat the name all the time. Both approaches, structural navigation as well as the keyword search, can be used together. Neither of them delivers an answer but both help to formulate questions more precisely and a concrete question in most cases suggests its answer, which then can be validated with further studies in the records.

The aims of archival description, therefore, are to lay bare as far as possible the underlying and unarticulated contexts of the records. The nonverbal way of presenting these contexts is designed for that purpose, because it does not suggest a particular understanding of what can be seen. It just opens up the records for being used as needed. "Open Archives–Open Eyes," with this sentence the former head of the archives of the Stasi Files in Germany, Joachim Gauck, pleaded for open access instead of closing and hiding away even highly problematic material like the secret service files of an authoritarian state. Open eyes are a prerequisite for inspection and interpretation, and history as a scientific discipline needs open sources facilitating open discussion on how they ought to be understood and how they can explain societal phenomena.

ARCHIVAL DESCRIPTION AND THE INTERNET

Archivists are in a profession that has a lot to gain from the new technologies of the Internet. The Internet is a tool that could not have been better invented for the purpose of opening archives. It is not only the fact that the Internet is open 7 days a week, 24 hours a day, and that it is independent of location. It is much more, because the Internet finally allows a use of information technologies in a way that is fully adapted to archival working and research methods. The Internet is navigation. Virtual navigation was the research technique used with legacy finding aids on paper. Finding aids were not read sequentially but they were studied and browsed back and forth. This can be done much more easily on the Internet. Furthermore, Internet technologies enhance the functionality of finding aids for this purpose because they offer new ways when compared to the traditional paper forms. As a pilot project, MidosaXML has realized some of them and has provided opportunities to think about further developments to use these new flexibilities.

Combined Research Strategies

Presentation on the Internet can offer combined and interchangeable search strategies. Internet-based tools allow navigation with a left-hand frame and a header together with keyword searching across one or a choice of several finding aids irrespective of the location of the collection as well as with index terms or browsing functions. It is possible to offer users flexible switches between both together with a high range of orientation marks and personalized search histories for retracing their own search strategy. Tools like MidosaXML offer the production of online finding aids including navigation, browsing, index term search and keyword search. The finding aids can be integrated into gateways like RLG's *Archival Resources*, which offers cross-searching over more than 45,000 finding aids via keywords as well as by using structure-based navigation inside the finding aids.[5]

Supplementary Information

The hypertext technology of the Internet allows the linking to supplementary information from the places in the finding aid were it is needed. This information may contain explanations of appraisal decisions and certain description methods or may announce plans for further availability of new parts of record groups. This data can be entered during the description work and then displayed when needed by activating a symbol indicating that supplementary information is available. MidosaXML, which can also produce hard copy finding aids from the same data, places the supplementary information into footnotes referenced to the descriptive unit or the header of a series in relation to which it was entered. There are other ways to present this information. In any case in digital finding aids such information, not being part of the description, but documenting what is done with the records, can be used as necessary without the physical restrictions of paper printouts.

Integration of Images

The same linking methods can be used to join images as illustrations to the texts. MidosaXML offers the possibility of entering the addresses and legends of a deliberately chosen number of images during the description. They are presented with text-links under the title and are opened in a separate window were they can be browsed or opened individually. Other ways to integrate images are possible. It might be the other way around, for instance in the case of digitization on demand. When users order digital reproductions with a certain resolution, they might be delivered inside the relevant part of the finding aid, so that the context is not lost. Or images integrated in their description might be used for experimental e-learning tools on the web site of a repository, so that users can prepare in advance for their visit to the reading room by working with example material online.

Easy Handling on the Desk

Besides the use of Internet technologies for presentation and greater ease of research, the same technologies offer even greater possibilities for the archivist's workbench, because they provide new ways to arrange information and to enhance the transparency of the archival processing. In MidosaXML, several features have been developed that benefit from the great flexibility of XML-based structures for the description work.

a. Building of the arrangement scheme can be done with drag and drop of single units, or even whole classification groups, placing them were they belong inside the scheme.
b. Classification headers can be numbered and renumbered automatically.
c. Elements and sections of finding aids are offered in the toolbox on the right-hand side and can be added, repeatedly if necessary, whenever needed.
d. Call numbers can be shown or hidden in the title line.
e. Descriptive units can be sorted by call number.
f. An export to HTML or print (RTF) can be made at any time to see the results of the work.
g. Supplementary information can be entered whenever wanted to document what was done during the processing or to explain appraisal decisions.

h. All parts of the finding aid can be edited including the entries for the title page and the introduction.
i. All texts can be formatted in a similar way to a word processor.

These and more functionality are made possible by using XML technology. It opens the way to deliver more information without overload for the user by assuring orientation through the layout and functionality of Web presentation.

MidosaXML– AN INNOVATIVE TOOL AND ITS PERSPECTIVES

One of the intentions of MidosaXML was to see what could be done with the newest technologies. It was designed as a small tool that allows flexible editing of finding aids as texts while they are in a structured form and are, therefore, manageable automatically. It should be possible to change the data as necessary while its presentation is controlled by style sheets for as many different forms as wanted.

From the beginnings of Midosa its philosophy was decentralisation. Today, for those who use it, MidosaXML presents a part of the workbench for archivists. As such it does not intend to replace comprehensive archival systems. MidosaXML is an application for 80 percent of day-to-day archival processing offering open interfaces for data exchange with other applications. As such it has open import and export facilities, using different formats. Data from databases can be imported, reworked and exported again, to integrate it (or eventually only parts of it) in the original (or other) database, such as an archives management system. Its character as a tool for professionals implies that it does not prescribe how to do the work. It is meant for the archivist, who knows professional working methods and feels responsible for the outcomes.

For the developers of Midosa, Midosa95 and MidosaXML, it has been an exciting opportunity to try out the innovative possibilities of the newest technologies for archival purposes independently of other costly systems developments. However, the road has not yet come to an end and many new fields wait to be exploited, such as the construction of integrated national or international gateways or enhanced methods to exchange data between archives as well as between different applications for different purposes in the management of archival repositories. The future for the past has just begun.

NOTES

1. Hans Booms, Society and the Formation of a Documentary Heritage, *Archivaria* 24 (1987), 69-107; translation of: *Gesellschaftsordnung und Überlieferungsbildung, Archivalische Zeitschrift* 68, 1972, 3-40.

2. Reinhart Koselleck, *Vergangene Zukunft: zur Semantik geschichtlicher Zeiten, Suhrkamp Taschenbuch Wissenschaft*, 757 (Frankfurt am Main: Suhrkamp, 1995), 204.

3. Raul Hilberg, *Sources of Holocaust Research: An Analysis* (Chicago: Ivan R. Dee, 2001), 31-32.

4. Angelika Menne-Haritz, *Business Processes: An Archival Science Approach to Collaborative Decision Making, Records, and Knowledge Management* (Dordrecht/Boston/London, 2004).

5. Further information about RLG's Archival Resources database can be found at http://www.rlg.org/en/page.php?Page_ID=120.

Online Finding Aids with BASYS-Fox in the Bundesarchiv, Germany

Oliver Sander

SUMMARY. This article discusses the process for the production of online finding aids with BASYS-Fox system and it describes the scope of application of EAD in the Bundesarchiv. In 2000, the project "Presentation of Online Finding Aids with the EAD system" was started at Bundesarchiv. The project was promoted by the German Science Foundation (Deutsche Forschungsgemeinschaft). The objectives were, first, to examine whether EAD could be applied to German archives, especially to the federal archives. Second, the possibilities for software development were to be assessed. BASYS-Fox is the result of this software development. Fox is an acronym for "Finding aids Online with XML." The production of finding aids with BASYS-Fox starts with an XML export from the archive database of the federal archives (BASYS-S). After the XML file is imported into the BASYS-Fox system, different elements, which at present are not available in the database, have to be added to the file. After the completion of these additions, the finding aid is published with BASYS-Fox. Publishing in this context means the pro-

---

Oliver Sander has been Deputy Head of Division G 1 in the Bundesarchiv since April 2003. He is responsible for conception and support of Archival IT-applications (BASYS-S, BASYS-Fox), record group forming, and publication of finding aids.

Address correspondence to: Oliver Sander, Potsdamer Str. 1, D-56075 Koblenz, Germany (E-mail: o.sander@barch.bund.de).

[Haworth co-indexing entry note]: "Online Finding Aids with BASYS-Fox in the Bundesarchiv, Germany." Sander, Oliver. Co-published simultaneously in *Journal of Archival Organization* (The Haworth Information Press, an imprint of The Haworth Press, Inc.) Vol. 3, No. 2/3, 2005, pp. 97-110; and: *Encoding Across Frontiers: Proceedings of the European Conference on Encoded Archival Description and Context (EAD and EAC), Paris, France, 7-8 October 2004* (ed: Bill Stockting, and Fabienne Queyroux) The Haworth Information Press, an imprint of The Haworth Press, Inc., 2005, pp. 97-110. Single or multiple copies of this article are available for a fee from The Haworth Document Delivery Service [1-800-HAWORTH, 9:00 a.m. - 5:00 p.m. (EST). E-mail address: docdelivery@haworthpress.com].

Available online at http://www.haworthpress.com/web/JAO

doi:10.1300/J201v03n02_08

duction of XML files according to EAD and to the local BArch DTD, which are saved in a file system. Access to these online finding aids is made possible by the classification scheme and via the Lucene search engine. At present there are about 200 online finding aids (list of Fox-Finding aids: http://www.bundesarchiv.de/foxpublic/index.html).

KEYWORDS. Archival description, BASYS-Fox, Bundesarchiv, EAD, Extensible Stylesheet Language, finding aids, online access, standardization, XML

INTRODUCTION

In 1970 the first seven finding aids were published by the Bundesarchiv. Since then access to the archival holdings has become easier, and now there are more than one hundred published finding aids available, some of which are illustrated in Figure 1. Editions of the minutes of the cabinet of the federal government and documents relating to German politics are another source of information for the public about material held in the Bundesarchiv.[1] Times change, however, and this affects the provision of access to archival information.

FIGURE 1. Bundsarchiv Published Finding Aids

THE BUNDESARCHIV AND ARCHIVAL IT-SYSTEMS: THE IMPACT OF EAD

Since the 1970s, finding aids published by the Bundesarchiv have been generated by IT programs. Beginning with a simple system named AKABDA (*Aktenabgabedatei*), the so-called "Thomson-system" was introduced in 1992. It was partly replaced in 2000 by a new system called BASYS-S (*BundesArchiv-IT-SYStem*). BASYS-S is a relational database system using Informix software. It consists of several modules and was drawn up as an integrated archival administration system. This powerful system is able to show the processing status of an archival object from its arrival in the record centre, via appraisal, description as (illustrated in Figure 2) and its use finally in the archive.

The federal archives have had a presence on the Internet since the summer of 1997. From the beginning the inventory guide was a key publication providing users with information about the holdings. The information available has recently been expanded by the presentation of detailed online finding aids.[2] At the moment we produce "conventional" finding aids in a Microsoft Word interface, but in the future we

FIGURE 2. BASYS-S: Module for Appraisal and Description

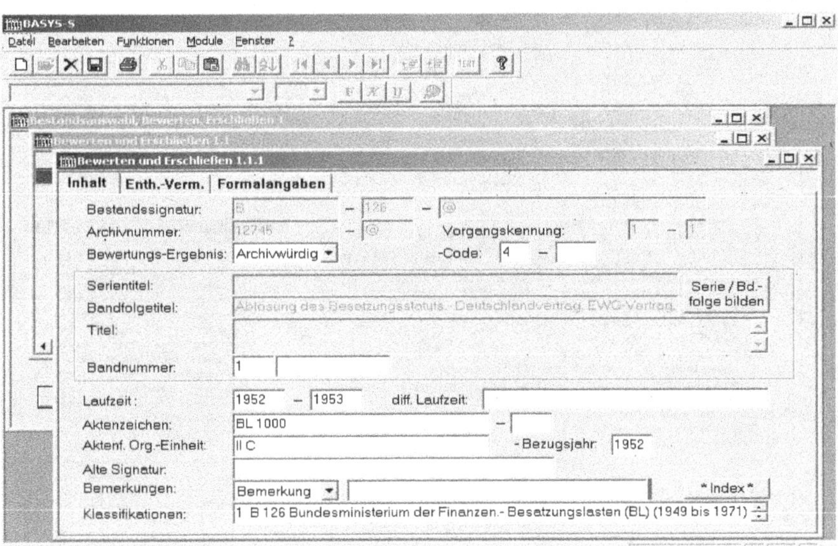

will also use XML and stylesheets for this purpose as shown in Figure 3. Before the development of BASYS-Fox (discussed below), the production of online inventories from the BASYS-S database was not that straightforward: records were exported in a CSV format, converted and manipulated in Microsoft Access and finally converted into a MySQL database. The introductions were added as PDF files. This process is illustrated in Figure 4.

ENCODED ARCHIVAL DESCRIPTION (EAD) PROJECT

Stimulated by a German American task group and a project sponsored by the German Science Foundation (Deutsche Forschungs-Gemeinschaft-DFG) for the further development of the use of the Internet for the presentation of access information to archives that began in 2000, the Bundesarchiv started to investigate Encoded Archival Description (EAD) more intensively.[3] The task group's final report recommended further investigation and a new project named "Presentation of Online Finding Aids with the EAD System" (*Präsentation von On-*

FIGURE 3. BASYS-S: "Classification/Finding Aids" Module and XML Export

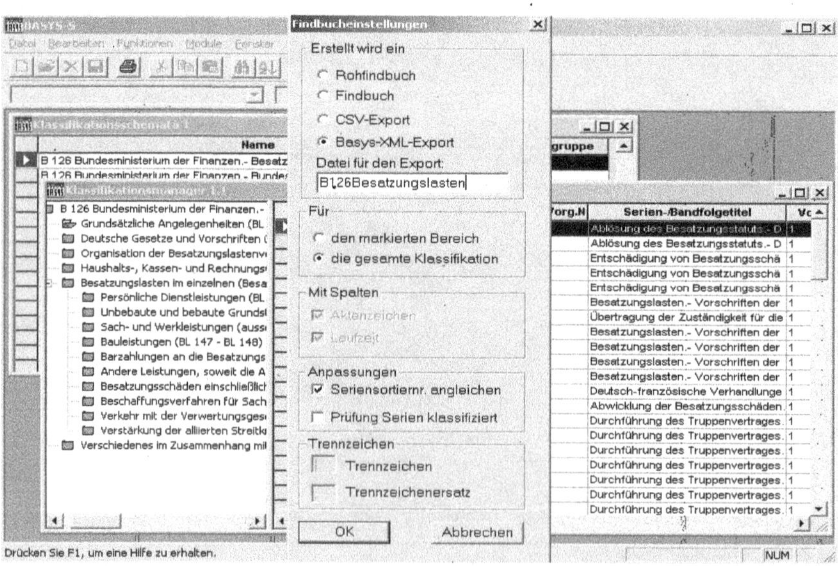

FIGURE 4. Bundsarchiv Database Workflow (2003)

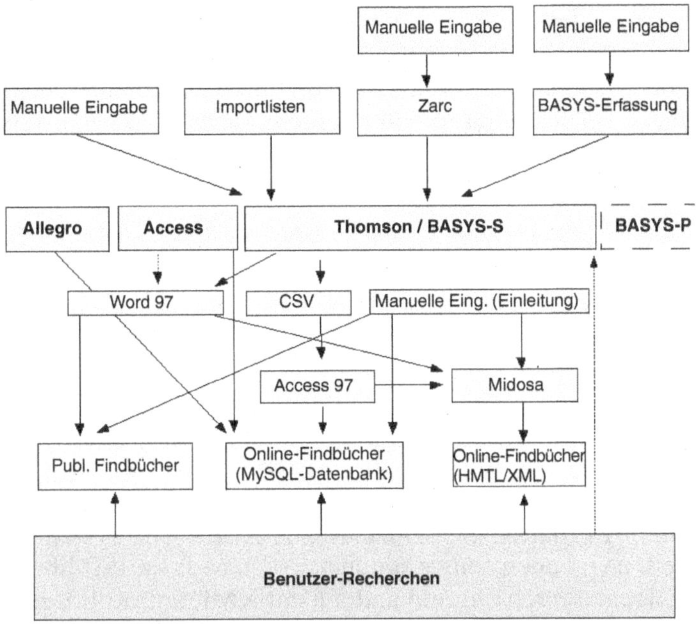

line-Findbüchern unter Berücksichtigung des EAD-Systems).[4] The work was in fact more exciting than the formal title led us to believe. The project was to develop tools which allow presentation conforming to EAD as well as a system that simplifies the production of online finding aids from the relational database of the federal archives. In 2001 a member of staff started work on the project.

In the context of this work, a mapping was made between EAD and the *Retrokonversion* DTD and the Midosa DTD,[5] with the support of the Public Record Office in London, the French National Archives and others. The idea that EAD might not only be suitable for data exchange but also for opening up the archives of the federal archives was also examined. While the data model of the federal archives can be translated to EAD, it does not map exactly reflecting differences in practices between Germany and the United States. The tradition of appraisal and description in German archives and especially in the Bundesarchiv differs in some ways from the one on which EAD is based. Consequently, some elements or attributes do not fully correspond with the elements and attributes available in EAD. The EAD-DTD, for example, includes the element abstract which we (and MidosaXML) have to use for a closer description of the title of a description unit. In Germany we used to call this "Enthält-Vermerk" the so-called Type ("includes" type). Given this, a DTD similar to, but not the same as, EAD was developed, which corresponds with the DTD developed in the context of another DFG project that dealt with the retroconversion of finding aids.[6]

THE BASYS-Fox SYSTEM

Technology

Another product of the aforementioned DFG project was a tool that enables us to convert existing finding aid instances from the relational database to EAD. The tool is called BASYS-Fox: Fox being an acronym for Finding aids Online with XML (*Findbücher Online mit XML*). The technology that BASYS-Fox uses is XML. The system is totally Web based, using open source products (such as Java, JSP-library Struts and the Lucene search engine) and a local XML editor. It is, therefore, independent of any proprietary operating system. This matches the intention of the German government to use open source software as much as possible. It also meets the demand of the DFG that other institutions should be able to use the system. With this in mind, we are planning to publish the source code with a GNU General Public License.

Workflow

The workflow for the BASYS-Fox system is illustrated in Figure 5. The steps in the workflow are as follows:

- The inventory is made up of the description and the classification component of the IT system of the federal archives (BASYS-S; see Figure 3).
- The inventory is exported in an XML format and is automatically uploaded to the processing server. This inventory is stored in a development database (Oracle) and the necessary metadata is automatically inserted.
- The second step is to open BASYS-Fox and to "feed" in the XML file, as shown in Figure 6.

- This "feed" divides the file in to two parts, information about the file itself ("dateiinfo") and the descriptive information ("findmittelinfo"), as illustrated in Figure 7.
- Some necessary information is not kept in the database and has to be added. This addition takes place in an external XML editor. The XML parts ("dateiinfo" and "findmittelinfo") have to be transported from the BASYS-Fox server to a local client, where they are edited, as shown in Figure 8. For the editing we use the French XML editor XMLmind (as seen in Figure 9), which has a German input mask, but one could use any other similar tool such as XML Spy or Morphon. If we decide to integrate this information in our database, we will be able to delete this step. To avoid problems with version control, only the introduction and the file information can be processed in the XML editor. Changes to the inventory can be carried out only in the database, but we do have a function to "re-feed" the inventory.
- After all additions have been made the XML parts are uploaded to BASYS-Fox, where links or images can be added.
- To enable quality control, it is possible to see the results in a preview, which shows the latest version.
- If one is happy with the result, the file can be given the status "ready" and final quality control is carried out by the responsible division.
- After checking, the inventory is released, at which point the EAD XML file is automatically produced for data exchange. Currently we let Research Libraries Group (RLG) index the files on our server and they provide access to them on their *Archival Resources* portal.[7]
- The XML files are saved in an XML file system. By an automatic routine our online presentation is updated every 30 minutes, after which the inventory can be searched.

Presentation

Online presentation of the BASYS-Fox finding aids, which follows the style guide of the Bundesarchiv, is divided into three frames, as shown in Figure 10:

- In the "head" frame the reference and title of the archival unit are shown and the classification group chosen is noted.

- In a "navigation" frame on the left-hand side, a summary of all the classification groups is presented. The list is expandable and collapsible and clicking on a particular group opens the units of description of that group in the main frame.
- In the main frame the units of description are presented in three columns (reference, title, date). To enable a wide-ranging overview detailed information for each unit is available by clicking on the link "view here for details" (*Detailansicht*).

For retrieval we use the open source search engine Lucene, which enables the cross-searching of all the finding aids produced with BASYS-Fox. We have a simple "Google" type search form and a compound search menu. The latter allows the selection of one or more finding aids and the qualification of searches by certain parts (finding aid information, classification or description of files) and special elements (date, reference number), etc. A hierarchical or relevance sort is also possible.

After starting a query (for example, "Paris" as shown in Figure 11), all hits are presented in an overview (*Trefferübersicht*), as seen in Figure 12. The hits can be sorted by relevance (the number of hits) (*Findmitteleinleitung*), classification and units of description (*Bestandsverzeichnis*) or hierarchically. A click on the numbers of hits opens a view of the hits in context (*Trefferansicht*). The detailed information with the highlighted hit can then be viewed.

FIGURE 5. Workflow of BASYS-Fox System

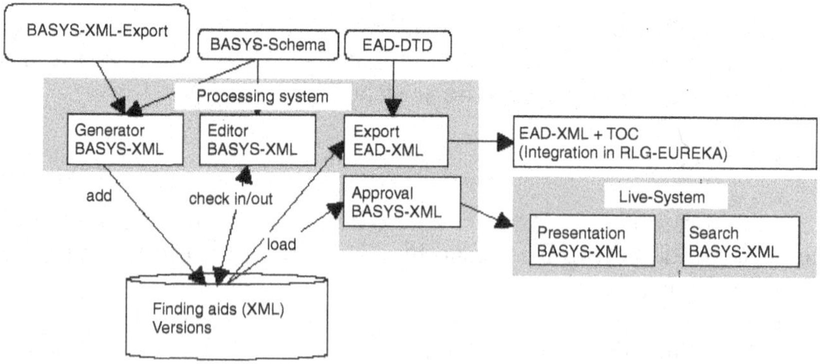

FIGURE 6. BASYS-Fox: Processing Menu: List of Finding Aids

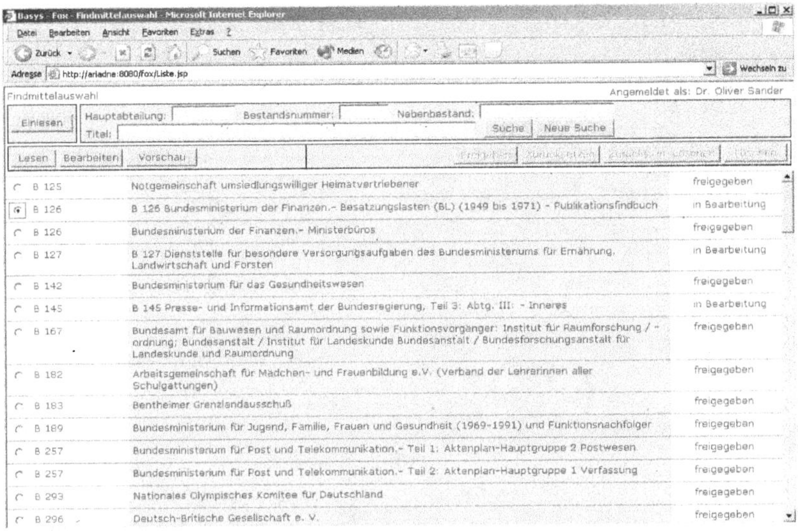

FIGURE 7. BASYS-Fox: Processing Menu

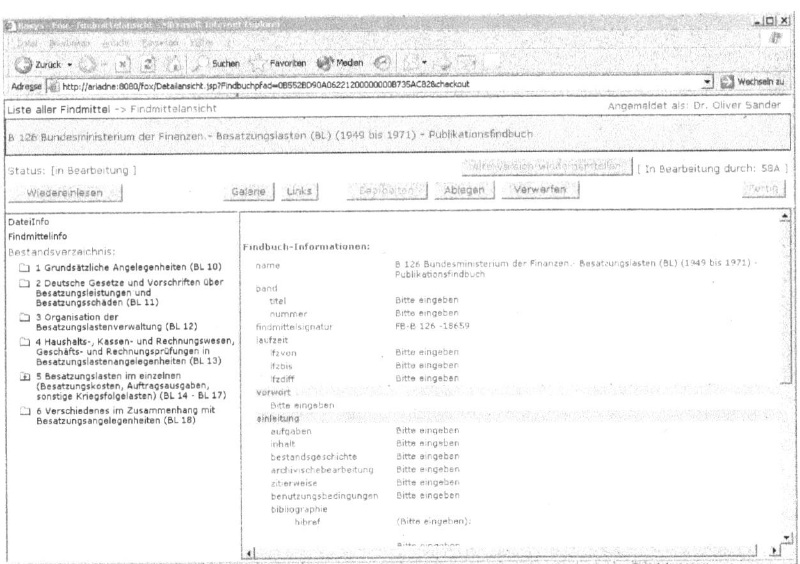

FIGURE 8. Download of an XML Part from BASYS-Fox

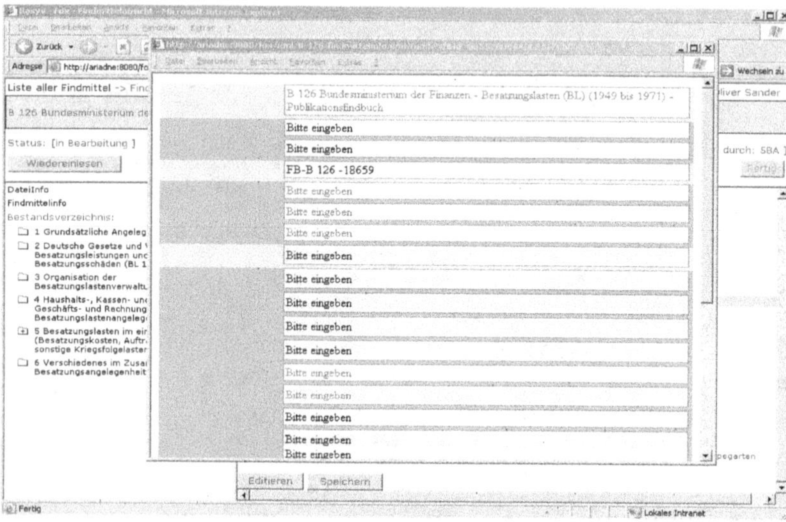

FIGURE 9. Completion of XML Parts with XMLmind

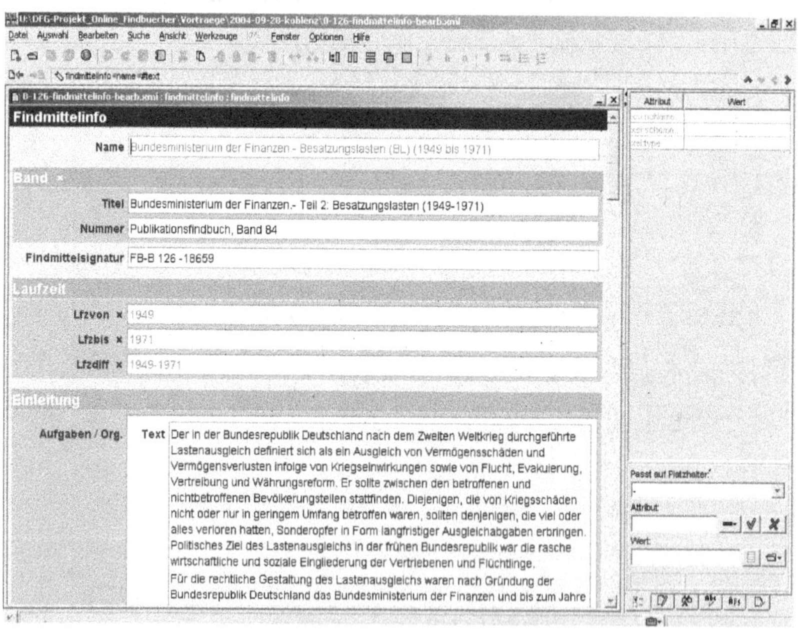

FIGURE 10. BASYS-Fox Presentation: Frames

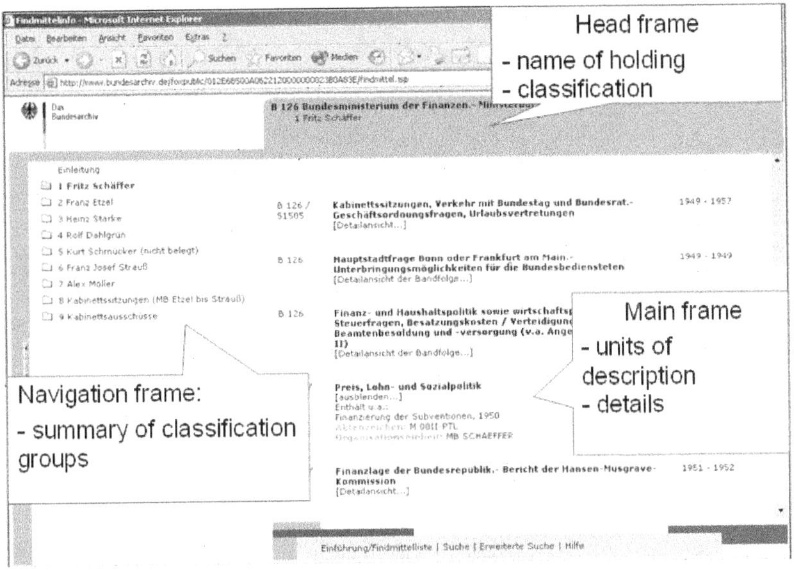

FIGURE 11. BASYS-Fox: Compound Search Menu: Step 1: Query for "Paris"

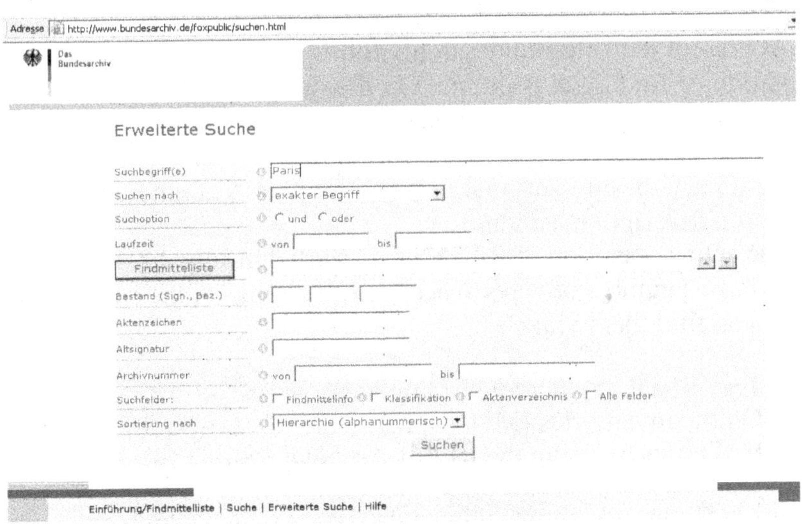

FIGURE 12. BASYS-Fox: Query for "Paris": Step 2: Hit List

Bundesarchiv - Sucheergebnisse - Microsoft Internet Explorer

Datei Bearbeiten Ansicht Favoriten Extras ?

Trefferübersicht

Sortierung: **Relevanz**

Findmittel	Findmittel-einleitung	Klassifi-kation	Aktenver-zeichnis
Nachlass Hans von Zwehl	3	0	0
Berater für den Marshallplan beim Vorsitzer des Verwaltungsrats des Vereinigten Wirtschaftsgebietes	2	1	13
Nachlass Eduard Fuchs	2	0	0
Reichsministerium für Wiederaufbau	1	0	25
Ministerium für Post- und Fernmeldewesen. - Teil 1 Postwertzeichen	1	0	4
Reichsverkehrsministerium. - Kraftverkehr, Luftschiffahrt, Hauptbüro und kleinere Strukturteile	1	0	2
Nachlass Paul Leverkuehn	1	0	1
Kolonialpolitisches Amt der NSDAP	1	0	1
Büro der Deutschen Geschäftsstelle des Marshallplanes und des Beauftragten für den Außenhandel der drei Länder der Französischen Zone	1	0	0
Kolonialwirtschaftliches Komitee	1	0	0
Bentheimer Grenzlandausschuß	1	0	0
/ R 2107 Oberfinanzpräsident Berlin-Brandenburg. - Außenstelle für feindliches Vermögen	1	0	0
Militärattachés	0	1	0
Reichskolonialamt	0	0	19
Bundesministerium für Jugend, Familie, Frauen und Gesundheit (1969-1991) und Funktionsnachfolger	0	0	8
Bundesministerium für Post und Telekommunikation.- Teil 1: Aktenplan-Hauptgruppe 2 Postwesen	0	0	7
Reichsfinanzministerium (Ve-WM)	0	0	7
Reichsverband der Deutschen Presse	0	0	5
Nachlass Theodor Heuss	0	0	5
Publikationstelle Berlin-Dahlem	0	0	4
Nachlass Paul Dickopf	0	0	4
Außenpolitisches Amt der NSDAP (APA)	0	0	3
Reichspropagandaleiter der NSDAP	0	0	2
Bundesministerium für das Gesundheitswesen	0	0	2
Deutsch-Britische Gesellschaft e. V.	0	0	1
Generalstaatsanwalt der DDR	0	0	1
Reichskanzleramt	0	0	1
Sonderbeauftragter für die Überprüfung des zweckmäßigen Kriegseinsatzes (OKW Stab z.b.V.)	0	0	1
Reichsbeauftragter für die deutsche Filmwirtschaft	0	0	1
Ministerium für Wirtschaft und Funktionsvorgänger	0	0	1

CONCLUSION

At present then the Bundesarchiv follows a dual strategy for the presentation of finding aids online. On the one hand, online finding aids based on BASYS-XML are presented on the Bundesarchiv Server. On the other hand, EAD XML is used as an external exchange format for integration with international portals and search engines. EAD is not used as a description standard.

The active operation of BASYS-Fox started in July 2004. Since then, users have a number of ways to access the holdings of the Bundesarchiv. They can find them via:

- Traditional publication finding aids
- Online inventories (Midosa, MidosaXML, BASYS-Fox) or
- EAD files by using the RLG's *Archival Resources*.

For the future we are planning a databased online administration system that has a three-tier architecture. With this online system we will–according to the present state of planning–create a system, which uses the well-founded German traditions of administration and description. According to the recommendations of the German American task group and following the experience we now have with BASYS-Fox and MidosaXML,[8] EAD will be used by the Bundesarchiv as an exchange format for the integration of our descriptive data in search engines and international platforms. At present EAD is not scheduled as an *internal* exchange format for the Internet application of the Bundesarchiv or for the description of our holdings. However, although EAD could play a useful role, more concrete planning is required for the planned German archive portal.

Access to the holdings of the Bundesarchiv has been made fundamentally easier by online presentation on the home page of the federal archives and international portals and networks, such as RLG's *Archival Resources*. Perhaps archival circles will remember printed finding aids in a melancholic way as things of the past.

NOTES

1. An online version of the cabinet minutes of the federal government has been available online since October 2003 at http://www.bundesarchiv.de/kabinettsprotokolle.

2. For online access to finding aids at the Bundesarchiv see http://www.bundesarchiv.de/bestaende_findmittel/findmittel_online/index.html.

3. Sigrun Eckelmann, Hans-Dieter Kreikamp, Angelika Menne-Haritz, Wilfried Reininghaus, "Neue Medien im Archiv: Online-Zugang und elektronische Aufzeichnungen," *Bericht über eine Studienreise nach Nordamerika, 10-21. Mai 1999* (*Veröffentlichungen der Archivschule Marburg*, Nr. 32), Marburg (2000).

4. See the report of "DFG-Projekt: Deutsch-amerikanische Arbeitsgruppe Online-Findmittel," *Der Archivar*, Jg 53 (2000), H 4, S 352f available online at http://www.uni-marburg.de/archivschule/daagead.pdf.

5. For a detailed discussion of the Midosa system see Angelika Menne-Haritz, "Enhancing the Effectiveness of Description with Innovative Tools–the Example of MidosaXML" in this volume, 83-95.

6. The Bundesarchiv XML-schema is available at http://www.bundesarchiv.de/aktuelles/projekte/00005/index.htm. The Workshop of the Northrhine Westphalia State archive on the DFG-Project "Development of Tools for Retroconversion of Archival Finding Aids," (September 2003), 22/23 available online at http://www.archive.nrw.de/dok/tagung-retro/.

7. Table of content for RLG-indexing at http://www.bundesarchiv.de/findbuecher/rlg_findm/table_of_content.htm. Further information about RLG's *Archival Resources* database can be found at http://www.rlg.org/en/page.php?Page_ID=120.

8. See report in 4 above, S 20.

SELECTED BIBLIOGRAPHY

Menne-Haritz, Angelika. "Archivische Erschließung–Methodische Aspekte einer Fachkompetenz," *Beiträge des 3. Archivwissenschaftlichen Kolloquiums der Archivschule Marburg*, Marburg (1999) (Veröffentlichungen der Archivschule Marburg, Bd 30).

______. "Online-Findbücher, Suchmaschinen und Portale," *Beiträge des 6. Archivwissenschaftlichen Kolloquiums der Archivschule Marburg*, Marburg (2002) (Veröffentlichungen der Archivschule Marburg, Bd 35).

Report "DFG-Projekt: Deutsch-amerikanische Fachkonzeption für die Präsentation von Online-Findmittel," in *Archivnachrichten, hrsg. von der Landesarchivdirektion Baden-Württemberg* 22 (2001), S 6.

Managing Building Permits Files at the Archives de Paris, France

Louis Faivre d'Arcier

SUMMARY. Collecting bulky series of paper materials happens very often in an institution as large as the Archives de Paris. Questions arise of how to give access to those materials and how to produce finding aids well suited to their many diverse uses. The numerous specific application programs that are used by the offices of origin of the archives can provide precious metadata for the archivist. Using the EAD DTD in order to preserve and recycle that information can be one way to solve a double problem: the description of modern serial paper-based public records and the enhancement of value for a certain type of electronic record. The use of the EAD DTD presented in this paper is a bit unusual in some ways. It reveals the DTD's capabilities as an archival interpretative tool for information created by different professional communities as well as its limitations as a tool for exchange of structured data.

Louis Faivre d'Arcier is Curator, Archives de Paris, 18 Boulevard Sérurier, F-75019 Paris, France (E-mail: louis.faivre_darcier@paris.fr) since 2001. He is in charge of automation and also responsible for collecting digital archives. He graduated from the École Nationale des Chartes with the degree of "archiviste-paléographe."

[Haworth co-indexing entry note]: "Managing Building Permits Files at the Archives de Paris, France." Faivre d'Arcier, Louis. Co-published simultaneously in *Journal of Archival Organization* (The Haworth Information Press, an imprint of The Haworth Press, Inc.) Vol. 3, No. 2/3, 2005, pp. 111-123; and: *Encoding Across Frontiers: Proceedings of the European Conference on Encoded Archival Description and Context (EAD and EAC), Paris, France, 7-8 October 2004* (ed: Bill Stockting, and Fabienne Queyroux) The Haworth Information Press, an imprint of The Haworth Press, Inc., 2005, pp. 111-123. Single or multiple copies of this article are available for a fee from The Haworth Document Delivery Service [1-800-HAWORTH, 9:00 a.m. - 5:00 p.m. (EST). E-mail address: docdelivery@haworthpress.com].

Available online at http://www.haworthpress.com/web/JAO

doi:10.1300/J201v03n02_09

KEYWORDS. Archival appraisal, EAD, Encoded Archival Description, electronic records, finding aids, public records

INTRODUCTION

The history of an archival institution such as the Archives de Paris[1]–which is both a city archives and an "Archives départementales"[2]–explains to a great extent the decisions made regarding its automation.

The Encoded Archival Description (EAD) DTD is not yet used on a daily basis at the Archives de Paris. The automation effort was first focused on control and management of the reading room and of the location list, an obvious choice given the number of paging requests: there are more than 700,000 boxes in the archives; about 180,000 paging requests happen per year, including 50,000 of original materials.

For the production of finding aids, common word-processing software has been used since the appearance of such products on the market. The main effort consisted of standardizing these finding aids, by using the *General International Standard of Archival Description (General)* (*ISAD(G)*) and the *International Standard Archival Authority Record for Corporate Bodies, Persons and Families* (*ISAAR(CPF)*)[3] as well as a standard filing plan, as the only efficient way to make up for a backlog in indexing.

The experiment conducted with GERCO (as the software used by the City of Paris for managing land use permits is named) partly takes place in this context. The goal is to preserve and reuse metadata produced by an administrative department in the course of its regular activities, in order to create a standardized finding aid that can be integrated with the information system of the Archives de Paris.

I shall begin by explaining the context, from the archives' perspective as well as from that of the administrative department. Then I shall present the possibilities of recovering useful data for the creation of a finding aid and the ways in which this data can be encoded in EAD. Finally, I shall discuss the capabilities and limitations of EAD for such a use–a use that appears to me inevitable.

THE CONTEXT

The Building Permits in Paper Format at the Archives de Paris

To this day the Archives de Paris preserve all building permits issued in Paris between about 1880 and 1998. This enormous series of about

100,000 files takes up more than 2 kilometers of shelf space. It is completed by a much smaller series of demolition permits (preserved only after appraisal). This material is the focus of much interest at the Archives de Paris, since approximately one out of ten users comes to the archives in order to view a building permit file. This group of users can be divided into two categories: first, researchers in the history of architecture or in a related field, who are looking for as much contextual information as possible; second, people conducting research on their own apartment building, who are mainly concerned with the accuracy of the finding aid.

Available documentation regarding building permits is still rather heterogeneous. Building permits have found their way to the archives in at least sixteen different transfers. For each recent transfer, a list was established, containing the following information: control number of the file, address of the building, date of the permit, and shelfmark. For the three oldest transfers, the description is quite vague: the finding aid mentions only the name of street or streets, without giving the exact address, which confuses users and leads to numerous unnecessary productions. The more recent transfer lists have more detail, because they were established by the controlling agency: a member of the Building Permit Department staff was inputting data in a spreadsheet and then printing the resulting table.

As a first attempt to correct this disparity in access tools, the oldest transfer list was turned into a card file, which gave details on existing plans, names of architects, and dates of the files. Unfortunately this card file was never completed. Another attempt consisted in exhaustively indexing pertinent information published in the *Bulletin municipal officiel*, for the period 1882-1985. This index, however, enabled users to make sure that a building permit had been issued, but not that the relevant file had actually been preserved.

More recently, systematic appraisal and arrangement of the pre-1988 files has begun, directed by Sandrine Aufray. An Access database (called CONPA) is being developed. This work will lead to the disposal of a large number of duplicates. This greatly simplifies perusal by researchers, by improving their understanding of the files, minimizing the handling and as a result enhancing physical preservation.

GERCO

Since 1988, the City of Paris Planning and Building Department has automated its procedures. The current software is named GERCO. The

City owns the software source code, which proved a happy circumstance for our project; the maintenance is outsourced.

As GERCO is a proprietary software package, a number of the out-of-the-box functionalities offered by its publisher are not used by the Building Permit Department, because of the local context. Indeed, in a city as densely built-up as Paris, the functionalities about creation of new developments or removal of trees are not used. Furthermore, for organizational reasons, other functionalities are left unused, for instance the management of permits for shop signs.

The software is used for administrative management tasks, such as processing applications for building permits, remodeling permits, demolition permits; processing declarations of works and declarations of renovations; and managing of related administrative litigation files. For each task, the main stages of the procedure are documented: dates of application, dates and types of decisions made on the file. The main parties are also documented: applicant, owner, and architect. Only post-1988 information is found in GERCO, as there was no retrospective keying of data. Two tables have been added to GERCO, at the archives' suggestion: transfer number and box number, which allows us to know whether a file is located in the intermediate storage room at the department, or has been transferred to the Archives.

Each night, the most important information is exported from GERCO to a published application, accessible via the City's Intranet, and used by the fellow administrative departments of the City. GERCO has been submitted for approval to the French Data Protection Authority. The processing of the nominal information thus created is regulated by a city bylaw, and no maximum delay for online publication is required.

All conditions were therefore met to facilitate the transfer of data from GERCO. On the one hand, the software processes information of great historical interest, the controlling agency knows the source code of the program, it is inclined to cooperate with the archives, and an export functionality is already implemented. On the other hand, there is great pressure from the public to access information on Parisian buildings.

RECOVERING THE DATA

Basic Principles

The advantages of GERCO are twofold for the Archives de Paris. Since the database describes the administrative procedure, it de facto describes the files that record that procedure. Among the files thus documented, some are preserved (all building permits effectively delivered, plus certain demolition permits); others are disposed of (everything else). For the preserved material, GERCO can serve as a finding aid, provided that a link to the archival shelfmark is added; for the destroyed material, GERCO can serve as a surrogate.

It seemed judicious to transfer the data in two separate sets, according to their separate goals:

- A set of a "finding aid" type, for records corresponding to the material actually preserved. To this effect, two fields were added to the original database: transfer number and box number. The retrospective keying of the information was done by the Planning and Building Department. For the transfer, the export criterion was the existence of a transfer number associated with the file.
- A set of a "documentary" type, which records correspond in fact to the sum of information about construction in Paris from 1988 to 2000. This set includes the data in the first set, along other types of information. Determining the chronological coverage for this data set has proved especially difficult. This particular transfer will not be discussed here.[4]

The data transfer was not followed by any destruction of data in the original GERCO database, since the Planning and Building Department wished to maintain its own direct access to the data transferred to the archives.

Appraisal of the Data

Which information should be retained? It did not seem judicious to keep all the tables of the original database, no more than all the records. After a few tentative experiments, we decided to take our lead from the information found in the published database available on the City's Intranet. This published database has a greatly simpler structure than the production database, the physical data model for which is about 500 pages long. Furthermore, a lot of information related to the management of internal administrative procedures (like the dates of transmission from one department to another, for instance) does not appear in the database available on the Intranet. Finally, only the fields really used in the production database are exported into the published database. In fact, the published database operates a selection between important data and the rest.

It was thus thought appropriate to use that structure as a model for the transfers to the Archives de Paris. The data transfer resulted in fifteen files; for each table of the Intranet GERCO system a .TXT file was produced, in which fields were separated by the "pipe" character (|). I shall not detail here all fifteen files, but simply present their main features. The main table (SUIVI) gathers identification information on the building permit files

- With that main table are associated secondary tables, that describe, for each building permit file, the stages of the procedure, the parties involved (SYNDIC, ARCHITECTE), the existence of a shelfmark (SUIVI CARTON), the street or streets concerned (SUIVI RUES), the decision or decisions made about the application (PROJA, CONFORMP), the stage or stages of the building operation (TRANCHES), the national identification number corresponding to the application file number assigned by the City of Paris (V1_SUIVI)
- Finally there are reference tables to clarify the various codes used in an individual application file: title of the person (QUAL, QUALMORAL), street (RUE), transfer number (VERSEMENT), type of application (TYPDO), type of decision (TYPAVIS).

We shall now examine the problem of reusing the data in the form of EAD files.

REUSING THE DATA

Underlying Principles and History of the Project

Choosing EAD as the retroconversion format for the data produced in the GERCO system was but one possible option. Before explaining our modus operandi, let us take a look at the other options:

- Doing nothing, and simply storing a CD packed with data until a user wants to see it. This option was obviously unsuitable, given the nature of the information, and the fact that the controlling agency also keeps its own data.

- Using a database software (Microsoft Access, for instance) in order to "recreate" a viewing system. This option would have added one more tier to the Archives information system, without being either durable or easy to use by a non-archivist.
- Transferring the data into an archival information management system–but we did not have one.

Besides the fact that all other possible options were problematic, the EAD DTD had a strong argument in its favor. It is a standardized solution that could in the future be integrated to any archival information management system selected by the archives.

In order to convert the data to XML, we decided to have a conversion program written for us. We never considered using XML editing software, because we wanted an automatic conversion, and the Archives de Paris do not currently use such software for their production of finding aids.

A call for bids[5] was published in July 2003. Five companies were approached, all of them having experience with XML. Three of them submitted proposals. One company appeared not to know EAD, since it wanted to bill the cost of learning the DTD. The choice between the other two companies was based on a combination of familiarity with the DTD and price. Work progressed in an exemplary manner, even faster than anticipated.

The project developed in two stages: during the first one (November-December 2003), we defined the conversion criteria to XML and we wrote, with the vendor, a mapping table; during the second phase (January-February 2004), the vendor wrote the conversion program and the archives put it to the test.

The Mapping Table

The conversion program allows the production of an EAD file from source files that come in part from the GERCO system and in part from the work of the Archives:

- The GERCO files were used to constitute the units of description at the lower levels;
- The files coming from the Archives were used for high-level information.

Besides, some information has been "hardcoded" in the XML file. We had to make decisions regarding the granularity of markup. In order not to make the resulting XML file too large, some GERCO fields were concatenated, while the DTD allows the encoding of such information separately (for instance, addresses and personal names).[6]

EVALUATION AND LESSONS OF THE EXPERIMENT

The EAD DTD as an Archival Interpretation of Specific Professional Data

The advantages of the conversion to EAD appeared more and more clearly as the project was making progress. The DTD allowed us, in fact, to move from a professional use and structure of data to a proper archival–or documentary–rendition.

This is, of course, particularly obvious regarding the information added to the original GERCO data during the conversion to EAD. The DTD requires some minimal contextual information in the EAD Header (<eadheader>) and Front Matter (<frontmatter>) elements. It also requires a description of the archival unit at its higher level. Because of these two requirements, the conversion program provides for adding two files that did not exist in the GERCO data export: a file "Introduction" (marked up as the high-level Abstract [abstract] element) and a file "Bibliography" (marked up as Bibliography [<bibliography>]).

For several types of information, the conversion produced a slight rearrangement of data, at the Archives' request. Mostly this involved making the GERCO table of street names compatible with those in the Conpa database table, since the GERCO table did not use a full typographical range; no distinction was made between capitals and lowercase, and diacritics were not used. It has been necessary to painstakingly compare the more than 7,000 entries in both tables.

Furthermore, the conversion in EAD has led us to think about new uses for the data. There are indeed several ways to identify a given building permit: an identification number specific to the administrative departments of the City, a national identification number, and the archival shelfmark. The latter number actually refers not to an intellectual unit, but to a container. At the Archives de Paris, building permits are stored in archival boxes (30 × 30 × 30 cm) that bear the shelfmark. All three types of information are found in GERCO. We decided to tag the local number with ID of the Unit (<unitid>), the shelfmark with Container (<container>), and to encode the national number within the Scope and Content (<scopecontent>) element, in as structured a format as possible. GERCO contains many different types of addresses. The DTD allows their tagging with the element Address (<address>), using for each line the element Address Line (<addressline>). We chose not to encode all addresses in such a detailed way, for fear of producing a large, over-encoded, XML file. In fact, we generally contented ourselves with putting the emphasis on the information most useful for research, namely the address of the building and the name of the architect, while the rest of the data was more summarily structured.

Finally, the conversion to EAD revealed the documentary interest of certain types of information. In the GERCO database, the tables PROJA and TRANCHES give detailed information on the main decisions made on a project. The encoding of that data with the element Chronology List <chronlist> resulted in a precise description of items within the administrative file, probably a lot more precise than it would have been if an archivist had had to write the finding aid "from scratch," by looking at the material itself.

However, if using the DTD in order to recover information exported from GERCO permits us to achieve a very detailed description, we are nevertheless dependent on the primary goal of the original database. The description may be very precise regarding the procedures, but is a lot less detailed regarding the documentary typology, precisely because GERCO was not designed to manage documents. For instance, there is no mention of plans in the original database, and consequently none either in the resulting finding aid. At the time of the conversion, it was decided not to add that information arbitrarily, and to leave a blank, rather than to risk leading the user on a false track.

A Few Limitations of the DTD

The conversion of the data to XML has led the archivists to add contextual information that did not exist in GERCO and that is certainly useful. But the experiment also demonstrated that the DTD is quite permissive, sometimes surprisingly so. The first surprise is the rather moderate amount of standardization. Regarding dates, for instance, it is the encoder's sole responsibility to choose a format and to stick with it!

Furthermore, it is permitted to give in the description of an archival unit many types of information in variable order.

Finally, certain types of information, though often present in modern public archives, are not taken into account in the DTD: for instance, identification numbers specific to the office of origin, so useful when a fonds is structured in several series that refer to each other.

Conversion also requires one to document precisely the *modus operandi* and the decisions made, in case of a future repetition.

Enhancing the Value of the Finding Aid

Conversion to EAD is not a goal in itself, but, as we saw earlier, a step in an automation project. The file resulting from conversion is much too large to be put online as such, since it is 17 MB in size, a rather imposing size for an XML file and in any case a lot more than the fifteen original tables (8 MB only).

At this point two possibilities for using the file are being assessed:

- Recovering the data in the archival information management system that will be selected by the Archives de Paris. This would be a good way to test the system for compatibility with EAD.
- Perhaps later, and depending on the relationship between the archival information system of the Archives and the Internet site of the City of Paris, there might be a direct publication of the XML file online via the City Web site.

In any case, the conversion of the data to XML was a good choice in the perspective of the integration of the GERCO data into the information system of the Archives.

CONCLUSION

Reuse of the GERCO data by incorporation within an EAD file is not only an experiment, but mainly a stage in the automation process of the Archives de Paris. This conversion can prove very enlightening, by its limitations as well as by its successes.

There is a palpable need for increased standardization that will perhaps lead to the transformation of the DTD into a XML schema. Beyond purely technical questions, it is very important to refine the way archivists use this tool, not only through best practice recommendations, but also through standardization of the export of finding aids. If that does not happen, there is a real danger of seeing practices diverge, which in itself might not be detrimental but will in the end create a problem for the use of the XML files thus produced.

NOTES

1. I thank all those who have contributed to the progress of the project: Sandrine Aufray especially, but also Marc Richaud, Marie-Andrée Corcuff, Valérie Brousselle, François Gasnault, Catherine Dhérent, Olivier Mijoint and Nelly Schwab.

2. Paris is both a city and one of the ninety-five "*départements*" (main administrative divisions) of France.

3. International Council on Archives, *ISAD(G): General International Standard Archival Description*, 2nd edition (Ottawa, 2000) is available at http://www.ica.org/biblio/isad_g_2e.pdf. International Council on Archives, *ISAAR(CPF): International Standard Archival Authority Record for Corporate Bodies, Persons and Families* (2004) is available at http://www.ica.org/biblio.php?pdocid=144.

4. L. Faivre d'Arcier, "De l'application 'métier' à l'instrument de recherche archivistique. Archivage des données de l'application de gestion des autorisations d'occupation des sols de la Ville de Paris," *Document Numérique*, 8 (2004): 51-62.

5. More exactly, we used the procedure called in French a "*marché sans formalité préalable*."

6. An extract of the XML/EAD mapping table will be found below at Appendix A.

APPENDIX A

Mapping Table of building permit data to EAD:

Ellipses are indicated by the sign (...). A few commentaries are placed between square brackets.

```
<?xml version="1.0" encoding="ISO-8859-1" ?>
<!DOCTYPE ead SYSTEM "ead.dtd">
<ead>
  <eadheader> (. . .)
[In this tag the Archives de Paris staff insert contextual information]
  </eadheader>
  <frontmatter> (. . .)
[Here too, information is provided by the Archives de Paris]
  </frontmatter>
  <archdesc level="fonds">
    <did>
      <abstract>Here comes a general presentation of the fonds, written by the Archives</abstract>
    </did>
    <bibliography>
    </bibliography>
    <dsc type="in-depth">
      <c level="item">
        <did>
          <container type="box" label="cote">Shelfmark </container>
          <unittitle>Building permit ; or Demolition permit ; or Remodeling permit </unittitle>
          <unitid label="dossier">control number of the application file</unitid>
          <unitdate type="inclusive">1980-1995 for instance: 1980 being the date of the oldest item within the whole application file, 1995 being the date of the most recent one [The notion of inclusive dates does not exist in the GERCO system. The content of this tag was created by a query programmed by the vendor in order to place here the oldest and the most recent dates found in the file] </unitdate>
          <origination><corpname>authority making the decision [City or State]</corpname></origination>
```

```
			</did>
			<scopecontent>
				<p>national identification number for the
application file: <p>
				<address>
					<addressline>street number</addressline>
					<addressline>type of street : street,
square, boulevard. . .</addressline>
					<addressline>name of the street
</addressline>
					<addressline>district ("arrondisse-
ment")</addressline>
					<addressline>PARIS</addressline>
				</address>
				<p>applicant : title + name (person)</p>
				<p>title + corporation</p>
				<p>address : address of the applicant + postal
code + city</p>
(. . . ) [Here can be found several addresses, in the same format]
				<p> architect: code of title<persname>architect's
name</persname></p>
				<p> address : architect's address - postal code +
city </p>
				<p>Subject:</p>
				<p>architectural program: </p>
				<p>administrative management of the application
file:
					<chronlist>
						<chronitem><date>date of
action</date><event>action </event></chronitem>
					</chronlist>
				</p>
			</scopecontent>
		</c>
	</archdesc>
</ead>
```

Concerning Descriptive Standards: A Partnership Between Public Archives and Private Collections in Geneva, Switzerland

Barbara Roth-Lochner
Didier Grange

SUMMARY. This paper presents the results of a partnership begun in 2002 in the field of archival description between the Geneva City Archives (AVG) and the Manuscripts Department of the Public and University Library of Geneva (BPU). This cooperation has allowed the creation of two computer applications, which share technical and conceptual foundations. Both *IDEA* (at the AVG) and *Odyssée* (at the

---

Barbara Roth-Lochner, PhD, is Editor of *Arbido*, and is on the Committee for the Certificate in Archival Studies (continuing education) of the Lausanne, Bern and Geneva Universities. She also teaches at Haute École de Gestion of Geneva, Bibliothéque Publique et Universitaire, Les Bastions, CH 1211 Genève 4, Switzerland (E-mail: barbara.roth@bpu.ville-ge.ch).

Didier Grange is City Archivist for Geneva and Chair, International Council on Archives Section of Records Management and Archival Professional Associations, Archives de la Ville de Genève, Palais Eynard, 4 rue de la Croix-Rouge, CH 1211 Genève 3, Switzerland (E-mail: didier.grange@seg.ville-ge.ch).

[Haworth co-indexing entry note]: "Concerning Descriptive Standards: A Partnership Between Public Archives and Private Collections in Geneva, Switzerland." Roth-Lochner, Barbara, and Didier Grange. Co-published simultaneously in *Journal of Archival Organization* (The Haworth Information Press, an imprint of The Haworth Press, Inc.) Vol. 3, No. 2/3, 2005, pp. 125-138; and: *Encoding Across Frontiers: Proceedings of the European Conference on Encoded Archival Description and Context (EAD and EAC), Paris, France, 7-8 October 2004* (ed: Bill Stockting, and Fabienne Queyroux) The Haworth Information Press, an imprint of The Haworth Press, Inc., 2005, pp. 125-138. Single or multiple copies of this article are available for a fee from The Haworth Document Delivery Service [1-800-HAWORTH, 9:00 a.m. - 5:00 p.m. (EST). E-mail address: docdelivery@haworthpress.com].

Available online at http://www.haworthpress.com/web/JAO

doi:10.1300/J201v03n02_10

BPU) are built with respect to international descriptive standards, notably *ISAD(G)*, as well as the combination of XML and EAD.

KEYWORDS. Archives de la Ville de Genève, Bibliothèque Publique et Universitaire de Genève, EAD, Encoded Archival Description, standardization, *ISAD(G)*

TWO INSTITUTIONS WITH DIFFERENCES AND SIMILARITIES

Differences

There was nothing driving our two institutions to work together in the field of automation. Indeed, they have very different traditions and they hold very different types of material. The Geneva City Archives (AVG) is a department created and run by a professional since 1986, that holds the administrative archives of the city, created in 1842, as well as a few fonds from individuals, companies or organizations.[1] The Manuscripts Department of the Public and University Library of Geneva, in existence since 1904,[2] holds a collection of single manuscripts–from Greek papyri to letters of contemporary writers–as well as a collection of about 500 fonds of family or personal archives, along with about 50 fonds from corporate bodies.

There are also many differences with regard to the descriptive practices of the two institutions. Given its relative newness, the AVG has always created its finding aids using word-processing programs. Many finding aids, therefore, took the form of Microsoft Word tables and about 6,000 pages of text have been produced in this way. The Manuscripts Department, being older, had other traditions. The cataloguing (to use a library term) was always detailed. The department as a consequence produced tens of thousands of typewritten or printed pages, along with several card files for indexes, mostly of names. Given that personal and family archives are of a more heterogeneous nature than series of administrative records produced by a well-defined entity, they require fuller description to reveal the information they contain.

Similarities

The archivists of both institutions are deeply convinced that the international descriptive standards elaborated by the International Council on Archives are necessary. We are certain that they are conducive to the professionalization of practices and to the promotion of contacts, including those with the users and the public for whom we are working. Another factor, in the field of administrative organization, has to be taken into account. The City of Geneva has centralized computer services, with an extremely competent staff. Such help can allow two separate departments like ours to develop common projects without any major financial outlay in this area. Last but not least, one should not underestimate the part played by the professional friendship that exists between the heads of the two repositories.

THE ROAD TO EAD

The Geneva City Archives has been interested in standardization of description for many years. In 1996, it produced inventories partly compliant with the *General International Standard of Archival Description (ISAD(G))*. The following year it published online descriptions of fonds, based on a mix of *ISAD(G)* and the Canadian standard, *Rules for Archival Description (RAD)*.[3] For her part, the Head of the Manuscripts Department wanted to make fonds processing practices more compliant with the principles of modern archival science, without demeaning, or getting rid of, the splendid heritage of traditional catalogues.

The evolution of both departments led us to look for the most convenient automated tool for the description of our fonds. The word processing programs used definitely had many advantages, but did not allow us to take full advantage of the possibilities presented by information technology in terms of the sharing of information (through the Internet), refined indexes and queries. Given this, the question of acquiring a commercial system dedicated to managing archives, and especially descriptions, was broached several times.

Commercial systems, however, also have well-known drawbacks:

- Their evolution and their lifespan depend entirely on a commercial company, the continued existence of which is uncertain
- Their acquisition and ongoing maintenance are expensive
- The user has absolutely no control over proprietary data structure formats.

These considerations led us to make the decision to develop our own system, taking great care to avoid these problems.

As early as 2001 we agreed to the features of the future system. It would allow:

- Using and respecting international standards
- Conversion of finding aids already created with Word, for the AVG[4]
- Creation of new finding aids through a simple data input interface that could be used by staff not necessarily fully trained in archival science
- Publication of all finding aids on the Web, at least for the AVG[5]
- Possibility of printing out finding aids.

For the reasons described above, we opted for a combination of *ISAD(G)* for the content of descriptions and we selected Encoded Archival Description (EAD) as XML for the digital format. Such a choice led to the creation of the *IDEA* (*Instrument de Description Électronique des Archives*) application, which allowed the online publication of the finding aids of the AVG in December 2003.

Rather than using all the possibilities offered by EAD for marking up finding aids, we inverted the perspective and deliberately placed *ISAD(G)* at the center of the process.[6] We therefore decided to limit the markup strictly to the fields defined by *ISAD(G)*. Even if such a decision was confining, it proved decisive for the rest of the process. It actually turned the standard into the spine on which the computer application had to rely. To the *ISAD(G)* outline were added index fields for corporate bodies, persons, places and subjects, plus two additional fields specifically intended for the Manuscripts Department: occupations and families.[7] Once the framework was defined, a consultant, Sarra Ben Lagha, elaborated a specific XML DTD, based on the structure of *ISAD(G)*.

For the staff that input the data, EAD is invisible. The input screen is divided in several parts; the archivist selects, in a predetermined order, the necessary fields, which carry an easily understandable label as illustrated in Figure 1. The fields appear without the EAD tags, which in their hard-coded form are likely to scare off many archivists. The validation procedure checks on the presence of the mandatory *ISAD(G)* fields. The hierarchy of the finding aid can be displayed from left to right with the mouse, or can be shown as a table, at the archivist's choice.

FIGURE 1. AVG, Data Input Screen for the Fonds of the Musée d'Art et d'Histoire of Geneva

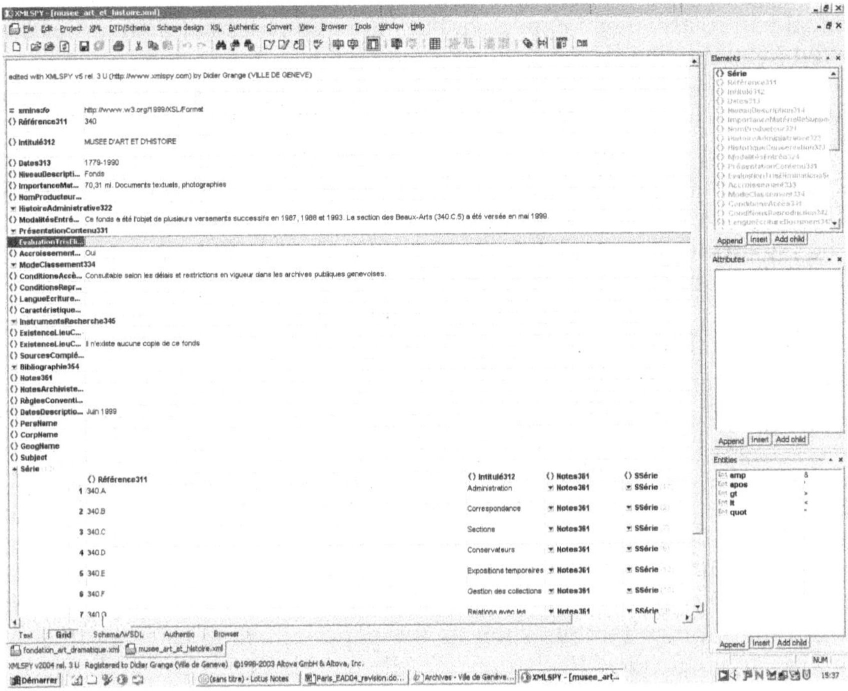

The consultant also invented a series of operations that enabled the conversion of the Word tables until then produced by the AVG into the new DTD, as well as the generation of EAD, HTML and PDF files. For reasons of cost and user-friendliness, she selected XML Spy as the editing software rather than XMetaL, even though the latter has been used by many archival institutions for several years.

Our colleague Vania Cavalli, from the Computer Department, conceived the Lotus Notes application[8] that stores and manages the XML, HTML and PDF files generated with XML Spy and with the tools invented by Sarra Ben Lagha. She also wrote the online help intended for users, and she designed for the AVG a module for the ordering of documents.

PROBLEMS ENCOUNTERED

Interestingly, the major problems we encountered were not of a technical nature as we had expected, but rather consisted of difficulties created by archival practices.

In the case of the AVG, the relative youth of the institution made the work easier. It has not been necessary to re-engineer many finding aids. The finding aids were not very heterogeneous as is often the case in older institutions where practices have evolved over time. The oldest finding aids, however, proved quite difficult to convert. In some cases the organization of a fonds had to be revised, since it did not correspond to the several levels of description found in *ISAD(G)*. The post-1996 finding aids, on the other hand, which were partially *ISAD(G)*-compliant, passed the hurdle successfully and were easily converted.

The Manuscripts Department, for its part, had to take into account decades, even centuries, of variant practice in its catalogues and finding aids. This not only meant that there was a great wealth of information but also the complexity of successive "layers" of methodological improvements. Such a context leads to the consideration of many options. Should the department, in its use of the *ISAD(G)*-XML/EAD tool, give priority to new finding aids? Should it, on the contrary, focus on older finding aids (mostly those of heavily used fonds and collections that make the library famous such as the papers of the protestant theologians, Jean-Jacques Rousseau, Ferdinand de Saussure and Nicolas Bouvier, etc.) by re-engineering and adapting them? Reason and sound management plead for the first option: indeed, why invest time in collections already processed and with existing finding aids, while so many others are waiting for attention? However, the second option has compelling strategic arguments in its favor: publishing on the Web finding aids of prestigious collections contributes to the fame and influence of the institution; rekeying an old finding aid while adapting it to the *ISAD(G)* standard takes less time than processing a new collection, even if the conversion requires professional archival competences. One must indeed keep in mind that the encoding in EAD of a description and its indexing are but the final stage of a long process, from identification, analysis, organization, and housing to finally attribution of shelfmarks.

Another difficulty for the Manuscripts Department came about due to the existence of numerous collections of manuscripts and autographs. Like all collections, due to the diverse provenance of their components and the deliberate planning of their gathering, they cannot be strictly defined as organic fonds. Some of them were formed by a scholar or an amateur in the course of his professional activities or his passion; these can be related to real fonds. Others were created by archivists and librarians for practical reasons, most often according to a common theme, for instance notes taken by students during academic lectures at the University of Geneva (some of which date back to the sixteenth century). However, only single items, acquired as such by the department, were treated in this way: notes found in a fonds of personal archives would never be extracted from it in order to *respect des fonds*. Describing such collections with *ISAD(G)*-XML/EAD does not offer, in our opinion, insuperable difficulties. One only needs to use the descriptive level "fonds" when establishing the description of the whole collection and to explain in which ways, by whom and when the collection was formed. Single items are then described at the file or item level. We believe that most users do not care if the information they are looking for belongs to an organic fonds or to an artificial collection of single items.

Other issues were more challenging for us. *ISAD(G)* requires one to always take into account the level of description, since each bit of information must be placed at the corresponding level. As a consequence, the AVG had to revise its practice and become a lot more rigorous. To give but one example, information about the appraisal of administrative records used to be placed in the introduction to the finding aid, whether it applied to the whole fonds or only to one of its parts. Now, only appraisal information regarding the whole fonds is mentioned at the highest level, while all other such information is mentioned at the relevant lower level (series, subseries, etc.).

We were also induced to reconsider the depth of description that we wanted to use for each fonds. This can depend on the size of a fonds, on the urgency of processing, and on the human resources available. It is always a crucial question when beginning the processing of a new fonds, especially if we are looking at the archives of a person with multiple activities. True, a certain invariability appears regarding the categories of documents that are found: legal documents (diplomas, notarial documents, contracts), correspondence, manuscripts related to the activities or occupations of the person (literary manuscripts, drafts for articles, conference papers, but also critical reviews on works by others), documentary files, autobiographical writings (diaries, personal or not, travel narratives). The larger and more complex the fonds is, the more tempted the archivist is to create series, subseries and sub-subseries. We believe that in this case the best is the enemy of the good, and that it is in the users' as well as the archivist's best interests not to multiply the levels of description, especially when the fonds is closed.

We all know that archivists are not experts when it comes to subject indexing. Working according to the principle of provenance and the occupations of the corporate bodies, families and persons, we guide the users willing to explore a particular subject along paths that are different from those used by librarians and documentalists. But in this age of information in which we live, can we go on sticking strictly to the great principles of archival science without making a few concessions to the legitimate wish of quickly finding information on a particular subject? In relation to this issue, being part of a great university library gives the Manuscripts Department an interesting potential for synergy. One must admit that our librarian colleagues do have, in the field of subject indexing, as well as in the field of standardization, a head start on archivists. It would be absurd to build a thesaurus of subject terms when one already exists for indexing printed material. Even if it does not cover all the specificities and complexities of archives, not to take inspiration from it would be counterproductive, especially if it includes, as does the thesaurus of the *Réseau Romand des Bibliothèques Universitaires* (*RERO*), periods and events (such as "Reformation" and "Russian revolution" for example).[9]

As in every similar project, difficulties have appeared that will sound familiar to colleagues. One must find time to proofread finding aids before and after their publication on the Internet, and to standardize the formats for dates, abbreviations and references, etc. Of course it is obvious, but is it always taken into consideration at the onset of a project? If the absence of rigor is not too much of a problem in paper-based finding aids, it is very damaging as soon as the finding aids become digital. Thus, the AVG and the Department of Manuscripts have each written a guide, progressively enriched and completed as the work moves forward, and validated by a project manager. Such tools for reference and quality control, shared by all staff members who arrange and describe fonds, will be regularly updated.

ASSESSMENT

Results

With regard to the AVG, we can say that all objectives have been reached. The Web pages presenting the finding aids of the Geneva City

Archives have been online since December 9, 2003, as shown in Figure 2. Each finding aid is available in three different formats: HTML, PDF and EAD.[10]

Web users can also use the Lotus Notes search engine to search across several or all of the finding aids. Search within a particular finding aid can be performed with the browser's search engine. Through an ad hoc module, researchers can also reserve the documents they wish to use before a visit to the reading room. Even if the *IDEA* application is not difficult to use, it nevertheless takes a bit of practice for an archivist to become familiar with certain functionalities. In order to capitalize on the experience gained by those involved in the project and to share common practices in the future, a short users' guide has been written. This

FIGURE 2. *IDEA*: Description of the Fonds of the Musée d'Art et d'Histoire of Geneva

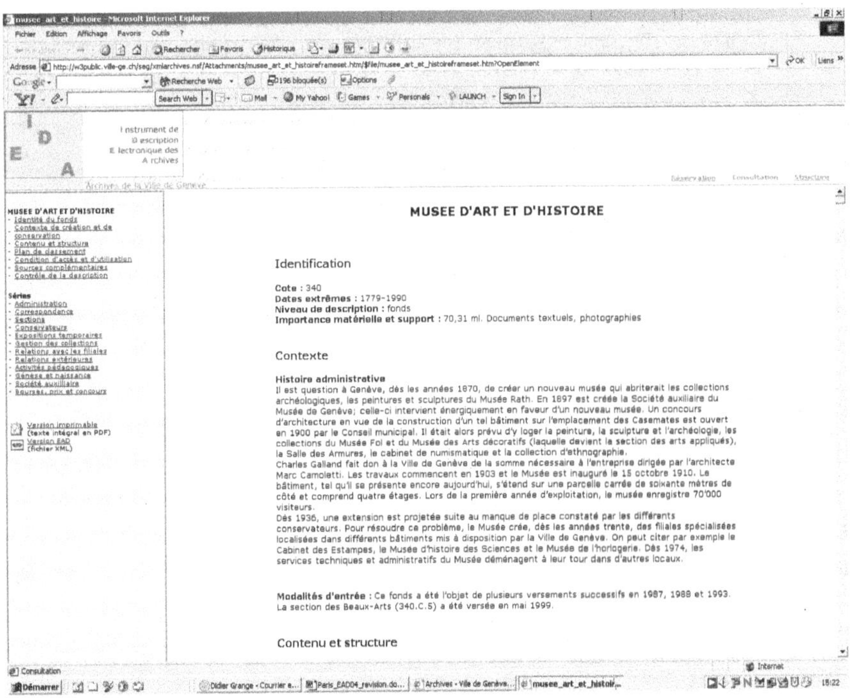

guide, which is constantly improved by the various parties, has become an indispensable tool.

As for the Manuscripts Department, it is still too early to assess the results. The effort is still too recent and the number of finding aids in digital format too small. The department suffers from a lack of human resources (which is not very original!), and would certainly have greatly benefited from more time from the specialist who adapted the AVG application. She could have, thereby, worked with the staff members during their first experiments and enlarged the database. However, the initial results of the *Odyssée* database are quite promising. In particular, it has been possible to reproduce, through a dedicated application, the considerable advantages of the cumulative card index of authors and addressees of correspondence, a research tool that is greatly appreciated and used on a daily basis by the department's patrons as can be seen in Figure 3.

FIGURE 3. *Odyssée*: Search by Authors and Addresses of Letters

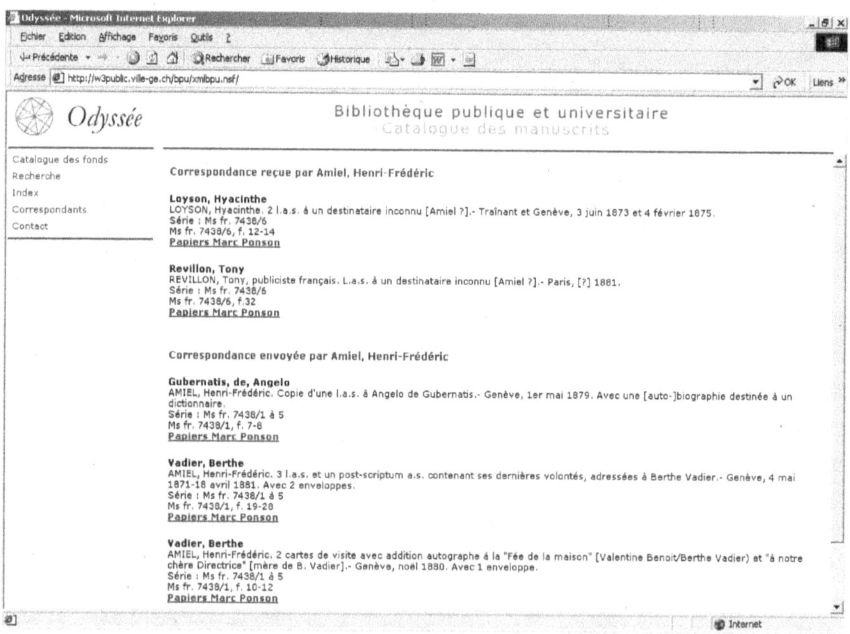

Lessons Learned

It is essential to clearly define the objectives at the beginning of the project and to remain pragmatic in the course of it. Too much perfectionism can quickly become crippling. One must accept the notion that neither the system nor the archival descriptions are frozen for eternity. Both can always be improved.

The experience of the AVG shows that it is important to re-engineer existing finding aids in order to automate their encoding as much as possible. Such a decision proceeds from a purely logical observation: one will always find more archivists capable of updating and improving old finding aids than archivists capable by themselves of marking up finding aids in EAD. We think it is preferable to adopt a restrictive approach to markup and limit ourselves to *ISAD(G)* fields, rather than using all the options offered by EAD, even if the latter would allow more precise descriptions. Finally, reflection must not be limited to the writing of finding aids but must embrace a wider field. With the development of new technologies, it is now possible to develop an application within a succession of projects that must lead archivists from writing traditional descriptions to creating more sophisticated finding aids, shared with others.

Perspectives

We do not want to stop where we are. Future developments are planned, in three directions: authority control, indexing and digitization.

In the near future, we wish to add to *IDEA* and *Odyssée* a new module related to the *International Standard Archival Authority Record for Corporate Bodies, Persons and Families* (*ISAAR(CPF)*),[11] of which the second edition was recently published, as well as to the Encoded Archival Context (EAC) DTD. In this context, the Manuscripts Department is very interested in the Linking and Exploring Authority Files (LEAF) project,[12] and wishes to establish a partnership with national institutions (Swiss National Library and Federal Archives) in order to standardize and share authority data from the time of its creation. This would be particularly useful for the authority records of persons and families, or of corporate bodies with a national dimension that have regional and local branches. In *IDEA* as well as in *Odyssée*, fields have been expressly set aside for indexing. However, our institutions are not yet ready to use them. Only a large project, funded on a secure basis, could one day allow us to start this work that requires greater resources.

It will also be necessary to plan a digitization campaign. Of course we do not want to digitize everything, but rather to select coherent and useful sets of material. For instance, the AVG are planning to digitize the official reports and statements produced by the City government and council since 1842 (*Comptes rendus de l'administration municipale*, *Procès-verbaux du Conseil administratif* and *Mémorial du Conseil municipal*). In the same vein, the Manuscripts Department wishes to establish links between EAD encoded descriptions and documents for which there is already a digital surrogate or that are heavily used.

CONCLUSION

The partnership between our two institutions has been very fruitful. Now that we have reached the end of this project, we think that the method of standardization is the right one. We now have at our disposal tools that are functional, stable and easy to use, and that permit us to describe our holdings in a satisfying way. Our approach, as well as our applications, could be implemented in other institutions in the City of Geneva and elsewhere. Other archives from different cantons[13] and cities, both in Switzerland and abroad, have shown interest in such a possibility.

It would indeed be very interesting in the future to create cross-institutional archival applications. Standardization could allow us to envision the creation of a real archival network on a regional, national or even international scale, following the Canadian example or another model yet to be created.[14] Indeed one could go further and expand the scope by developing descriptive projects that would also include libraries and museums, so that users could find complementary information kept in these different institutions. To limit ourselves to the case of Geneva alone, for example, the Manuscripts Department wishes to include in its descriptions links to the *RERO* catalogue for books and articles published by a person whose archives it keeps, as well as for publications relating to that person. Other links can be created with the database of Geneva museums and iconographic collections, MusInfo,[15] to direct users to portraits, photographs, or even objects which once belonged to a scientist or a writer. This approach could prove very promising and could open new perspectives, for professionals as well as the public.

AUTHORS' NOTES

Barbara Roth-Lochner studied at the University of Geneva, where she gained a licence in history in 1976, a degree in numerical computation in 1980, and a PhD in 1994. After being Deputy State Archivist at the State Archives of Geneva from 1981 to 2001, she became curator of the Department of Manuscripts of the Geneva Library. She is editor of the professional journal *Arbido* and sits on the scientific committee for the certificate in archival studies (continuing education) of the Lausanne, Bern and Geneva Universities. Barbara also teaches archival science at the Haute École de Gestion of Geneva (section Information and Documentation), at the CESID and for the certificate in archival studies Bibliothèque Publique et Universitaire, Les Bastions.

Didier Grange holds a licence in history (1989) and in classical archaeology (1991) from the University of Geneva. He has been the City Archivist for Geneva since 1995. He chairs the International Council on Archives Section of Records Management and Archival Professional Associations (2004-2008). He has taught at the Haute École de Gestion of Geneva (section Information and Documentation), at the CESID and for the certificate in archival studies (continuing education) of the Lausanne, Bern and Geneva universities.

NOTES

1. For further information about the Geneva City Archives see http://www.ville-ge.ch/archives.

2. For further information about the Manuscripts Department of the Public and University Library of Geneva see http://www.ville-ge.ch/bpu/manusc/f/manusc.htm.

3. Didier Grange and Jean-Manuel Grob, "Quand ISAD(G) rencontre Internet. Constitution d'un état des fonds aux Archives de la Ville de Genève," Arbido 9, 1997, 11-12. See also International Council on Archives, *ISAD(G): General International Standard Archival Description*, 2nd edition (Ottawa, 2000), available at http://www.ica.org/biblio/isad_g_2e.pdf.

4. Finding aids have been keyed or transferred in Word format for many years, so that they would form a homogenous set when retroconversion became possible.

5. The AVG created its Web site in 1997; an Intranet for the City employees opened in 1999.

6. In its second edition.

7. In order to account for the great diversity of private archives, two additional levels were included in the DTD used by the Manuscripts Department.

8. The Lotus Notes platform is commonly used in the administrative departments of the City of Geneva to manage databases of documents. It was selected for its flexibility and its adaptability, but it would be possible to use another database.

9. The *RERO* vocabulary is available on the site of the *Réseau des Bibliothèques de Suisse Occidentale*, at: http://www.rero.ch.

10. Several finding aids were not published online in their complete version. For confidentiality reasons, for instance when a description mentions a legal dispute with a person, we had to create two series of files, one with full descriptions, for internal use, the other "sanitized" for the public. Fortunately only a very small number of finding aids are concerned.

11. International Council on Archives, *ISAAR(CPF): International Standard Archival Authority Record for Corporate Bodies, Persons and Families* (2004) is available at http://www.ica.org/biblio.php?pdocid=144.

12. For further information about the Linking and Exploring Authority Files (LEAF) project, see http://www.crxnet.com/leaf/index.html.

13. A "canton" is the main administrative subdivision in Switzerland.

14. For details on the Canadian project, see http://www.archivescanada.ca/fr/index.html.

15. For further information about the database of Geneva museums and iconographic collections, MusInfo, see http://www.ville-ge.ch/musinfo/.

The *Metrica Regni* Project: The Polish Experience of EAD

Hubert Wajs

SUMMARY. The fonds of Crown Chancery Public Register (*Metrica Regni*) was chosen for the pilot project to introduce Encoded Archival Description (EAD) because of its historical value, typical archival structure and existing finding aids. The rights and privileges granted by Polish kings were recorded in the Register. The oldest books in the series of registrations (*Libri Inscriptionum*) began in the middle of the fifteenth century. This paper discusses how the Polish EAD project was completed from the fall of 2003 by the staff of the Central Archives of Historical Records in Warsaw. It started with the theoretical background and ended with practical work with a Polish HTML editor–"*Pajączek*" (Little Spider). The data were prepared and exported from a Microsoft Access database and a Microsoft Word editor into an XML file. After validations and corrections, the stylesheet from the "EAD Cookbook" was adopted as a delivery method. On 29 July 2004 the first version of the inventory of Crown Chancery Public Register in EAD was published on the Web site of the Central Archives of Historical Records.

Hubert Wajs is Head, Central Archives of Historical Records, Warsaw, Poland (E-mail: hubert.w@wp.pl).

[Haworth co-indexing entry note]: "The *Metrica Regni* Project: The Polish Experience of EAD." Wajs, Hubert. Co-published simultaneously in *Journal of Archival Organization* (The Haworth Information Press, an imprint of The Haworth Press, Inc.) Vol. 3, No. 2/3, 2005, pp. 139-146; and: *Encoding Across Frontiers: Proceedings of the European Conference on Encoded Archival Description and Context (EAD and EAC), Paris, France, 7-8 October 2004* (ed: Bill Stockting, and Fabienne Queyroux) The Haworth Information Press, an imprint of The Haworth Press, Inc., 2005, pp. 139-146. Single or multiple copies of this article are available for a fee from The Haworth Document Delivery Service [1-800-HAWORTH, 9:00 a.m. - 5:00 p.m. (EST). E-mail address: docdelivery@haworthpress.com].

Available online at http://www.haworthpress.com/web/JAO

doi:10.1300/J201v03n02_11

KEYWORDS. EAD, Encoded Archival Description, finding aids, Polish Chancery, retrospective conversion, standardization

At the Fifteenth International Congress on Archives recently held in Vienna, I spoke about the Polish experience with Encoded Archival Description (EAD).[1] In this paper, however, I will not only present the story of how the Polish EAD project was completed, but also ask some questions about EAD. First of all, I would like to express my thanks and acknowledge my debt to the many archivist colleagues who have helped me on my road to EAD. I had the chance to exchange opinions on EAD with Swedish, German, Dutch and English archivists and I wonder, or even doubt, if one could do it alone.

In archives or in repositories, we keep not only records (as our holdings), but finding aids as well, in order to know what these records are about. Nowadays these finding aids (inventories, registers, catalogues, etcetera) and, of course, the archival holdings, should be easily accessible for all. Inventories should be presented in electronic format on the Web, to guarantee easy access to the records. Descriptive information is a key to the holdings. Without inventories, access–which is right now one of the most important issues for archives–would be not possible.[2] "EAD . . . is the first data structure standard to provide the means to distribute over the Internet detailed information about archival collections and fonds"–as one can read in the preface to the *EAD Application Guidelines*.[3] This is what EAD is for. In Polish archives only a small fraction of existing finding aids are in electronic format. I hope–and here I am rather optimistic–it is around 15 percent of all our inventories. The rest still have to be put into electronic format–we call it retrospective conversion. And once again, EAD is just for such activities.

Retrospective conversion seems important for archives with a "long history" or historical archives. The Central Archives of Historical Records in Warsaw, where I am working, is one of them. By historical archives I mean non-accruing holdings of medieval or more recent date, where appraisal was done by history itself. The first, important issue to be considered is the way of describing the record. With all due respect to what former generations of archivists have done, I wonder if without additional work old inventories could be easily encoded according to EAD standards. Old descriptive practice did not include many basic elements, like information about physical description, language, former identification number, record creator or–which is not their fault–other copies (microfilms), bibliography, and published editions. These elements seem essential today for a proper finding aid and can be standardized thanks to the *General International Standard of Archival Description* (*ISAD(G)*).[4] Very often in old inventories only one level of description was done and others still need to be prepared. Old inventories–and in the Central Archives of Historical Records some of them are 100 years old–need verification. Another problem is that of former or old identification numbers. It could be an old chancellery number (or numbers) even from the sixteenth century or a former archival number, sometimes both. On Daniel Pitti's suggestion I managed to solve it using two ID of the Unit tags (<unitid>): one <unitid label ="Sygn"> and another <unitid type ="former">.

Because of its great historical value, typical archival structure (series, files [volumes], and items) and existing finding aids,[5] the fonds of the Crown Chancery Public Register (*Metrica Regni*) was chosen for the pilot project to introduce EAD. The rights and privileges granted by Polish kings were recorded–probably from the end of the fourteenth century–in the volumes of the Crown Chancery Public Register. The oldest from the series of registrations (*Libri Inscriptionum*) began in the middle of the fifteenth century and the series continues until the fall of the Polish Republic at the very end of the eighteenth century. In these volumes were written copies of all the important royal charters of permanent value such as those relating to the donation of estates and landed properties, and nominations for offices, and military ranks, etcetera. There are also highly detailed registers for each record (including an abstract or brief notes describing to what each and every record refers) from the earliest part of that series, which is from the second half of the fifteenth century to the 1570s. These registers or "summaries"–*Matricularum Regni Poloniae Summaria*–were systematically edited during the last century.[6] Another series, which gathers diplomatic records from the beginning of the sixteenth century, is called legations (*Libri Legationum*). In the seventeenth century, the Chancery began a series for the registration of records that were sealed in Crown Chancery (*Sigillata*) and in the eighteenth century, other volumes for Chancellery records were issued by Chancellors. The fonds also contains the records (volumes) of the kings' courts of justice but this part was mostly destroyed during the Second World War. The language of the majority of the volumes (and records), except perhaps in the eighteenth century, was Latin, but there were also records in Polish, German and Old Ruthenian. There are 790 volumes in all the series, and in registrations there are 361 volumes, as shown in Table 1. For the first half of the sixteenth century alone there are about 30,000 records in 90 volumes.

TABLE 1. Structure of the Fonds of *Metrica Regni*

Name of series	Dates	Volumes
Libri Inscriptionum	1447-1794	361
Libri Legationum	1501-1761	41
Sigillata	1658-1794	44
Kanclerskie (Chancellery records)	1735-1794	117
„Metryka Ruska"	1569-1673	31
„Metryka Mazowiecka"	1414-1526	21
Sądy: Asesorski, Relacyjny i Sejmowy (Kings' high courts of justice)	1591-1744 [1795]	23
Sąd Referendarski (Kings' court of justice for royal estates)	1582, 1591-1794	65

The project was started in the fall of 2003. The initial idea was simply to rewrite the existing inventory partly into a Microsoft Word editor and partly into a Microsoft Access database at the series and file (volume) levels; that is the EAD component wrappers, <c01 level="series"> and <c02 level="file">. The general information at the series level was rewritten into a Word editor and using "paste and copy" put inside the EAD wrappers: Scope and Content (<scopecontent>), Biography or History (<bioghist>), and Bibliography (<bibliography>), etc. In the same way the introduction to the whole fonds was rewritten and put inside the Archival Description (<archdesc>) wrapper. Table 2 presents the crosswalk for the conversion from the database to an XML file for the file (volume) level.

The input of data was partly done in the Central Archives of Historical Records by a member of staff (Ms. Katarzyna Janowska-Kucio), partly by a person sent by the labour office as part of her half-year practice in the Archives (Ms. Aleksandra Siwek), and partly by students from one of the high schools in Warsaw (Wyższa Szkoła Pedagogiczna Związku Nauczycielstwa Polskiego). The most important part of the task, that is the proofreading, checking of accuracy and correction of errors, was done by archivists: Ms. Urszula Kacperczyk, Mr. Michał Kulecki, Ms. Inga Stembrowicz and myself. At the beginning of 2004 it was possible to add highly detailed, item-level abstracts of the single records, as nested Component wrappers (<c03 level="item">), for the oldest volumes from the fifteenth century. These volumes and records are in Latin. The input of that data was done by a person sent by the labour office (Mr. Witold Poletyło). The Central Archives of Historical

TABLE 2. EAD–ISAD(G): Database Fields for File Level

No	EADname after conversion	ISAD(G) v2	Type of the field	Polish name of the field
1	<unitid>	ISAD 3.1.1	Numeric	*Sygnatura*
2	<unitdate>	ISAD 3.1.3	Note	*Daty*
3	<unittitle>	ISAD 3.1.2	Note	*Tytuł*
4	<langmaterial>	ISAD 3.4.3	Text 50	*Język*
5	<unitid type="former">	ISAD 3.1.1	Note	*Dawne sygn.*
6	<physdesc>	ISAD 3.1.5	Test 250	*Opis zewnętrzny*
7	<scopecontent>	ISAD 3.3.1	Note	*Zawartość/treść*
8	<note>	ISAD 3.6.1	Text 250	*Uwagi*
9	<accessrestrict>	ISAD 3.4.1	Text 250	*Udostępnianie*
10	<altformavail>	ISAD 3.5.2	Text 50	*Mikrofilm*

Records began cooperation with the seminar of Professor Wojciech Krawczuk, who is currently the leading expert in the field of kings' chancery during the early modern period,[7] and his students from the Jagiellon University in Krakow. He also published registers for three seventeenth century volumes; his abstracts were written in Polish. We hope to broaden this cooperation into a collaborative grant project. "Quite easily"–because they are in printed format–we could integrate around 42,000 abstracts into our finding aids. Money is the only missing element. It would also be possible to add digitized images of the original pages of the volumes into the EAD description. This idea, though very interesting, requires much more money, work (scanning from black and white microfilms), hardware (disc space) and software (browsers). Examples of such an undertaking, based on the chosen volume *Metrica Regni* 16 (MK 16), will be available soon on the Web site of the other project.

I think that some theoretical and conceptual work is needed for a good start to any project. The introduction of *ISAD(G)* in 1995 as a schema for description in the Central Archives of Historical Records was very useful and helpful. In 2000 Poland held a conference dedicated to EAD where Peter Horsman told us about his ideas (*pro et contra*) in a paper entitled "EAD–Magic Word or Terror?" In the spring of 2003 we had two conferences (one domestic and the other one international) on EAD, within the framework of the "Delos" project.[8] The papers were published both in paper and electronic format on the Web site of the Central Archives of Historical Records. Among them there is a translation of RLG's *Best Practice Guidelines for Encoded Archival Description*, which I did on the suggestion of Bill Stockting.[9] This was the theoretical base and background for further application.

Regarding the technical side of the project, the most important source of information are the Web sites of the Library of Congress dedicated to EAD and the Society of American Archivists' EAD Roundtable site, currently hosted by The Institute for Advanced Technology in the Humanities at the University of Virginia.[10] Here one can find the basic information needed to work with EAD, as well as download the DTD for the second version of EAD (EAD 2002). One can also find two eminent works of Michael J. Fox, the "EAD Cookbook" and stylesheets (for both the first and the second versions of EAD) as well as examples of how to use EAD and, last but not least, the *EAD Tag Library*, which is necessary to consult to develop one's EAD structure or template. The means of presentation of EAD files online depends on your ideas and could be achieved in different ways, such as the use of Extensible Stylesheet Language (XSL), Cascading Style Sheets (CSS) or HTML. After visiting the Library of Congress Web site dedicated to EAD all one needs to build a template is an XML editor. One of the recommended products is XMetaL, which was, however, a bit too expensive for my archival institution. I used a Polish HTML editor known as "*Pajączek*" (Little Spider), as it can read XML tags as well.

The next step was the input of (structured) data. The data can be extracted from the Access database directly into an EAD template, as it is structured according to ISAD(G) (see Table 2). The data from the Access database was exported into an XML file automatically. Some changes were made before export, such as making the names of the fields in the database the same as those of the related EAD tags. Other changes were made in the HTML editor, such as putting Paragraph (<p>) tags after a <scopecontent> tag, etc., by means of the "find and replace" function. Dates and structure were corrected and checked during all these steps. When an XML file was ready, it needed to be validated against the EAD DTD. I used–on Daniel Pitti's suggestion–the freeware *xmlvalid* by Elcel Technology Ltd, which is an MS/DOS product. After a series of validations and corrections, the last thing to be done was presentation. I used–with small changes–Michael Fox's stylesheet for the first version of EAD as a delivery method. On 29 July 2004 the inventory of Crown Chancery Public Register in EAD was visible on the Web site of the Central Archives of Historical Records.[11] It was an XML file with an XSL stylesheet. There are no search engines or any other indexing tools so far.

The first inventory in EAD still needs a lot of additional work. There are item-level descriptions for only eight volumes, and the item level description for the next hundred volumes could be done quite easily. There are, however, more then 350 volumes in the series of registrations. While the other finding aids will be presented soon–I hope–some questions still remain. For archives with historical holdings, hierarchical description down to the item level seems important, not only for archivists but also for the users. It is beneficial to have a hierarchical structure of description, but at which level is the place for the <scopecontent> wrapper and which for the Abstract (<abstract>) wrapper? My solution is to use the <abstract> tag at the bottom (item level), as it is a single record, because in the volumes the content is diverse. I have already discussed the issue of the former identification numbers above.

Another problem is who will do the data input for retrospective conversion. In this project the input was partly done by a person sent by the labour office. Preparation of inventories and control of the input is needed and it means money. Of course there are some technical matters, like which software to look at. While technical, this issue may also be philosophical. Peter Horsman in Florence in June 2001, speaking on "E-Term," observed that, "in the archival community, often due to the lack of appropriate budget, there is much of do-it-yourself attitude. [. . .] Without being impolite–EAD is a modern example of such an approach."[12] I am myself a good example of such a solution and it was no coincidence that at the Vienna Congress I presented the Polish experience of EAD as "Bob the Builder." Obviously, this is the best way to understand EAD. The next step, however–in my opinion–should be the development of software that enables the archivist to use EAD without knowing it.

AUTHOR NOTE

Hubert Wajs has been Head of the Central Archives of Historical Records in Warsaw, since 1998. He has participated in projects and working groups concerning automation, standards for archival description, Encoded Archival Description (EAD) and electronic records. He has translated the international standard ISAD(G) into Polish and written some articles and reviews on electronic records for the journals *Archeion* and *Polish Archivist*.

NOTES

1. The full text from the ICA Congress in Vienna (http://www.agad.archiwa.gov.pl/ead/polish_road.html) and the presentation (http://www.agad.archiwa.gov.pl/ead/polish_road.ppt) are on the Web site of the Central Archives of Historical Records.

2. Angelika Menne-Haritz, "Access–the Reformulation of an Archival Paradigm," *Archival Science No 1* (2001), 57-82; Polish translation in *Archieon* No 104 (2002) 68-95.

3. *Encoded Archival Description Application Guidelines* available at http://lcweb.loc.gov/ead/ag/aghome.html.

4. International Council on Archives, *ISAD(G): General International Standard Archival Description*, 2nd edition (Ottawa, 2000) is available at http://www.ica.org/biblio/isad_g_2e.pdf.

5. Opracowały Irena Sułkowska-Kurasiowa i Maria Woźniakowa, *Inwentarz Metryki Koronnej, Ksiegi wpisów i dekretów polskiej kancelarii królewskiej z lat 1447-1795* (Warszwa, 1973).

6. T Wierzbowski and others ed., *Matricularum Regni Poloniae Summaria*, Vol. I-VI (Warszawa, 1905-1999).

7. W. Krawczuk, *Metryka Koronna za Zygmunta III Wazy* (Kraków 1995); W. Krawczuk, *Metrykanci koronni. Rozwój registratury centralnej od XVI do XVIII wieku* (Kraków 2002); W. Krawczuk opr., "Księga wpisów podkanclerzego Tomasza Zamoyskiego z lat 1628-1635," *Sumariusz Metryki Koronnej.*, Seria Nowa, t. I (Kraków, 1999); A. Kot, W. Krawczuk, M. Kulecki, A. Sokół, G. Spyrka opr., "Księga wpisów kanclerza Jana Zamoyskiego MK 133 z Archiwum Głównego Akt Dawnych w Warszawie z lat 1587-1595," *Sumariusz Metryki Koronnej.*, Seria Nowa, t. II, (Kraków, 2001).

8. More information on DELOS (Network on Excellence on Digital Libraries) can be found at http://www.delos.info/.

9. *Archiwa w postaci cyfrowej. Standaryzacja. Od ISAD(G) do EAD. Materiały międzynarodowych warsztatów Delos CEE* [Proceedings of the International Delos CEE Workshop, "Standardization. From ISAD(G) to EAD. Implementation and Best Practice"], pod. red. E. Rosowskiej (Warszawa, 2003)–Wskazówki dotyczące "dobrych praktyk" przy wdrażaniu EAD opracowane przez grupę doradczą RLG, s. 77-100. Both of which are available online at http://www.agad.archiwa.gov.pl/ead/ead.html.

10. The official EAD site can be found at http://www.loc.gov/ead/ead.html. The EAD roundtable site found at http://www.iath.virginia.edu/ead/index.html.

11. The finding aid can be seen at http://www.agad.archiwa.gov.pl/pomoce/MKINw.xml.

12. Peter Horsman, E-TERM. Report to the Sixth European Conference on Archives, Florence, 2 June 2001. I have a copy by the courtesy of the author.

Controlling the Production of EAD Encoded Documents, Extracting Metadata and Publishing Them on the Web: Methods and Tools, France

Florence Clavaud
Martin Sévigny

SUMMARY. This article presents four projects geared towards providing the community of EAD users with methods and tools to control the quality of archival finding aids, to extract metadata from them in Dublin Core and qualified Dublin Core for use in OAI-PMH repositories, and to

Florence Clavaud is Archivist and Consultant with Anaphore. She is a member of the AFNOR working Groups of Experts on the EAD and EAC DTDs and sits on the board of ADNX.

Martin Sévigny is Consultant and Partner, AJLSM, Bordeaux, France.

[Haworth co-indexing entry note]: "Controlling the Production of EAD Encoded Documents, Extracting Metadata and Publishing Them on the Web: Methods and Tools, France." Clavaud, Florence, and Martin Sévigny. Co-published simultaneously in *Journal of Archival Organization* (The Haworth Information Press, an imprint of The Haworth Press, Inc.) Vol. 3, No. 2/3, 2005, pp. 147-169; and: *Encoding Across Frontiers: Proceedings of the European Conference on Encoded Archival Description and Context (EAD and EAC), Paris, France, 7-8 October 2004* (ed: Bill Stockting, and Fabienne Queyroux) The Haworth Information Press, an imprint of The Haworth Press, Inc., 2005, pp. 147-169. Single or multiple copies of this article are available for a fee from The Haworth Document Delivery Service [1-800-HAWORTH, 9:00 a.m. - 5:00 p.m. (EST). E-mail address: docdelivery@haworthpress.com].

Available online at http://www.haworthpress.com/web/JAO

doi:10.1300/J201v03n02_12

publish them on the Web along with the digital images produced by digitization of the material described. The first two projects were conducted in 2004 by the Centre Historique des Archives Nationales together with AJLSM and resulted in the writing of reports and programs. The other projects are PLEADE and Navimages, which consist of open source applications that allow the building of Web-based search and viewing applications. All these tools can be used by archivists to create a complete publishing suite.

KEYWORDS. Digitization, Dublin Core, EAD, Encoded Archival Description, finding aids, Navimages, OAI-PMH, Open Archives Initiative: Protocol for Metadata Harvesting, open source software, PLEADE, standardization

INTRODUCTION

For a number of archival institutions, using the Encoded Archival Description (EAD) DTD is now a common and well-established practice. If such a fortunate institution has already gone beyond the stage of debating whether they should use EAD or not, they will then find themselves facing other questions, looking for tools or methods that allow them to go further in their use of EAD or improve their current practices and the quality of their results.

In this article, we will present tools and methods that can be helpful in three cases. First, to ensure quality control in the production of EAD encoded documents. Second, to extract metadata from EAD instances to use in other contexts. Third, to publish finding aids in EAD format, as well as, if wished, digital versions of the material described in the finding aids.

The three projects have a common goal, which is to present the community of EAD users with elements of reflection along with the technical means to enable production throughout the whole editorial workflow process.

The tools thus elaborated use technological standards and have been conceived to serve as many people as possible, just as they are, or, as is more likely, after being adapted to a local context. This is the reason why the publishing applications PLEADE and Navimages have, from their beginnings in 2003, been based on open source free software under a GNU GPL license.[1] It was recently decided to also place under open source license the quality control and Open Archives Initiative Protocol for Metadata Harvesting (OAI-PMH) metadata production tools, so that they can be used by anyone interested.

The first two parts of this article describe projects conducted in partnership by the Centre Historique des Archives Nationales de France (CHAN) and the company AJLSM. This same company is also the main author of the programs PLEADE and Navimages, described in the third section, of which the CHAN is one of the main users.

AN ENVIRONMENT TO CONTROL THE PRODUCTION OF EAD ENCODED DOCUMENTS

The CHAN holds, processes and gives public access to the central archives of the French state from its origins to 1958, the archives of public organizations of national interest, the archives of Parisian notaries, and a great number of private fonds. It began using the EAD DTD in 2000. Today the results of this effort remain modest when compared to the vast amount of printed or typewritten finding aids still awaiting conversion. Only a few members of staff use the DTD and produce EAD encoded finding aids. This situation can be explained, as is usually the case, by various human, financial and technical factors.

From 2003, however, production has increased significantly, and there are now numerous EAD finding aids. Several projects have also been initiated, geared towards the *systematic use of EAD* for the description of certain fonds (those relating to the Napoleonic period, archives of notaries, and oral archives deposited by the Fondation pour la Mémoire de la Déportation (FMD)).[2] A few of these fonds are currently being digitized. The EAD finding aids were initially published on the CHAN's Internet site in a static HTML version. They are now systematically published, along with their associated images, in an application built around PLEADE and Navimages and available through the intranet of the Ministry of Culture and Communication.

The CHAN has reached a point where it can legitimately be said that its work with EAD has become more industrial than experimental. The project described here, therefore, concerns whole groups of finding aids, which were produced in various ways by various staff members.

A number of finding aids stem from traditional documentary databases, from which a set of records is extracted, prepared and processed by an XSLT program, in order to be turned into an EAD document. As these databases most often describe archival material at the item or file level, the resulting finding aids are analytical, with precise indexes, and their hierarchical structure needs to be carefully checked.

Others are produced by conversion of word-processed files or of published paper-based finding aids. Several vendors have already worked for the CHAN, converting in a semiautomatic way general guides and inventories. A contract has just been signed to encode 11,000 pages of published printed finding aids. The files thus produced have a less detailed structure, and certain elements (references, dates, description levels, indexes, internal cross-references, etcetera) have to be manually checked or inserted by institutional staff.

A third method of production is to create finding aids directly in EAD, by using an English-language XML editor to which a specific French interface has been added.[3] The CHAN decided in 2001 to use an editor rather than a database management system, both because at that time no existing system was fully satisfactory and because the greatest flexibility was sought during a time of experiment. This direct production is practiced at the CHAN by the IT department, author of numerous finding aids and responsible for their online publication, by a few archivists in the various specialized departments, and by students in archival science completing their degree with a training period at the CHAN. Archives of notaries and oral archives of the FMD are described in this way, which gives the author of the finding aid complete control of the work. The EAD documents thus produced are potentially very different in their structure and content. All documents produced in EAD are proofread using the same XML editor.

The corpus of finding aids is therefore quite diverse, consisting of documents produced in several ways, by various staff or vendors, concerning several different types of archival material, and presenting different levels of analysis and structure. On top of this variability, one can remark that the level of expertise in EAD has risen since the first experiments in 2000, so that the first finding aids produced do not have the same quality as the more recent ones. These older electronic finding aids have all been updated to EAD 2002, and several of them have also been reworked. However, differences remain, especially with regard to the content of certain elements and the indexing.

Now it is essential for the CHAN to ensure homogeneity of the finding aids. More generally, this is a required condition in any archival institution in order to make finding aids easily understood by the public. A minimum of consistency is necessary, for example, in the naming of the EAD files, in noting the level of description, in keying the identifiers of the archival material or access or reproduction information, and in indexing the material in order to build correct cumulative indexes.

The IT department has been very keen on this question for several years, and carefully proofreads all EAD documents before publishing them. In 2003 great effort was put into gathering all the best practices and explaining them in an application guide. The guide is available on the Internet,[4] as a set of HTML pages with hyperlinks to appendices constituting document-type specific sub-guides.

It was felt necessary to go further and give the guide a practical form in the shape of automated computer applications, which would help check that the EAD documents comply with the recommendations and quality criteria enunciated in the guide. The finding aids had to comply with the EAD DTD. The checking tools had to be easy to use, preferably by the authors of the finding aids themselves, and should return clear information. From the start the CHAN also wanted to be able to customize these tools or have them adapted in-line with the evolution of the finding aids or of different projects; it was wished that other institutions facing the same need could do the same as well. These requirements meant that the programs had to be written in open source code or under free license.

The CHAN commissioned the company AJLSM for the task and the programs were delivered in September 2004. They were accompanied by a report that explained the issue, presented the various possible methods and solutions depending on the quality desired, and described the tools and their use. These tools can function by running a simple script on a computer or a server equipped with a Java virtual machine and the results can be viewed via a Web browser.

Given the nature of the constraints to be implemented and the state of the art of the standards, the project actually resulted in the creation of a set of separate tools, each one working on a specific constraint level.

The first tool is an XML schema called "EAD-chan," obtained by turning the EAD DTD into a schema and adding to it a number of constraints on the syntax of the finding aids. These constraints are about:

- The content of certain elements: The Date (<date>) and Date of the Unit (<unitdate>) elements, for example, must have a "normal" attribute, and the attribute value must be a character string compliant with the standard ISO 8601. The "href" attribute of the

Extended Reference (<extref>), Digital Archival Object (<dao>) and Digital Archival Object Location (<daoloc>) elements must contain a URI. The "otherlevel" attribute in certain Component (<c>) elements comes with a closed list of values. Indexing elements, when they are used in narrative text, must have a "normal" attribute duly completed.
- The structure of the finding aids: The schema, for example, imposes the use of Component (<c>) elements instead of numbered components (<c01>, <c02>, etc.).

This tool is strictly a validation tool. It has not been possible to use it in order to implement all the constraints that had been defined, since it would have strayed too far from the original DTD. One of the limits met with was the impossibility of controlling the content of elements of a mixed-content model. It was impossible, for instance, to define one or several possible values for the Subtitle (<subtitle>) element or to enforce the keying of a character string in the Title Proper of the Finding Aid (<titleproper>) element.

In order to complete the constraints, it has been considered, though without implementation, to add new functionality to the XMetaL production environment. Links could be offered towards external vocabularies, such as authority lists of terms for certain attribute values, while continuing to allow the keying of free text. The interface could also integrate certain pages of the application guide that could be called up when inserting a particular element for example.

The other quality criteria defined by the CHAN have been treated in a different way, through the use of the XPath and XSLT standards. A set of programs were produced that analyze EAD documents and are used, therefore, after their creation.

The first one was written with Schematron[5] and serves to create an HTML file which lists the discrepancies with respect to the coded rules. It signals, for example, if a required element is missing or empty, or if one of the attributes is missing ("level" or "otherlevel" for components (<c>)), if the hierarchy of levels is illogical (for instance a fonds described within a series) or if the structure is flat (when more than a hundred Component (<c>) elements are siblings).

The Report Card program recently published by the Research Libraries Group (RLG) has the same objective.[6] It gives a report on the compliancy of an EAD document with the RLG EAD Best Practice Guidelines,[7] established with the goal of standardizing encoding practices before the loading of EAD documents into one of the online services offered by the Group.

The second program gives a report on reading the EAD document. The idea is not to alert authors about anomalies, but to provide a global picture of the EAD document. The table of contents is reconstituted, along with a list of any indexing elements and their content, or a list of linking elements. Such a report is especially helpful in the case of large and complex finding aids with many access points and numerous links to digital surrogates. In the case of the CHAN, it is particularly useful in view of checking the accuracy of the links with respect to publication in the PLEADE/Navimages interface.

The third program deals with the analysis of a set of documents stored in the same directory. It verifies that EAD identifiers are unique (in the elements Encoded Archival Description (<ead>), EAD Header (<eadheader>) and EAD Identifier (<eadid>)), that links between documents are consistent, and that external links are accurate (the program sends an alert when a URL produces a 404 error).

The last two programs provide the XPath paths of the analyzed EAD documents. These XPath expressions can later be used by software, such as XMLSpy, to reach an element needing examination easily. In the future one could imagine better integration with the production tools used by the CHAN.

While all these programs have been tested, it is still too early to evaluate their benefits accurately. They are, however, extremely useful for the IT department that collects, manages and publishes the EAD documents. They complement the production platform based on XMetaL quite well. Several of them will probably be used by other departments as well, with the goal of promoting and facilitating the use of EAD. It is quite probable that they will evolve along with the application guidelines. Being written largely in XML and XSLT, they can be easily updated. The checking and analysis programs could easily be used by other archival institutions as well, whether they use the same XML editor, a different one, or a database management system.

Should the DTD itself evolve into a schema or another model, parts of these programs would still remain useful. Another project is conducted at the CHAN, to create a management platform based on a XML database. If this platform is conceived and implemented, some of its functionality could replace some of the constraints expressed in the programs; at the same time, segments of the programs could certainly be integrated within the platform.

EXTRACTION OF METADATA FROM EAD DOCUMENTS

The second project presented in this article concerns what happens after the production of the EAD documents.

The CHAN wanted to study the possibility of "producing metadata that could adequately represent its EAD finding aids in documentary portals." Documentary portal means here, in a now classic sense, an online application intended for the public, in which descriptions of diverse resources, most often held in different locations, are gathered, according to a theme, a historical period, a place, a type of resource, etcetera. In such applications, it is quite conceivable to find archival material. A portal may concern only archival material, or it may include also descriptions of museum or library collections, in order to allow searching across all these sectors. In any case archive users should be able to save precious time by querying these portals, which should at least allow them to easily identify and locate relevant fonds, that are unique and often scattered in an unpredictable way by accidents of history.

Such portals are beginning to appear in France,[8] either purely devoted to archival material or gathering material from diverse cultural heritage institutions. Given the wealth and the national importance of the CHAN's collections, it was time to consider the presence of its EAD finding aids in such portals.

The CHAN has also created a large number of databases describing archival material at item or file level; several of these databases are available online. There is also an historical library, which will be open to the public in the near future. The CHAN, then, can consider in the coming years the creation of its own portal to give access to the whole of its data. Finally, the CHAN is one of the five repositories of the National Archives, which are located in different parts of the country and have specific or complementary missions, while forming only one legal entity. This entity might also create its own portal in the future.

The project described here happened at the same time as the one discussed above. It involved the same parties, and used the same finding aids that were compliant with the CHAN application guidelines. The goal was to produce metadata to constitute an OAI-PMH repository. This data exchange protocol,[9] still recent but widely used and functional, has many advantages, including leaving each producing entity with control of its own metadata and projects; it is well suited to a distributed technical architecture. Since the CHAN already had a Web application built with PLEADE to allow the viewing of its finding aids, using the OAI protocol appeared the best solution.

Given the diversity of the CHAN finding aids, and the fact that no specific portal was targeted but rather that a generic need was felt, it was decided that metadata would be produced only in qualified and simple Dublin Core formats, the latter being the format required by the OAI-PMH protocol. The decision to produce metadata in qualified Dublin Core, a more detailed format, was made because of the richness of the EAD documents, especially in relation to the indexing elements and the links between resources. One should note that the simple Dublin Core records are produced from a first extraction in qualified Dublin Core; this production line approach allows one to easily target other formats in the future.

As for the previous project, AJLSM wrote a report presenting the issue in the fall of 2004, offering a mapping between EAD and the two targeted data models (Dublin Core and qualified Dublin Core), and explaining the production methods for this metadata. With the report came XSLT programs that allowed the automatic production of Dublin Core metadata from an EAD instance, in a static way, by running a script.

Parts of the report, notably the crosswalk between EAD and qualified Dublin Core,[10] were included in the online documentation of the PLEADE project; at the same time, the XSLT programs have been adapted and included in the PLEADE software, which from now on offers an OAI repository. That way, while waiting for the diffusion of the report and of the programs under a free license, PLEADE users or people who consult its documentation can already take advantage of the results. For this reason, only a few major aspects of this work are presented in this article.

Representing an EAD document as XML metadata compliant with the Dublin Core model is a complex problem, particularly because of the hierarchical structure of an EAD document. Each level serves to describe a given unit, from the highest level to the item or file level, without repeating information from one level to the next; the hierarchy may vary from one finding aid to the other. This problem is currently studied in other institutions, and several projects are very advanced, especially at the University of Illinois in the United States.[11]

In the CHAN project, it was desired that each user of the program should be able to represent any level of description that he or she would deem relevant by as many Dublin Core records. Among the description levels, the program processes systematically the level of the finding aid itself (segment EAD Header (<eadheader>)) as well as the highest level of archival description (segment Archival Description (<archdesc>)) up to and excluding the element Description of Subordinate Components (<dsc>) element.

With respect to the other component levels (<c> elements), the person using the program may choose to create a Dublin Core record for:

- numbered or unnumbered components at a given hierarchical level, for instance the second highest level, or the second and the fourth;
- components at a given descriptive level, indicated by the value of the "level" attribute: for instance the fonds, or the fonds, sub fonds and series;
- specific elements, for instance <c> or <c01>.

At an intermediate stage of the process, before the creation of the metadata, the program will modify the EAD document by adding to each of the selected elements an "encodinganalog" attribute with the value "oai:resource." This automatic marking can be preceded by manual marking of any component (<c>) that would be deemed relevant but that would not correspond to the defined criteria.

It was necessary to include a system to give identifiers to each of the archival resources represented by a Dublin Core record. The process implemented works in this way:

- If the component (<c>) or numbered component (<c01>, <c02>, etc.) does not have an identifier ("id" attribute), the XSLT program will give one to it, and thus modify the original EAD document.
- This identifier will include the identifier of the finding aid, which is supposed to be unique within the CHAN as well as outside as it includes country and repository codes.

This process works well. One problem, though, especially in the context of a dynamic application, is that the identifiers are valid only as long as the program is not applied again to the same EAD document. The identifiers are perennial only when they exist before the execution of the program. This is one more argument in favor of systematically attributing an identifier to a component (<c>) at the time of production of the finding aid, and making sure that the production and checking tools facilitate this.

It was also proposed, and implemented in the program, to establish links between the generated Dublin Core records, with the <dc:rela-

tion> element in Dublin Core or the <dcterms:isPartOf> in qualified Dublin Core.

The program has been written to produce automatically XML elements according to the crosswalk table defined by the study in each Dublin Core or qualified Dublin Core record. In the Dublin Core record corresponding to the finding aid itself, for example, the element <dc:creator> will contain the text found in the Author (<author>) element in the EAD Header (<eadheader>) of the original EAD document. In a Dublin Core record corresponding to any level of archival description (<archdesc> or <c>), the element <dc:creator> will contain the text found in the "normal" attribute of the elements Personal Name (<persname>), Corporate Name (<corpname>), Family Name (<famname>) or Name (<name>) that can be found in the origination element (<origination>). If these elements are empty, the program will take the information from the immediate ancestor of the one being processed.

If the user wishes to mark explicitly that an EAD element should be processed in a specific way, not defined by the crosswalk table, he or she can include in the relevant element of the original EAD document an attribute that gives the name of the targeted Dublin Core (or qualified Dublin Core) element and its URI, for example:

```
<subject encodinganalog=http://purl.org/dc/elements/1.1/subject> 1914-1918
war</subject>
```

Finally, the user can also indicate to the program that he or she wants the content of the indexing elements present in a component's ancestors to be inherited in the DC record.

At this point, the programs are completely functional, in their static as well as in their dynamic version. The PLEADE application at the CHAN includes today an OAI-PMH repository containing Dublin Core and qualified Dublin Core metadata produced from each of the published finding aids.

The great flexibility of these tools really allows one to adjust the process to the structure and content of each finding aid, which also supposes one knows these characteristics well.

It would certainly be possible to go further and to look for different or more specific criteria for the selection of the units,[12] or to allow the simultaneous choice of several criteria (for instance a hierarchical level and a descriptive level). It would probably be useful to implement, among the possibilities for explicit marking, a way to exclude (and not only to include) an EAD element or a component (<c>) from the automatic selection defined. One could also foresee the limiting of the extraction for a given Dublin Core element (for instance, <dc:description>) to the first 150 or 200 characters found in the source EAD element (in this case, Scope and Content [<scopecontent>], which can be very long like all other EAD elements with a textual content). All these changes can be implemented by anyone familiar with XSLT.

The metadata thus produced is potentially very rich. To go further, one should study its real use in a portal. Circulation of the report and of the programs and their use by repositories other than the CHAN could allow the testing of its relevance in a number of different contexts.

Within the context of a more advanced project, a recent user survey conducted in the United States[13] showed that portal users, even sophisticated ones, had trouble in interpreting the archival information they found and understanding that the original material itself was not accessible online. The survey concluded that it was important to give context to the information, by providing information about the repositories holding the material.

In this case as in others, the issue with portals will not necessarily be one of understanding only. Before studying the various uses of such portals and their impact on users' research strategies, effort must be made in relation to the data itself. It will become necessary to provide a common definition, agreed upon by each contributing repository, of the content of the Dublin Core elements, or to define and use a common vocabulary for this content. In French archival repositories alone, indexing practices and forms of terms are quite variable, national controlled vocabularies are few and do not cover all the needs, and authority lists do exist, but only at a local level. Such a project brings one back logically to the question of standardizing the content of finding aids. This issue cannot possibly be resolved in any satisfactory way if the experience, knowledge and practices of other professional communities in the field of cultural heritage are not taken into account.

In the case of more specialized portals, it is probable that only a part of the Dublin Core records will be kept. For instance, in the future European portal MICHAEL (Multilingual Inventory of Cultural Heritage in Europe) dealing with digital cultural heritage,[14] only the Dublin Core records corresponding to fonds or collection levels will be used. It is thus reasonable to suppose that in most cases the number of elements or the number of levels will be partial. The metadata already created by the CHAN project could, however, serve as a starting point for thinking about future use.

If a portal is conceived to describe specific types of documents, the Dublin Core format might not be adequate. Another system of metadata could in this case be added to the first one, and specific programs be written. This will happen for the portal of digital sound recordings that is being developed by the *Institut de Recherche et Coordination Acoustique/Musique* (IRCAM)[15] for the French Ministry of Culture. The basic model of metadata has a hierarchy limited to four levels, and includes the description of persons, medium and digital resources.

PLEADE AND NAVIMAGES, TOOLS FOR PUBLISHING EAD ENCODED DOCUMENTS

The third section of this article deals with a technical application devoted to publishing EAD encoded finding aids along with the associated bodies of digital images. It is in fact the last link in the editorial chain. It is composed of an application, PLEADE, and a toolbox, Navimages. Like most of the open source software projects available under a GNU GPL license, both PLEADE and Navimages have a Web site[16] giving access to a downloading page, a discussion list, and documentation in French and in English. Interested readers should consult these Web sites for more information.

PLEADE: EAD on the Web

The history of PLEADE is very recent. The software sprung from a totally private initiative of the companies AJLSM and Anaphore, which envisioned the project in 2003 and invested in its development. French and foreign users also contribute to the evolution of the software, by submitting their problems, questions and suggestions through the discussion list. The CHAN, one of the institutional users, has also sponsored, in 2004, the development of functionality it needed for its own use but which is of general interest. An active community therefore, supports this software. Version 1.0 was released in August 2004; version 1.1 will appear in 2005.

PLEADE is devoted to the publication of EAD documents.[17] It includes a search engine[18] that can find a character string or an expression either in the whole XML textual flow or in most of the EAD elements previously indexed separately. PLEADE serves to build a dynamic Web application: the final user only needs a Web browser and a connection to the Web server where the application is installed, in an Internet or intranet environment. PLEADE is multilingual. The user and search interface can be offered in as many languages as necessary, and the software can publish and exploit EAD documents written in different languages. The software is highly configurable. The application administrator can, by editing configuration files written in XML, modify easily the content of static pages, and create search forms, etcetera. When publishing documents the user can select, in the publication form, parameters well suited to the finding aid or to a set of finding aids. PLEADE is also adaptable: all of its components are under free license, and the source code (in Java, XSLT and XML) is accessible. PLEADE works on the SDX platform,[19] which is itself composed of free software and based on the Cocoon publication environment.

The main functionalities of PLEADE, that is its basic characteristics, are as follows:

- PLEADE allows the creation of a complete Web site, with static pages (home pages, information and help pages, etcetera). This site may of course be given its own graphic design.
- One can define a classification of the finding aids, with as many sets and subsets as wished. The depth of the classification is theoretically unlimited, and easy to change. This is done by editing a few XML configuration files, which provide the publication form with the indexing parameters. In other words, a subset of EAD documents can be presented and searched separately from the rest; a given EAD document can belong to as many sets or subsets as desired. This permits one to give more visibility, temporarily or for a longer time, to a group of EAD documents related to an exhibition, a theme, or a type of material, etcetera.
- The search engine allows simple and Boolean searching. It can search separately the content of each EAD element (for instance Title of the Unit (<unittitle>), Subject (<subject>), and Genre/Physical Characteristic (<genreform>)), while also taking into account the presence of certain attributes.[20] It will display to the final user documentary units produced by the fragmentation of EAD documents, rather than whole EAD documents. This permits the easy location and display in any given finding aid of the content of the one component (<c>) element describing an archival item about the city of Lyons, for example, if the keyword "Lyon" has been indexed in a Geographic Name (<geogname>) element and if, at the publishing stage, it has been decided to index the Geo-

graphic Name elements and to fragment the document at the item level.

- Search results are displayed along with the context, that is the essential information on the source finding aid (in a frame at the top part of the screen), the basic information[21] about any parent, or even children, of the unit and the table of contents of the finding aid. The information context and the table of contents allow users to navigate within the finding aid. If the finding aid has indexes, the navigation can also use lists of descriptors.
- Presentation of the content of the units can be defined at the publication stage. For instance, one can choose to present information in a table form, and to establish a list of labels for displaying the contents of certain elements (for example, displaying a label "Name of the notary" before the content of the Origination (<origination>) element in finding aids describing archives of notaries).

In the next version of PLEADE (1.1), other functionality will be implemented,[22] especially:

- Definition and creation of an OAI-PMH repository storing Dublin Core and qualified Dublin Core metadata, according to the methods and principles described above.
- Integration and exploitation of thesauri or hierarchical authority lists.
- Possible definition of sorting criteria for search results different from the relevancy criteria used by the search engine: for instance, according to the content of an element (date, shelf mark, etcetera).

In the future other improvements will certainly be implemented. Creation of a publication and viewing module for authority records encoded in EAC is already envisioned for 2005. Currently, there are only a few services built with PLEADE available on the Internet (others are available only on intranets). Examples are the application of the Denver Public Library (Colorado),[23] and the application of the Centre des Archives d'Outre-Mer (Aix-en-Provence, France; one of the five sites of the Archives Nationales de France).[24]

Navimages: Viewing Series of Digital Images

Navimages is a toolbox for organizing, processing, making accessible and viewing large collections of digital images. It is particularly well suited to publication of digitized cultural heritage, and even better suited for archival collections completely or partially digitized.[25] Navimages is a free application (under GPL license) sponsored by the Direction des Archives de France and developed by the company AJLSM.[26]

Navimages offers a flexible, open and standardized environment, as it is developed with XML and XSLT. It is composed of three modules:

- The collector, for organizing and processing the images from a repartition file or an inventory, or an EAD file;
- The database, for researching and navigating the descriptions of the images;
- The viewer, for navigating within a series of images and visualizing individual images in an Internet, intranet or local environment.

The collector has two main functionalities:

- It stores images by organizing them as a file system, in which each subdirectory constitutes a subseries of images. This way, images can be viewed directly from a storage medium (hard disk, CD-ROM), without necessarily using a dynamic environment. These hierarchies of files can be built easily by automatic processes. Furthermore, an XML document present in each directory contains the metadata describing the images and can be used independently of Navimages.
- It processes images: several types of processing are possible, in particular conversion of format, changing size, and fragmentation (mosaic) so that several views or versions of a same image can be offered. The processing is done with the software ImageMagick.[27] One can easily add metadata to the original images as well as to the images resulting from the processing. Processing can be applied to a whole collection of images or only to a subset, defined by technical characteristics (weight, size, files names, format, etcetera).

The database module allows interaction with a search engine or a database so that structured image descriptions can be searched, navigated and linked to corresponding images. This module allows the loading of a relational database, and can also offer navigation through the various series of images within a collection via automatically generated HTML pages.

The viewer is integrated with a Web browser equipped with a plug-in supporting the Scalable Vector Graphics (SVG) format. Since SVG is based on XML, the viewer can be customized on the fly in a dynamic environment, for instance to adjust itself to users' preferences or to be adapted to different types of images. A configuration for the dynamic environment Cocoon (used by the SDX platform and, therefore, by PLEADE) is delivered with the tool, but naturally other configurations are possible.

The functionalities offered by the viewer are:

- For navigating within a series: go to the next or previous image; go to the nth next or previous image; go to the first or last image.
- For navigating between series (provided that the series viewed possesses subseries or is itself a subseries): go to the first image of the parent series; go to the first image of one of the child series, by choosing it from a list.
- For viewing an image (available functionality depending on the processes carried out by the collector): display one or the other of the available versions, by choosing from a list; display a mosaic in order to choose a tile; go from one tile to another; display the image in real size; display the image so that it is completely visible on the screen; scroll through an image; zoom forward or backward; zoom on a selected part of the image; display a reduced view (magnifier), in order to see right away which part of the image is visible on the screen; turn the image through 90 degrees; change the background color of the viewer to improve the vision of the image details; print the image as seen on the screen; download the original image; display online help.

Two examples illustrate the advantages of this tool.

An archival institution contracts the digitization of part of its fonds. CD-ROMs are delivered, which contain both images and an inventory file listing the images and providing a minimal description (shelf mark, date or identifier, for instance). The project manager configures the Navimages collector so that, first, images are organized by date and shelf mark in a file system, and second, they are turned into a lower definition version, in preparation for their viewing on the Web. The manager runs the collector for each CD-ROM: images are automatically organized and processed, a static viewing environment is created, and from this point the whole collection can be viewed and navigated with the Navimages viewer.

Another archival institution produces an EAD document describing a fonds. This fonds is digitized, resulting in a large amount of images more or less organized. Only the naming system of the files follows the viewing order of the documents. The project manager includes in the EAD file links, not to individual images, but to series of images corresponding to a description unit, by specifying the first and last image of the series. He then runs the Navimages collector, which will analyze the EAD file and organize the images according to the structure of the EAD document and the nature of the included links. Later, the digitized fonds can be viewed in a static way, as in the previous scenario; but it can also be viewed in the PLEADE environment, directly linked to the EAD document.

This second scenario emphasizes not only the link between EAD documents and Navimages, but also the link between PLEADE and Navimages.[28] These tools constitute a very interesting pair for the large-scale publication of an archival fonds that has been digitized and described in compliance with archival practices and standards.

The database of the *Archives Canada-France* project uses Navimages in order to publish digitized documents described in EAD.[29] Figures 1, 2 and 3 also illustrate some of the viewer's functionality.

FIGURE 1. Navimages Viewer: Lower Definition Image of Map

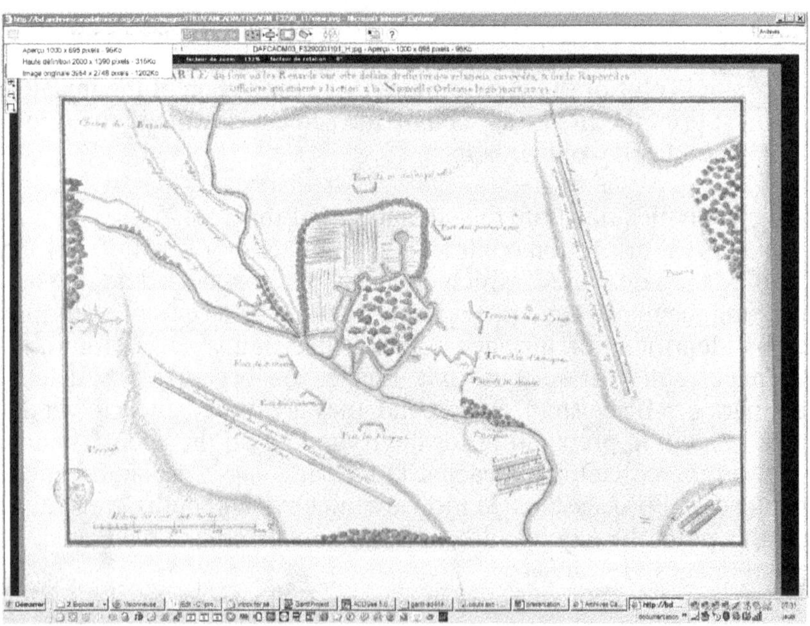

FIGURE 2. Navimages Viewer: Zoom Function

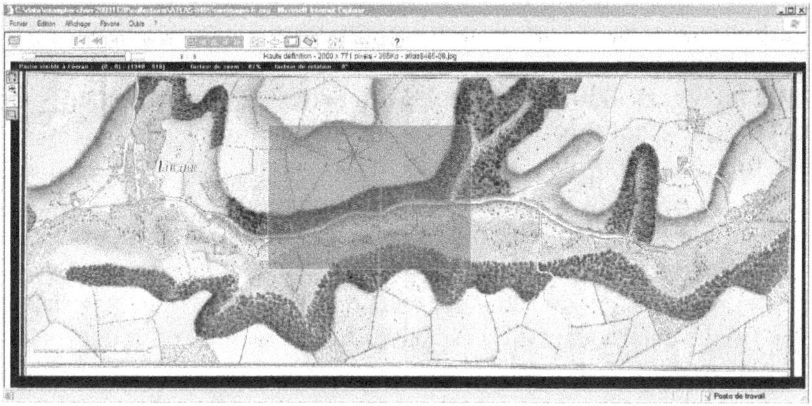

FIGURE 3. Navimages: *Etat civil des Français d'Algérie* (Centre des Archives d'Outre-Mer at Aix-en-Provence, France): Pages from an Identity Records Register

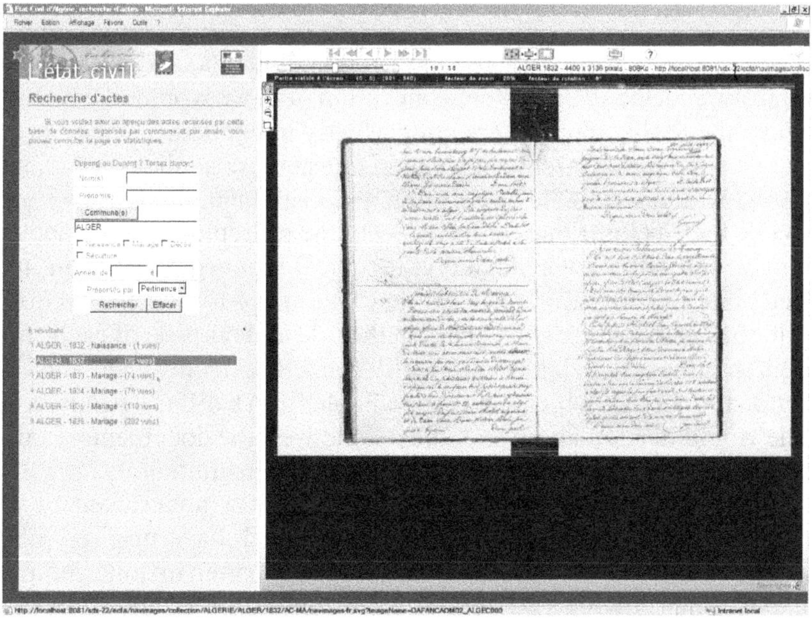

The Navimages viewer offers several versions of the same image, with a scrolling menu. In the example shown in Figure 1, for an antique map digitized with a high definition, the user is presented by default with the lowest definition version, but he or she can also select two versions with higher definition and obtain a better quality. Navimages also offers all the usual functionalities associated with image viewers. Figure 2, for example, illustrates the ability to zoom on a part of an image. Figure 3 comes from the application *Etat civil des Français d'Algérie*, published on the intranet of the Centre des Archives d'Outre-Mer at Aix-en-Provence in France. It illustrates the close interaction between a database supplied by Navimages and the viewing of the material described in the database, in this case pages from a identity records register.

CONCLUSION

Although the three projects discussed in this article may seem quite heterogeneous, they share the same goal: to provide the archival community with open, standardized and perennial solutions, to exploit EAD encoded archival descriptions and digitized archival material in the best way.

These projects were initiated in different contexts, and even if they stem from a perfectly consistent conception (and we would like to insist on this), the tools produced are not perfectly integrated. This is a problem: at this point, the archivist wishing to use these applications cannot simply download a single application and install and use it.

While then a closer integration is desirable it should be implemented, however, in both a conceptual and technical manner. Even if an integrated suite of tools was released that were easy to use, the archivist would still need to understand clearly the role and purpose of each component, to assess which ones are really needed, to identify any missing functionality or that which may be available from a different source. He or she would need to know and understand well the documentary environment and the various automated tools that constitute it.

Such integration efforts could be sponsored or undertaken by the large institutions which use these tools, or which have inspired them. They themselves need to think about integration, often in quite complex contexts. The growing EAD community could gain greatly from their reflection and its results, should they be willing to share them.

AUTHORS' NOTES

Florence Clavaud is an archivist specializing in information technology. She worked for 14 years at the Centre Historique des Archives Nationales de France in Paris, where, from 2000 to 2004, she was Head of the IT department. She managed digitization projects and carried out the implementation of the EAD and EAC DTDs. She is currently a consultant with the company Anaphore (http://www.arkheia.net), which publishes the archival management system Arkhéïa and offers various services to archive repositories. Florence is a member of the AFNOR Working Groups of Experts on the EAD and EAC DTDs and sits on the board of ADNX (Association pour la Documentation Numérique en XML, http://www.adnx.org).

Martin Sévigny is consultant and partner in the company AJLSM, located in Bordeaux, France (http://www.ajlsm.com). AJLSM specializes in data processing and information management technology, more particularly in the use of XML for offering open, durable and standardized solutions. Martin has contributed over many years to numerous projects concerning the EAD DTD as it is used in France in the areas of training, consulting, conception and development of tools. He sits on the board of ADNX (Association pour la Documentation Numérique en XML, http://www.adnx.org).

NOTES

1. GNU General Public License, see http://www.gnu.org/copyleft/gpl.html.

2. For more information on these projects, see the relevant pages in the CHAN's EAD application guidelines, at: http://www.archivesnationales.culture.gouv.fr/chan/chan/infopro/fr/projets/projetsspecifiq/index.html.

3. XMetaL by the company Blast Radius (http://www.blastradius.com), in its version Author, with a French configuration now under a LGPL license; it can be downloaded at: http://www.archivesnationales.culture.gouv.fr/chan/chan/infopro/infopro.htm.

4. For the CHAN best practices guidelines see http://www.archivesnationales.culture.gouv.fr/chan/chan/infopro/fr/index.html.

5. Schematron is a set of standards and tools to define the rules with which an XML document can comply, completing those that can be expressed in a DTD or a schema, because they are based on Xpath expressions, and to verify that an XML document meets the rules. For further information see http://www.ascc.net/xml/schematron.

6. For RLG's EAD Report Card see http://www.rlg.org/en/page.php?Page_ID=20513.

7. See RLG's EAD Best Practice Guidelines at http://www.rlg.org/en/page.php?Page_ID=450.

8. For example the portal *Aquitaine Patrimoines*; a prototype is available at: http://demo.ajlsm.com/sdx-bnsa/pa-portail/. It uses the OAI-PMH protocol to recover information on the cultural heritage of Aquitaine; one can find descriptive information on archival material kept at the Archives Départementales du Lot-et-Garonne.

9. For more information about the Open Archives Initiative Protocol for Metadata Harvesting (OAI-PMH), see: http://www.openarchives.org/.

10. A page devoted to the OAI repository in PLEADE is available at http://www.pleade.org/fr/documentation/descriptions/entrepot-oai.html. It explains concepts and problems, and gives a link to the crosswalk table between elements of qualified Dublin Core and EAD elements.

11. See the OAI portal project of this university online at http://oai.grainger.uiuc.edu/. See also, Christopher J. Prom and G. Thomas Habing, "Using the Open Archives Initiative Protocols with EAD," in: G. Marchionini, W. Hersch eds, *JCDL 2002: Proceedings of the Second Joint Conference on Digital Libraries, July 14-18, 2002* (New York, Association for Computing Machinery), 171-180 available online at http://oai.grainger.uiuc.edu/presentations.htm.

12. It would be interesting, for example, to study the results of the processing if the program took into account only components with a Scope and Content (<scopecontent>) element and/or indexing elements.

13. S. L. Shreeves and C. M. Kirkham, "Experiences of educators using a portal of aggregated metadata," Journal of Digital Information 5:3, 2004, Article No. 290, 2004-09-09, available at: http://jodi.ecs.soton.ac.uk/Articles/v05/i03/Shreeves/.

14. See the official project Web site at http://www.michael-culture.org/.

15. For further information about the Institut de Recherche et Coordination Acoustique/Musique see http://www.ircam.fr.

16. The PLEADE Web site is available at http://www.pleade.org/. The Navimages Web site is available at http://sdx.archivesdefrance.culture.gouv.fr/gpl/navimages/. The documentation of the PLEADE project gives useful information for implementing Navimages: see http://www.pleade.org/fr/documentation/descriptions/navimages.html.

17. Compliant with both EAD 1.0 and EAD 2002.

18. The search engine at the heart of PLEADE is Jakarta Lucene (http://jakarta.apache.org/lucene/docs/index.html).

19. SDX (http://www.adnx.org/sdx/) is a search engine and publication tool for bodies of XML documents, in a Web environment. SDX is now supported and offered by ADNX, Association pour la Documentation Numérique en XML (http://www.adnx.org/).

20. If the "normal" attribute is used, its value will be indexed instead of the content of the element; if certain EAD elements have a "source" attribute giving the name of a controlled vocabulary, PLEADE can index these elements separately.

21. The title, shelf mark and date of the described material, for example, will compose a "title" for PLEADE; the names of the elements selected for this purpose can be defined at the publication stage.

22. Much of this functionalities, like the definition and use of an OAI repository, is actually already present in the source code, available through the CVS protocol, before it is included in an official version.

23. For the Denver Public Library application see http://eadsrv.denver.lib.co.us:8080/sdx/pl/?l=en.

24. For the application of the Centre des Archives d'Outre-Mer see http://www.archivesnationales.culture.gouv.fr/caom/fr/index_irel.html.

25. One can see an instance of a small digital collection, prepared and published with Navimages at: http://sdx.archivesdefrance.culture.gouv.fr/gpl/navimages/examples/viewer/static/DROITS-HOMME/navimages-fr.svg.

26. See also Martin Sévigny, Frédéric Glorieux, and Florence Clavaud, "Navimages, Un environnement web pour la consultation de grandes collections de documents numérisés," *Document Numérique* 7, Nos. 3-4, (2003), 85-102.

27. For further information on ImageMagick see http://www.imagemagick.org/.

28. The PLEADE documentation gives a complete description of the functionality and configuration necessary to make it and the Navimages programs work together: see http://pleade.org/fr/documentation/descriptions/navimages.html.

29. The *Archives Canada-France* project can be found at http://bd.archives canadafrance.org/.

Using a Software Package to Publish EAD Encoded Finding Aids: A Practical Approach and Gradual Implementation at the Archives Départementales de la Côte-d'Or, France

Anthony Devarrewaere
Aude Roelly

SUMMARY. The Archives Départementales de la Côte-d'Or chose as a priority for its automation plan the acquisition of a search engine, to publish online archival descriptions and the library catalogue. The Archives deliberately opted for a practical approach, using for the encoding of the finding aids an automatic data export from an archival

---

Anthony Devarrewaere is Archivist and has worked at the Archives Départementales de la Côte-d'Or since 1992. He is in charge of automation and supervises the implementation of the EAD DTD.

Aude Roelly is Deputy Head of the Archives Départementales de la Côte-d'Or since 2002. She is a graduate of the École Nationale des Chartes with the title of archivist-paleographer, and was curator at the Centre des Archives du Monde du Travail (Archives Nationales) in Roubaix from 1996 to 2001.

[Haworth co-indexing entry note]: "Using a Software Package to Publish EAD Encoded Finding Aids: A Practical Approach and Gradual Implementation at the Archives Départementales de la Côte-d'Or, France." Devarrewaere, Anthony, and Aude Roelly. Co-published simultaneously in *Journal of Archival Organization* (The Haworth Information Press, an imprint of The Haworth Press, Inc.) Vol. 3, No. 2/3, 2005, pp. 171-181; and: *Encoding Across Frontiers: Proceedings of the European Conference on Encoded Archival Description and Context (EAD and EAC), Paris, France, 7-8 October 2004* (ed: Bill Stockting, and Fabienne Queyroux) The Haworth Information Press, an imprint of The Haworth Press, Inc., 2005, pp. 171-181. Single or multiple copies of this article are available for a fee from The Haworth Document Delivery Service [1-800-HAWORTH, 9:00 a.m. - 5:00 p.m. (EST). E-mail address: docdelivery@haworthpress.com].

Available online at http://www.haworthpress.com/web/JAO

doi:10.1300/J201v03n02_13

management system and for their publishing commercial software, selected on the basis of simplicity of use and efficiency rather than flexibility.

KEYWORDS. Archives Départementales de la Côte-d'Or, EAD, Encoded Archival Description, online finding aids

THE CONTEXT

The Archives Départementales de la Côte-d'Or began producing finding aids encoded in Encoded Archival Description (EAD) and looking for a suitable search engine in a context particularly remarkable for its diversity. There was indeed diversity among the archive users, in their expectations and their abilities to use modern information technology; diversity in the available finding aids; and finally, diversity in the mastery of EAD by the members of staff. The Archives Départementales de la Côte-d'Or is a middle-sized local institution[1] that certainly does not enjoy overabundance of means to conduct its mission. Of a staff of twenty-four, none of them work full-time on information technology and this limitation has had a strong impact on the decisions that were made.

The majority of the archives' users are amateur genealogists (55 percent) and academic researchers (37 percent); there are also a number of staff members from the depositing agencies. The experience and expectations of these different kinds of users with regard to new information technology are quite diverse. Generally speaking, those who are the least familiar with information technology are the administrative staff, who mainly want to find quickly a document that they had transferred to the archives. For the time being they make use of the transfer lists in paper format. Academic users are usually quite familiar with computerized databases, though a few students appear rather timid, disconcerted by a search engine and even worried that they may miss information. Their queries are often extremely focused; very few students think in terms of archival provenance and manage to formulate their questions accordingly. Genealogists are in general quite comfortable with computers, and often even hope to directly access digitized material.

The finding aids available at the archives are of many different types. A guide published in 1984 gives a general approach to the collections. The pre-World War II fonds and collections are for the most part arranged and described in finding aids that sometimes even give item-level details. Modern public records accessioned after 1982 arrived systematically accompanied by transfer lists. These lists are not available in the reading room. The shelfmark system often does not follow the official plan. For instance, there is a continuously numbered series referred to as "SM" or "*Supplément moderne*," that gathers archives accessioned after 1934 dating from 1800 to 1940. There is also a series referred to as "*W continu*" for modern administrative records transferred before 1982. For these two "series" idiosyncratic to Archives Départementales de la Côte-d'Or, descriptions are written on cards that are either available in the reading room or only upon request. Access to collections is not exactly easy, therefore, for the inexperienced user, perhaps even for the user familiar with other archival institutions facing different constraints. For this reason, the reference service is one of the archives' top priorities. Using a search engine would mean eliminating such mediation and it was, therefore, of the utmost importance to achieve the greatest possible clarity in the presentation and rendition of finding aids by a search engine.

All automation projects at the Archives need to be approved by the Department of Automation and Computer Management ("Service Organisation Informatique") of the Conseil Général de la Côte-d'Or.[2] The Department has a project manager who is responsible for all applications specific to the Archives; there is also a manager overseeing all hardware. Each year the department holds a meeting in order to assess the various automation projects of the four departments funded by the Conseil Général (the Archives Départementales being one of them). Only the projects deemed as priorities are sponsored.

OBJECTIVES

In this context, the Archives Départementales de la Côte-d'Or decided at the beginning of 2002 that the acquisition of a search engine was the priority within its automation project.

Since 1991, the archives had worked with several modules of the Arkhéïa archival information management system, for the control and management of the reading room and the location list. The acquisition of the description module was already planned. This module has the advantage of allowing the export of data in different formats, including HTML and XML. As the *Direction des Archives de France* had officially recommended using EAD as XML,[3] the Archives selected XML as the export format. Admittedly, EAD is used in a limited way, since the encoding is done automatically by the Arkhéïa program. It fits well, however, with the archives' desire, despite its limited human resources, to have simple finding aids and to get to work quickly with EAD. From the beginning the archives judged that production of digital finding aids, and especially of EAD encoded finding aids, was not an end in itself and that it was necessary to consider the implications of their online publication at the time of their creation.

The wider goal of the project was to facilitate access to finding aids and have only one system for managing the archival and library collections.

With regard to the library material, the idea was to improve access to existing catalogues. The historical collection had a catalogue on card files for public use, and on a Microsoft Works database for staff use. The administrative collection and the documentation center had their catalogues on Works databases, which the public could not access in the reading room. In fact, the very existence of these databases was a well-kept secret, and precious few users could boast of knowing about them. The objective for the archival collections was to offer easier and more exhaustive searching across all the finding aids at the same time (i.e., the finding aids available in the reading room as well as the more remote ones on card files). There was also a wish to make the transfer lists better known and used.

Improving access to all that data from the reading room was in our minds only a prelude to wider dissemination on the Internet. Another project, therefore, was launched in parallel: the creation of an Internet site, which should be completed in 2005.

ACQUISITION OF A SEARCH ENGINE

In September 2002, the specification of requirements for the search engine was finalized. It specified that:

- The proposed system should satisfy the general public's needs for clarity and simplicity of use, as well as the demands of sophisticated users to conduct more complex searches.

- All commands and functions of the search engine should be listed and explained very clearly.
- The display of search results should also allow the viewing of results in their context.

We were therefore looking not for a purely documentary product, but for a program really adapted to archival research. We had set aside a budget of 40,000 euros. Given the narrowness of the market at that time, it was not surprising that only two proposals were submitted. Users of both proposed products were contacted, and there were also commercial demonstrations. The two products were very different from each other. The first one resembled a toolbox offering many attractive possibilities; the publication of EAD encoded documents, however, was at that stage in development and not yet fully functional. The many options of the product led us to think that perhaps the expected simplicity of use for the public might be difficult to achieve, and that the product could prove cumbersome for our needs. The other product, ActionArchive, by the company Anticipaction, appeared a lot more formatted, probably more limited but nevertheless better suited to the needs expressed in the specification of requirements. More importantly, it offered the viewing of EAD documents in its standard version.

It would certainly have been possible to try and get more proposals, or even wait for the tools promised by the *Direction des Archives de France* on the Proximus platform, announced in June 2002 as being ready in 2003.[4] But we did not want to keep producing digital finding aids without having the ability to view them. The decision was made in December 2002, therefore, to select the ActionArchive product.

ADAPTING AN EXISTING PRODUCT

Adapting ActionArchive to our requirements took a long time, but allowed us, after careful thinking and work, to obtain a search engine that fulfills our expectations quite well.

The first challenge consisted of making ActionArchive capable of exploiting all the EAD tags, or at least, all of them used by the Arkhéïa automatic encoding. This was but a first step, since we also needed to decide how the data would be displayed on screen. The work on the archival finding aids was finalized in August 2003. A table was drawn up, listing the various tags, the labels under which the data should be displayed, and their order of appearance on the screen. In several cases, the terminology and the order of *ISAD(G)* or EAD had been rejected, insofar as they seemed obscure for users: for instance, we used the word "availability" instead of "conditions governing access" as in *ISAD(G)* or "access restrictions" as in EAD. Particular care and attention were given to allocating information to the several frames on the screen, in order to provide a logical way of navigation. This first phase was hardly completed before it became necessary to update the results to include the changes introduced by the 2002 version of the EAD DTD.

One problem with ActionArchive–as with other search engines–is that the user does not get an overview of the contents of the database. He or she, not knowing exactly the extent or nature of the material being queried, is, therefore, not in a position to assess correctly search results–or their absence. Until all existing finding aids were available via ActionArchive, it seemed to us of primary importance to explain in detail the contents of the database, at a stage prior to the query. This was made even more necessary as the population of the database was carried out in a random manner. Indeed, in the beginning all finding aids already in electronic format were integrated, having been easily converted to EAD as XML thanks to the automatic export function of Arkhéïa. To this almost random retroconversion set were added the recent transfer lists (now created in electronic format by the offices of origin), all the new finding aids currently produced by the archives, along with the results of a more planned retroconversion program focused at first on the inventories of the deposited town archives, a series very often requested by the public.

PRESENTATION OF THE ActionArchive SOFTWARE

General Characteristics

ActionArchive is a proprietary software, which offers corrective and iterative support. The only rights licensed users have are rights to use the product. Specific adaptations, corrections of bugs and improvements are provided only by the publisher. The software, currently in version 5, can nevertheless benefit from the experience and suggestions of its users (currently an informal club of six "*archives départementales*," two city archives and one private company). It is mainly used in intranets.

ActionArchive is a Web-based application developed specifically around the search engine Searchserver (by Hummingbird) in order to exploit XML files exported by the Arkheïa module (by the company

Anaphore). It is, therefore, meant to offer Arkheïa users an integrated system, from production to publication, based on XML and EAD. The system was progressively updated, following the continuous improvement of the XML exports offered by Arkheïa. Today, EAD 2002 is theoretically supported, but in practice it is so only within the limits of the tags used by the Arkheïa module.

Documentary Functions

Organization of Finding Aids

Finding aids are integrated with the database as soon as they are indexed. Each EAD document is treated as a whole, without any possibility of splitting. The EAD files corresponding to the library catalogue undergo an indexing process different from the one applied to the files corresponding to archival finding aids. In the end, two separate groups of finding aids are formed: one for bibliographical resources, the other for archival resources.

Search and Queries

Two modes of search are available, a simple search and a structured search.

The simple search mode is a free text search for words and phrases in the EAD documents. The contents of the elements EAD Header (<eadheader>), Archival Description (<archdesc>), as well as all the Components (<c>) included in Description of Subordinate Components (<dsc>) are explored. However, the text encoded in certain tags, corresponding to management information (Arrangement (<arrangement>) or Acquisition Information (<acqinfo>), etc.), is excluded from the search, in order to avoid unnecessary "noise" for the user. For instance, a query on Dijon will not bring back as results the occurrences of "Dijon" found in the Address Line (<addressline>) tags used in the publication statement of a finding aid.

The structured search mode offers, for each of the two groups, "Archives" and "Library," a specific search form with a number of predefined fields (shelfmark, title, author, date, content, etc.), thus allowing a more precise search. It is possible to combine several fields; the search will then bring results only if the several fields are present within the same component, at only one hierarchical level. From the search form, the user can also access alphabetical lists of index terms associated with the descriptions and marked up as Controlled Access Headings (<controlaccess>) elements. These lists (subject, title, author, etc.) are constituted progressively, as further XML files are integrated to ActionArchive. Both search modes use the common functionalities of the search engine: Boolean operators and truncations, equivalencies (between capitals and lowercase, etc.) and grammatical analysis (singular/plural, masculine/feminine). Furthermore, it is possible to refine a search. One can by successive queries search on several occurrences found in the same archival unit. This function is especially useful in the free text mode, as it allows a user to refocus a query that was initially badly formulated or too general. Predefined queries can be prepared by the Archives and saved in the system for the public. They are mainly used to present users with "mini-guides" to resources constituted by finding aids grouped with a common index term placed by the encoder at the highest level (<archdesc>).

Consultation

The navigation mode uses three frames.

After a query, the left frame displays in a table the list of finding aids, in order of decreasing number of hits.

The central frame has several purposes during the display of a finding aid. According to the request (display either of general information or of detailed results), it can serve, through generation of dynamic HTML pages, to display either the general overview (<eadheader> and <archdesc>) or the Description of Components (<dsc>). In this latter case, the system will by default apply a filter: it will offer to visualize only the Components (<c>) (with title, scope and content, shelfmark and dates) which correspond to hits. It is, however, possible to upload the whole finding aid, if wished.

The right frame is available at all times in order to display, via hypertext links, the rest of the data associated with the Component (<c>) displayed in the central frame (data other than title and scope and content), as well as the controlled access terms. When the user elects to display the whole finding aid in the central frame, the right frame serves to display the filing plan. This filing plan, comparable to the table of contents of paper-based finding aids, can unfold itself synchronically with the navigation in the finding aid. It comprises only the five hierarchical levels of titles offered by the Arkhéïa module.

In order to facilitate navigation and provide as many explanations as possible, all the buttons of the interface have a "pop-up" help text.

Management Functionalities

Management of Users

ActionArchives allows managers of the system to define groups of users in order to allocate each group specific rights. Several types of rights are available, so that separate profiles can be created for patrons and staff. In this way, it is possible to give a regular user the ability to save his queries for later use. One can also select a shelfmark from the search results and request production of the material via automatic sending to the reading room management module.

Reports on Connections and Statistics

Active connections can be automatically monitored in real time, which is very useful as the license limits the number of simultaneous connections. The statistical functions, though rather basic, allow staff to look at the history of connections and lists of failed queries and of the most heavily used finding aids.

Management of Finding Aids and Thesauri

To carry out the indexing of a finding aid in the database, one only needs to upload the file in the correct repertory (one for the archival resources, one for the bibliographic resources). Indexing can be started either directly from the interface, by authorized users, or by a scheduled routine. The finding aids reserved for an internal audience can be published in the application while remaining inaccessible for the public. This allows the staff to "test" finding aids in progress or to access sensitive personal data. The module ActionThesaurus can be paired with ActionArchive in order to use thesauri as searching aids. One can manage several thesauri and associate a particular thesaurus to a specific search field.[5] It is also possible to use a thesaurus with hierarchical relationships. In the public user interface it is possible to search not only on the selected index term, but also on the hierarchically dependent terms.

CONCLUSION

As happens in every automation project, cooperation of an institution with a commercial company on the one hand and with the IT services of the administrative governing body on the other hand is a difficult path, often full of pitfalls. Each of the three partners is strongly tempted to blame the other two whenever there is a problem. The close cooperation between the Archives Départementales de la Côte-d'Or and the other archives using the same software (in particular the great help received from Mr. Heckmann and Ms. Baudat at the Archives Départementales de Vendée) has allowed the placing of problems in a wider context enabling their origin, whether stemming from us or the software, to be identified.

After almost two years of work with our search engine, several conclusions were reached:

- Attempting to separate form and content in a finding aid appears to be a too theoretical approach. It can be useful, for instance, to design finding aids so that the resulting XML files are not too large and, therefore, not too slow in loading. Also, the nature of the system impacts on the writing of the descriptions, since searching across a number of fields only produces results if the search terms are found within the same component.
- As with every project, the outcome can be only correctly assessed by taking into account the limited time and money available. Given our constraints, the results we achieved, even if they are perfectible, seem to us quite satisfying.

There are still then many possibilities for improvement of Action-Archives. One can mention in particular the desire to put more emphasis on the predefined searches, to modify the display of results for library resources and iconography, to better manage the links between and within finding aids, as well as with an image-viewing system, and to allow the printing of search results. All these improvements will necessarily require discussion among the software users, the definition of priorities, and an agreement with the company, Anticipaction.

Before we move to that stage, the launching of the public interface in our reading room gives us the opportunity to observe the reactions of our patrons, to learn more about their behavior and strategies in front of a computer, and as a consequence to adjust our own practices. This necessary period of evaluation is already a very important asset in our reflection about the future online publication of our finding aids and the service we provide to our users.

NOTES

1. In France, the main administrative subdivisions are called "*départements*"; there are ninety-five of them in metropolitan territory. All public archives of a "*département*" find their way to an archival repository, *the Archives Départementales*, funded by the "*département*" but placed under the scientific control of the Direction des Archives de France. Côte-d'Or is part of Burgundy and the *Archives Départementales* are located in Dijon.

2. The *Conseil Général* is the elected council that runs a "*département*."

3. In an official notification dated June 21, 2001.

4. The Proximus project was never completed, as the call for bids received no proposals.

5. For instance the field "subject of modern series" to the thesaurus "W," which is the official thesaurus used in France for administrative archives produced after the Second World War.

Different Strokes for Different Folks: Presenting EAD in Three UK Online Catalogues

Amanda Hill
Bill Stockting
Sarah Higgins

SUMMARY. This article discusses three different online services providing federated access to finding aids relating to archives found in a number of repositories: the Archives Hub, Access to Archives (A2A) and Navigational Aids for the History of Science, Technology and the Envi-

---

Amanda Hill has managed the Archives Hub service since 2001. She is a member of the committee of the EAD/Data Exchange Group of the UK Society of Archivists and is involved in providing training in EAD and XML for archivists in the UK.

Bill Stockting became the Senior Editor for the Access to Archives (A2A) Programme in 2000. He has presented papers and trained fellow professionals in archival description standards and EAD in the United States and across Europe. Mr. Stockting is a member of the EAD Working Group and RLG's EAD Advisory Group as well as Chair of the EAD/Data Exchange Group of the UK Society of Archivists.

Sarah Higgins has worked at Edinburgh University Library as Project Archivist with responsibility for IT implementation and worked on a number of projects since 2000. She recently completed the Diploma in Archive Administration and took on the new role of Metadata Coordinator for the Library.

[Haworth co-indexing entry note]: "*Different Strokes for Different Folks*: Presenting EAD in Three UK Online Catalogues." Hill, Amanda, Bill Stockting, and Sarah Higgins. Co-published simultaneously in *Journal of Archival Organization* (The Haworth Information Press, an imprint of The Haworth Press, Inc.) Vol. 3, No. 2/3, 2005, pp. 183-206; and: *Encoding Across Frontiers: Proceedings of the European Conference on Encoded Archival Description and Context (EAD and EAC), Paris, France, 7-8 October 2004* (ed: Bill Stockting, and Fabienne Queyroux) The Haworth Information Press, an imprint of The Haworth Press, Inc., 2005, pp. 183-206. Single or multiple copies of this article are available for a fee from The Haworth Document Delivery Service [1-800-HAWORTH, 9:00 a.m. - 5:00 p.m. (EST). E-mail address: docdelivery@haworthpress.com].

Available online at http://www.haworthpress.com/web/JAO

doi:10.1300/J201v03n02_14

ronment (NAHSTE). While the scale of the services is very different, a significant similarity is the key role of Encoded Archival Description (EAD). The flexibility of EAD is clearly shown by the different ways it is used for the creation, storage, indexing, searching and presentation of finding aids online reflecting the differing needs of the contributors and users of each service involved.

KEYWORDS. Access to Archives programme, A2A, Archives Hub, EAD, Encoded Archival Description, end users, NAHSTE, Navigational Aids for the History of Science, Technology and the Environment, online access, presentation systems

INTRODUCTION

In the United Kingdom, Encoded Archival Description (EAD) has particularly found use as a tool facilitating the capture and presentation of standardized archival finding aids online. What follows is a discussion of the use of EAD in three services, which are very different in scope, that enable federated access to finding aids relating to archives found in a number of repositories: the Archives Hub, Access to Archives (A2A) and Navigational Aids for the History of Science, Technology and the Environment (NAHSTE).

THE ARCHIVES HUB

The Archives Hub was established in 1999 as a 'proof of concept' project, to investigate the feasibility of creating an online union catalogue of archival descriptions held in UK universities and colleges. The project was funded by the Joint Information Systems Committee (JISC)[1] and overseen by the Consortium of University Research Libraries (CURL).[2] The Cheshire Development Team, based in the Special Collections and Archives division of the University of Liverpool, developed an EAD SGML repository with Web and Z39.50 interfaces that is capable of displaying full EAD finding aids.

The project went forward as a service in 2000, based at MIMAS,[3] a national data center that is funded by the JISC and is situated within Manchester Computing at the University of Manchester. Universities and colleges throughout the United Kingdom were invited to bid for funds, which would be used to create collection level descriptions of archive holdings. Over the course of the service, over £800,000 (€1.2 million) has been awarded to UK educational institutions for this purpose.

The focus for the Archives Hub has been on creating descriptions at collection, or fonds, level. The intention was to create an accurate map of the archives available in the tertiary education sector, with the possibility of creating full archival descriptions at a later date. Quality has always been of prime importance, with detailed guidelines prepared for contributors[4] and the appointment of a Data Editor whose task is to check the consistency of the descriptions. The service currently contains over 18,000 archival descriptions from over 80 institutions throughout the United Kingdom.

An online data creation template, structured according to the elements of the *General International Standard of Archival Description*: (*ISAD(G)*),[5] was created to help contributors construct their descriptions.[6] This template includes links to the data creation guidelines for the eleven elements whose inclusion is mandatory for Archives Hub descriptions. A new template for the creation of EAD 2002 has recently been made available for contributors.[7]

To date, contributors have had to send the EAD files created using the template to the Archives Hub team, who check them and then load them into the SGML repository. The service is about to move to a new model, which gives archives and libraries the option of hosting their EAD files locally, while still making them available through the main Archives Hub (see Figure 1). The Spokes software, as it is known, provides a Web interface to the local EAD files (similar to that of the main Archives Hub) and provides Z39.50 access to the indexes of the data. These indexes are harvested on a daily basis by the main Archives Hub and are then combined with the indexes from the other Spokes and the main Hub, to create a 'meta-index' of all the available data. This is then searchable by users of the Archives Hub. The Spokes are not, therefore, actively cross-searched by the system: it is only at the point when a user wishes to view a description that a Spoke is contacted by the central Hub. Figure 1 shows the architecture of the system.

FIGURE 1. Archives Hub: Diagram of Distributed Architecture

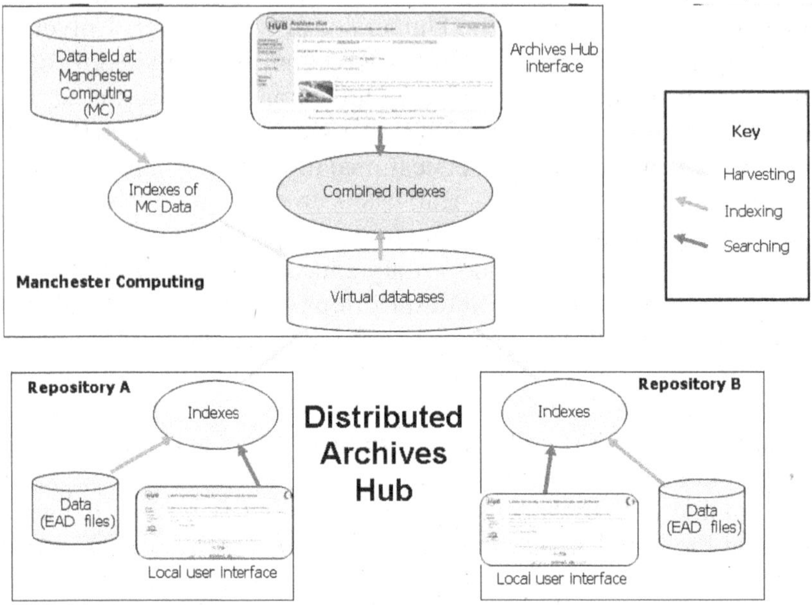

The system is currently undergoing comprehensive testing and fine-tuning. It is planned that the distributed version of the Archives Hub will be live in 2005. For contributing institutions the distributed architecture provides greater control over their data: they are able to add, edit and delete their files themselves. Their data could also be reused in other systems that are able to use the Z39.50 protocol to access the files. The software also provides a Web interface to the archives for local users. Most importantly, perhaps, the Spokes software is available free of charge to non-profit-making organizations![8]

ACCESS TO ARCHIVES–A2A

Introduction

Like both the other projects being discussed in this article, Access to Archives, or simply A2A, is an online database providing federated access, in this case to finding aids from over 390 holders of archives across England, including museums and libraries as well as traditional record offices. The discussion here will focus on the role of EAD within A2A and a more general description of the programme as a whole can be found elsewhere.[9]

There are differences in the way EAD is used in A2A when compared to the other projects discussed here, which reflect the different goals of A2A as a whole and the different ways of working of our contributors. Nevertheless, the key point here is that EAD has a central role in A2A as the carrier of standardized electronic descriptions of archives from their creation, their return to online repositories and their searching and presentation online.

Finding Aid Creation

A primary purpose of the A2A Programme is to be a vehicle for the retroconversion of the legacy finding aids of our contributors, in order to create the necessary content for the emerging UK national archives network. In this respect the Programme has been mainly interested in capturing detailed multilevel finding aids rather than collection-level descriptions, although these are accepted where more detailed data is unavailable. These finding aids include both the paper catalogues and lists found in public searchrooms, as well as electronic catalogues in non-standardized forms, that is word processing, spreadsheet and database files that have no explicit conformance to archival standards. By mid-2005 we will have converted the equivalent of over 1 million pages of finding aids amounting to about 95,000 archive collections.

Whether retroconversion is carried out in-house or by keying contractors, the product of the conversion is an EAD file conforming to the standard A2A template.[10] A2A is still working with EAD 1.0 and in SGML. Unlike the Archives Hub project then our contributors do not create the EAD files themselves; they simply provide us with copies of the paper or electronic lists, which are then converted to the EAD template.

The encoding in the template basically conforms to RLG's Best Practice Guidelines[11] and enables the structuring of the content of the finding aid in accordance with the descriptive standards for the Programme. The relationship to these standards is made explicit within the template by use of the appropriate attributes.

The data found in the EAD Header relating to the finding aid as a resource in its own right is mapped to the simple Dublin Core (DC) metadata set by use of the "relatedencoding" attribute of the EAD Header (<eadheader>) tag. Each metadata element is then mapped using the "encodinganalog" attribute. As there is not a direct map between EAD and DC some elements are given using Note (<note>) tags.[12]

The descriptive part of the finding aid (Archival Description–<archdesc>) is mapped to *ISAD(G)*, which is the Programme's key descriptive standard. Each EAD element is mapped to its related *ISAD(G)* element, in a similar way to the mapping to DC in the EAD Header. The structure of the multilevel finding aids is maintained in EAD by use of the level attribute of the Archival Description (<archdesc>) and Component (<c>) tags, which is set to the appropriate *ISAD(G)* level (fonds, series, file, etc.).

The forms of the names of creators wrapped within the Origination (<origination>) tag, and of the names of people, families, organizations, and places wrapped within the Controlled Access (<controlaccess>) tag are controlled by national rules that (as A2A still uses the first version of EAD) are noted in the "source" attribute of the relevant EAD name tag.[13] Subject terms are controlled by the UNESCO thesaurus, which is similarly noted.[14]

When we wish to give access to digital versions of the archives described, we make use of EAD's Digital Archival Object Group (<daogrp>) and associated tags. Finally, we note the text of the repository name in the Repository (<repository>) tag and also note the UK code for repositories in the "repositorycode" attribute for the Archival Description (<archdesc>) and Component (<c>) tags.[15]

Storage and Editing

The result of the A2A conversion process then is an EAD file with data conforming to the Programme's standards. As A2A is not the ultimate destination of the data, which is owned by A2A contributors, there has been no need for the development of extensive (and expensive) editorial facilities. The files are simply stored as EAD and their quality is checked by viewing them in an SGML editor. The contributors check the files online once they have been loaded into the A2A database. The little editing of files necessary, mainly on those elements holding authority-controlled data that forms the basis of indexing for searching, is also carried out in the SGML editor.

Exchange of EAD Files

The final step in the retroconversion process is, of course, the return of the standardized electronic data to the contributing repositories for their own purposes.

Many of these repositories have invested in proprietary archival management systems. These relational database systems are based on a core cataloguing module structured in line with *ISAD(G)*. As A2A's standardized EAD finding aids have the necessary structure, the data they carry is simply imported into these databases and thereby becomes the contributors' master version. The version held on the A2A database then effectively becomes a copy. Amendments and additions can then be made to the finding aids, updated versions of which can then be re-exported as EAD to A2A to replace the earlier version online.

There remain some contributors to A2A who don't yet have electronic systems and A2A's EAD files, therefore, remain the master data in these cases, until the time that electronic systems are acquired.

A2A Database

The EAD files also form the basis of the A2A online database. EAD files as SGML are converted to XML. After some initial pre-processing and validation of data (especially that used as the basis for indexing and searching), they are loaded into an XML document management system: a customized version of IXIASoft's TextML server, by employing bespoke Perl programs.[16]

This system then uses the standardized structure of the finding aids captured by EAD to create indexes, which form the basis for user searching via online forms written as active server pages (ASP). Finding aids found in response to a search are presented to users in one of three different views by conversion from XML to HTML by means of stylesheets written in Extensible Stylesheet Language (XSLT).

The user functionality in the database clearly reflects the standardized data structure captured in the EAD files and is best illustrated by a closer look at the A2A database.[17]

The main search page has a "google" like keyword or phrase search box, which is based on an index of the EAD elements representing

ISAD(G)'s main descriptive elements (scope and content, title, etc.). As can be seen in Figure 2, searches can be qualified by the repository name, which can be found via a drop-down list, as can the region in which records are held, data for which comes from the EAD Header. Finally there is also a search by creation dates, based on indexes of the data found in EAD's Date of the Unit (<unitdate>) tag.

An extended search screen provides searches based on indexes of the data held in a number of other EAD tags. There is one by creator, based on an index of all the names contained in the EAD Origination (<origination>) tag as well as searches by archive category[18] and theme, again based on indexes of the metadata held in the EAD Header.

Finally, we also offer a "People, Places and Subjects" search as illustrated in Figure 3. The "People" search is based on indexes created by combining the data held as creator names with the names of persons, families and organizations found in the appropriate EAD name tag (<persname>, etc.) within the Controlled Access Headings of the EAD

FIGURE 2. A2A Standard Search Screen

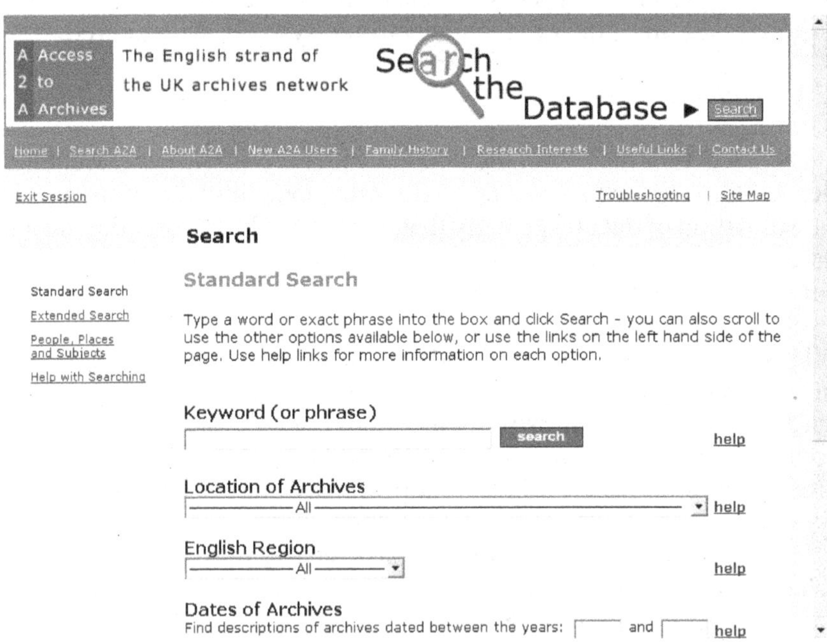

FIGURE 3. A2A People, Places and Subjects Search Screen

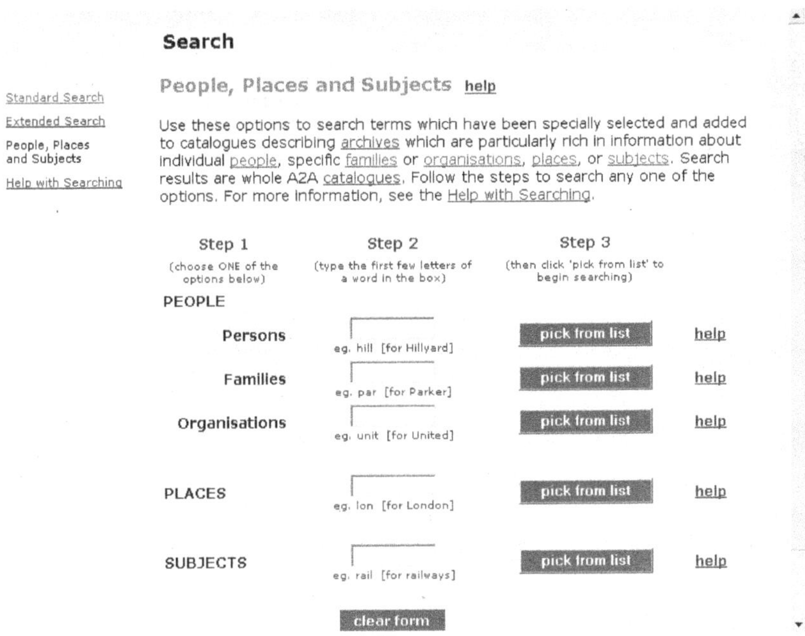

finding aid. Places and subject searches are similarly created as indexes from the EAD Geographic Name (<geogname>) and Subject (<subject>) tags respectively, again as found wrapped within the Controlled Access area.

In response to a keyword or phrase search, as that for 'windmill' at the English Heritage National Monuments Record shown in Figure 4, users get a list of all the catalogues on A2A that include the keyword or phrase, with a note of the number of hits as shown in Figure 5.

When a catalogue is chosen from the hit list, users are taken to the context view of the catalogue, which is one of the three views of the EAD finding aids that is created on request via an XSLT stylesheet. Rather than showing the whole finding aid, the context view lists each highlighted instance of the keyword or phrase searched for. With this is the basic information that users need in order to decide if they want to see or copy the record in question: reference, date and description (title and/or scope and content). For each highlighted hit, as illustrated

FIGURE 4. A2A Standard Search for 'Windmill'

in Figure 6, contextual information about any parent records is given (here for example is the fonds title and reference) to ensure that, even without seeing the whole catalogue, users are given enough of the context of a particular record to understand its nature.

If users decide they want to take their investigation further, they can click on the repository name, which has been placed at the top of the page by the stylesheet, and activate a link (based on the contents of the "repositorycode" attribute of the <archdesc> tag), which brings up online contact information for the repository. If there are links to the actual digital objects described in the catalogue by way of <daogrp> tags in the EAD file then the stylesheet displays a link and the user can click to see the image in a new window.

At the top of the context view page can be seen links to the other views offered of each catalogue. While the context view is that seen most often by users, and indeed very few choose to look at any other view, they may move to look at the whole catalogue, which can be

FIGURE 5. A2A Hit List for Search on 'Windmill'

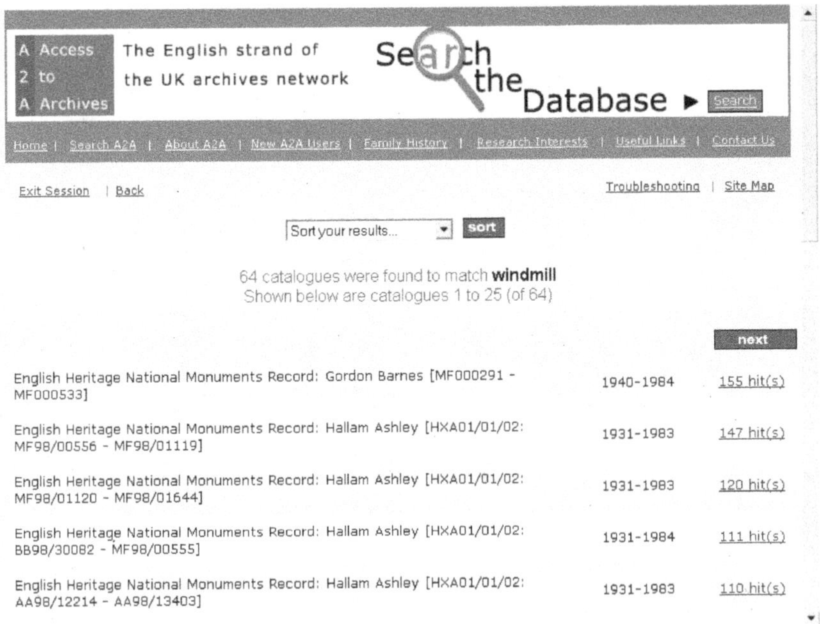

browsed. Finally, there is also the table of contents view. This simply shows the structure of the finding aid, with a note of the archival level, and gives basic information at file and item level as seen in Figure 7. It is not designed for users, but for our contributors as a useful view for them to have when they quality control the catalogues online in the A2A database.

NAVIGATIONAL AIDS FOR THE HISTORY OF SCIENCE, TECHNOLOGY AND THE ENVIRONMENT–NAHSTE

Introduction

Navigational Aids for the History of Science, Technology and the Environment (NAHSTE)[19] was a small-scale portal-based collaborative archival cataloguing project, which aimed to deliver topic-based hi-

FIGURE 6. A2A Context View of Search on 'Windmill' in the Finding Aid to the Records of Eric De Mare

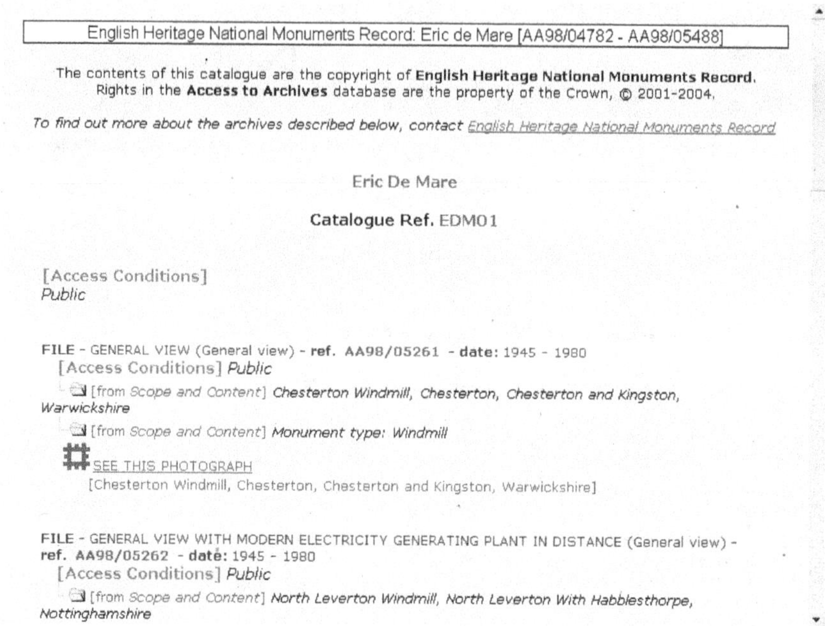
English Heritage National Monuments Record: Eric de Mare [AA98/04782 - AA98/05488]

The contents of this catalogue are the copyright of **English Heritage National Monuments Record.** Rights in the **Access to Archives** database are the property of the Crown, © 2001-2004.

To find out more about the archives described below, contact English Heritage National Monuments Record

Eric De Mare

Catalogue Ref. EDM01

[Access Conditions]
Public

FILE - GENERAL VIEW (General view) - **ref. AA98/05261** - **date:** 1945 - 1980
[Access Conditions] *Public*
[from *Scope and Content*] *Chesterton Windmill, Chesterton, Chesterton and Kingston, Warwickshire*
[from *Scope and Content*] *Monument type: Windmill*
SEE THIS PHOTOGRAPH
[Chesterton Windmill, Chesterton, Chesterton and Kingston, Warwickshire]

FILE - GENERAL VIEW WITH MODERN ELECTRICITY GENERATING PLANT IN DISTANCE (General view) - **ref. AA98/05262** - **date:** 1945 - 1980
[Access Conditions] *Public*
[from *Scope and Content*] *North Leverton Windmill, North Leverton With Habblesthorpe, Nottinghamshire*

erarchical archival catalogues, and a suite of additional research tools, to the Higher Education community.

This was achieved through careful data modeling and data creation methodologies, with EAD at the core. These methodologies continue to be used for further projects within Edinburgh University Library, and the data created will form the basis of a new online repository catalogue.

Partners

Funded by the Research Support Libraries Programme (RSLP),[20] the project ran from January 2000 until October 2002. It was led by Edinburgh University Library in collaboration with Glasgow University Archive Services and Heriot-Watt University Archive, Records Management and Museum Service.

FIGURE 7. A2A Table of Contents View of the Finding Aid to the Records of Eric De Mare

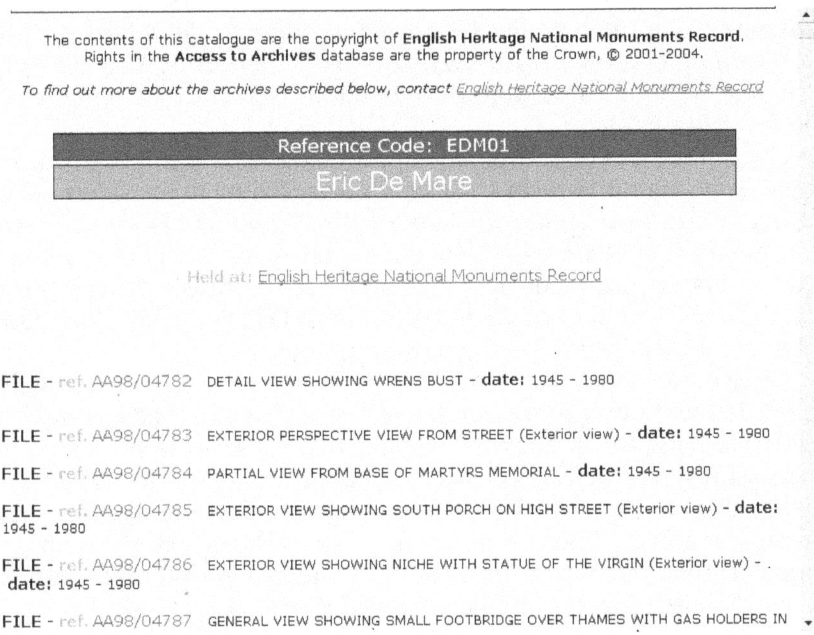

The contents of this catalogue are the copyright of **English Heritage National Monuments Record**.
Rights in the **Access to Archives** database are the property of the Crown, © 2001-2004.

To find out more about the archives described below, contact English Heritage National Monuments Record

Reference Code: EDM01

Eric De Mare

Held at: English Heritage National Monuments Record

FILE - ref. AA98/04782 DETAIL VIEW SHOWING WRENS BUST - **date:** 1945 - 1980

FILE - ref. AA98/04783 EXTERIOR PERSPECTIVE VIEW FROM STREET (Exterior view) - **date:** 1945 - 1980

FILE - ref. AA98/04784 PARTIAL VIEW FROM BASE OF MARTYRS MEMORIAL - **date:** 1945 - 1980

FILE - ref. AA98/04785 EXTERIOR VIEW SHOWING SOUTH PORCH ON HIGH STREET (Exterior view) - **date:** 1945 - 1980

FILE - ref. AA98/04786 EXTERIOR VIEW SHOWING NICHE WITH STATUE OF THE VIRGIN (Exterior view) - . **date:** 1945 - 1980

FILE - ref. AA98/04787 GENERAL VIEW SHOWING SMALL FOOTBRIDGE OVER THAMES WITH GAS HOLDERS IN

Project Aims

The Project's aims were to:

- catalogue outstanding collections of archives and manuscripts, relevant to the history of science, technology and the environment, held across the three collaborators;
- to cross-link catalogue entries to related Scottish scientific historical records;
- to stimulate increased research by making catalogue entries, and additional tools, fully accessible on the World Wide Web.

Data Components

At an early stage a number of data components were identified for inclusion in the project. Careful data modeling established their interrelationships, and informed future technical development, as illustrated in Figure 8.

The core data components were hierarchical archival descriptions structured according to the *General International Standard Archival Description*, edition 2 (*ISAD(G)*) and marked up using EAD. A set of strict cataloguing rules were developed, to ensure consistency across the descriptions.[21]

Three packages of additional support data were also provided. Personal name authority records, structured according to the *International Standard Archival Authority Record for Corporate Bodies, Persons and Families (ISAAR(CPF))*[22] were included for around one hundred individuals. As Encoded Archival Context (EAC) was still in early draft form, these were marked-up in an in-house DTD of XML, facilitating interoperability with the archival descriptions.

Three online themes and sources essays, giving further contextual information and ideas for research use, were written by academics[23] already studying the collections catalogued. These were presented at a successful symposium day, held by the project in November 2000. Also included were "informed links" to related collections held by other Scottish archives. These were marked up in Hypertext Mark-up Language (HTML) and hyperlinked to the archival descriptions through the Related Units of Description element of *ISAD(G)*.

FIGURE 8. NAHSTE Project: Data Architecture

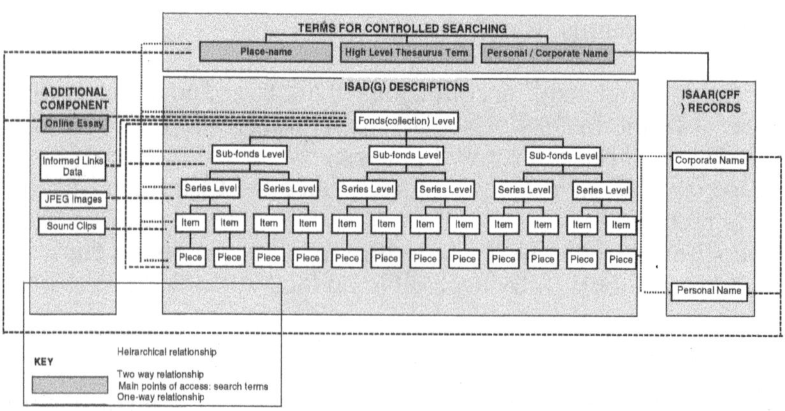

A gallery of exemplar images of documents from the collections was included along with sound-clips from the Edinburgh University Library collection Records of the Science Studies Oral History Project, in which eminent living scientists are interviewed concerning their careers.

Web Site Functionality and Development

The project's data model, which was developed in conjunction with the Gateway to Archives of Scottish Higher Education Project (GASHE)[24] led by Glasgow University Archive Services, demanded Internet delivery with seamless browsing, free-text searching and structured searching, within and across all data components.

Web delivery was undertaken by EDINA National Data Centre,[25] using Perl[26] scripts to perform XML to XHTML transformations and create cross-linked indices from the access points recorded in the <controlaccess> wrapper tags, and the *ISAAR(CPF)* records.

Data Authoring

XMetal2 software was chosen for data authoring due to its competitive price and compatibility with the EAD Cookbook.[27] In addition, peer support was readily available due to an existing body of archival users.

The majority of the project's archival descriptions were to be created from scratch with little possibility of data entry automation or retroconversion. Data authors would all be based at the University of Edinburgh. With this information, an XML consultant advised using raw XML for data creation, rather than providing templates that hide it from the creator. This flexible methodology would reap future benefits by ensuring that all staff were familiar with EAD, enabling easy creation of hierarchical levels of description, enabling the use of occasional tag sets in individual descriptions for specific purposes (e.g., inserting an image), and removing any need for a post-authoring editor.

Templates, which exposed the raw XML, were devised to ensure consistent use of EAD for all levels of description. Specifications for these were informed by other UK Higher Education usage, particularly the Archives Hub,[28] to ensure future interoperability within the sector. The fonds level description template used NAHSTE's full EAD set. EAD Header (<eadheader>), Front Matter (<frontmatter>) and Archival Description (<archdesc>) tags were wrapped in the Encoded Archival Description (<ead>) tag. Tags within Archival Description

(<archdesc>) used the EAD to *ISAD(G)* crosswalks published in the EAD Application Guidelines, with some minor modifications to take account of the changes in the second edition of *ISAD(G)*. Provision for the inclusion of access points was made through addition of a set of nested Controlled Access (<controlaccess>) tags, which would allow indexes to be separated into subjects, people, organizations and places. Provision for the inclusion of lower levels of description was made through the incorporation of the Descriptive of Subordinate Components (<dsc>) tag at the end of the Archival Description (<archdesc>) section. Different levels of description were nested within this, using the Component (<c>) tag in conjunction with the "level" attribute.

A number of methods were used to ensure that the correct tags were populated with the correct data by the authors. Navigation was facilitated though a Cascading Style Sheet (CSS)[29] which controlled the XMetal display in the "Tags on view." Background colors differentiated sections of the document. Incidental tags, which were added manually by the data author, were colored. Elements and attributes, which required a constant value, were pre-populated, while the remainder were flagged as requiring data entry, the former through the Visual Basic highlighted "replace text" command. Comments, for deletion, throughout the template, referred to a step-by-step authoring manual as illustrated in Figures 9 and 10.

Macros were devised for automatically inserting the tag sequences required for:

- series and item level descriptions–according to the *ISAD(G)* multi-level description rules;
- related units of description–hyperlinks to the "informed links";
- full bibliographic references to books, journals, Web sites, concise bibliographic references (title and date only), and images.

Tag sets for different types of bibliographic references enabled inclusion of detailed information regarding sources or related academic works, while enabling a full bibliography to be extracted if required. These tag sets were later used in the Rebuilding the City: the Percy Johnson-Marshall Collection[30] to cross reference manuscript material with a database of published material held in the collection. Figure 11 shows the EAD set for some completed bibliographic references, while Figure 12 shows the bibliographic references displayed on the Internet.

FIGURE 9. NAHSTE: Fonds Level Template Prior to Data Entry–"Tags on View"

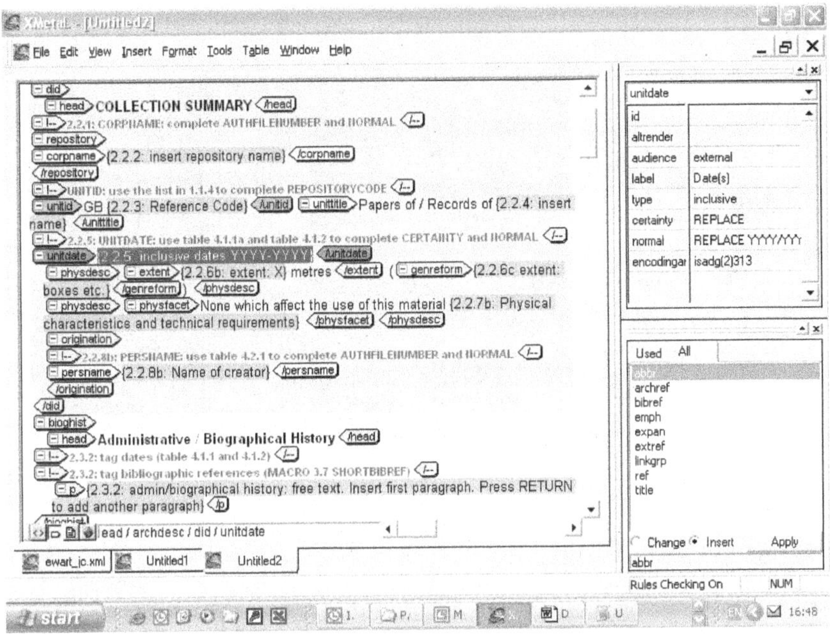

The Digital Archival Object Group (<daogrp>) wrapper was used to include digital image thumbnails in some descriptions. The path to a thumbnail was included in the "href" attribute of the Digital Archival Object Location (<daoloc>) tag. Perl scripts were used to read the end of this path and embed the images in the online description. The scripts also created hyperlinks to an enlarged image, from both the embedded thumbnail and the caption held in the Digital Archival Object Description (<daodesc>) tag, as illustrated in Figures 13 and 14.

Indexing

Controlled vocabulary for structured searching was included, with access terms assigned to each *ISAD(G)* description, at every level of the hierarchy. Subjects and place names were chosen from Library of Congress Subject Headings, in line with Edinburgh University Library's (EUL)

FIGURE 10. NAHSTE: Fonds Level Template After Data Entry–"Tags on View"

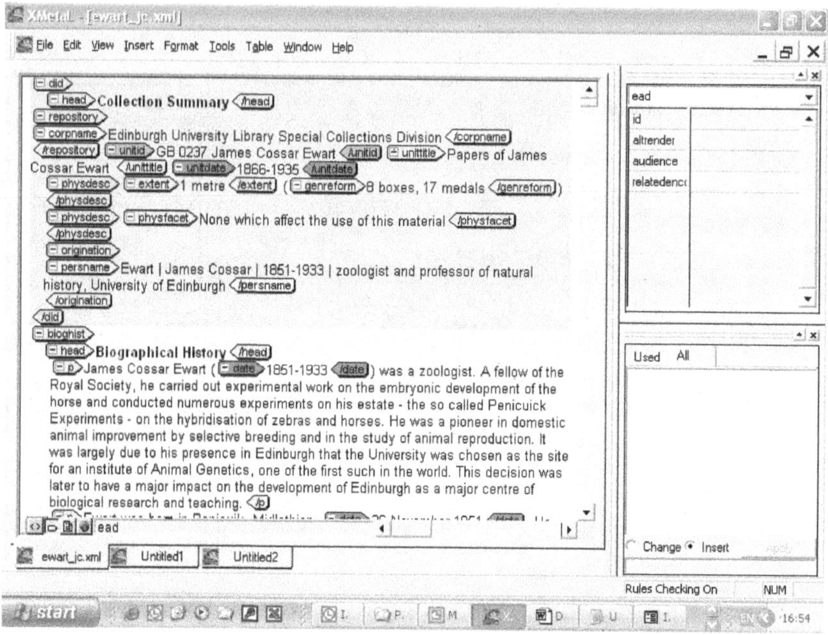

cataloguing policy. Personal and Corporate names were constructed according to the UK National Council on Archives Rules for the Construction of Personal, Place and Corporate Names (NCA Rules). Access points were recorded in a database to ensure that each term was assigned a unique identifier. This was used in the "authfilenumber" attribute of the Personal Name (<persname>), Corporate Name (<corpname>), Subject (<subject>) and Geographic Name (<geogname>) tags, to enable indices to be generated by a Perl script for structured searching.

Further EAD Work Planned

Edinburgh University Library updated the NAHSTE methodology to EAD 2002 immediately after its publication. The new templates and scripts were used for two further projects: The Baillie Project[31] and Re-

FIGURE 11. NAHSTE: EAD for Bibliographic References

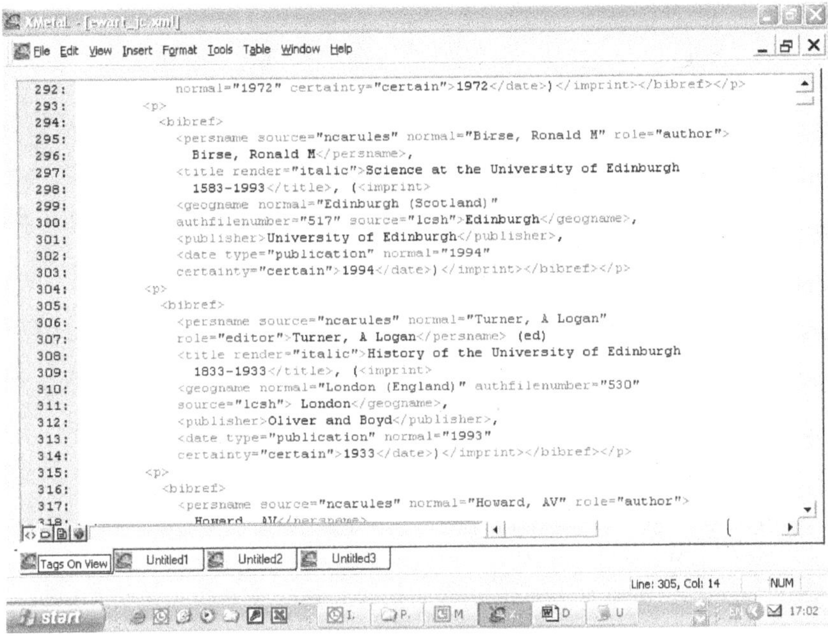

building the City: the Percy Johnson-Marshall Project. The former catalogued the papers of John Baillie, a Scottish theologian and former Moderator of the Church of Scotland. The latter catalogued the eclectic collection of Percy Johnson-Marshall, the University's former Professor of Urban Design and Regional Planning.

It is now proposed to move away from the provision of separate portals for different collections or projects. Instead it is planned to use the descriptions created for the three projects, along with those created for the Archives Hub and the GASHE Project, as the basis of a new online catalogue covering all the archival collections held in Edinburgh University Library. This will be delivered through a library wide implementation of Endeavor's ENCompass Solutions software.[32]

In conjunction with Endeavor's LinkFinder*Plus* Software, this will allow all digital resources held, licensed or created by Edinburgh University Library to be cross-searched in a one stop portal. Library catalogues, digital collections, e-prints and digital journals

FIGURE 12. Rebuilding the City: The Percy Johnson-Marshall Collection: Bibliographic References

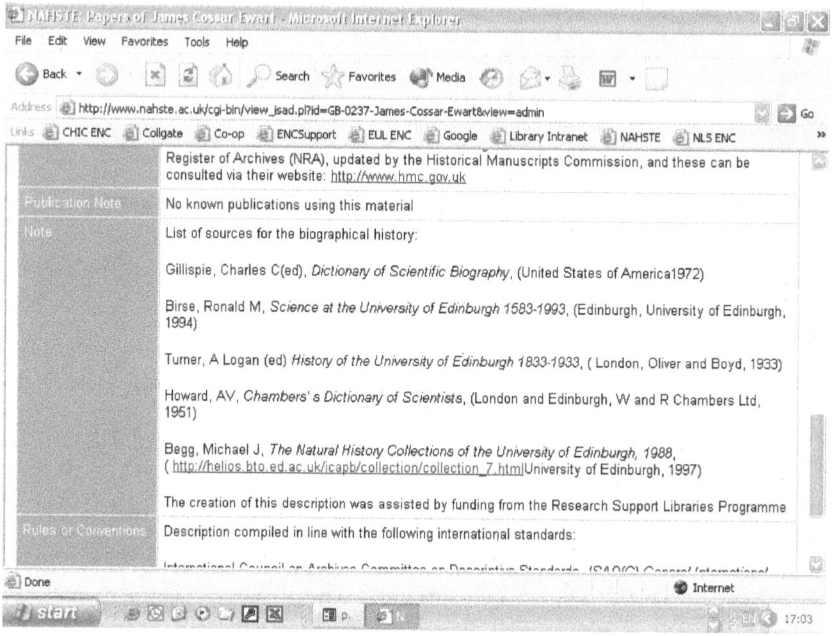

will be cross-searched through a mixture of Z39.50 connections, XML gateways, OAI harvesting, linkage to other software packages and data held locally. This brings new challenges. EAD files, created to different specifications and in different versions, for different original purposes, have to be integrated into one union catalogue without losing functionality. Cross-searching in ENCompass is achieved through crosswalks between standards, and these need to be implemented, and in some cases devised, to enable EAD data to be searched to the lowest hierarchical levels.

CONCLUSION

Despite the differences exhibited by the services discussed above, reflecting their different needs, EAD has proved a very effective tool. The

FIGURE 13. NAHSTE: EAD Markup for the Inclusion of Digital Images

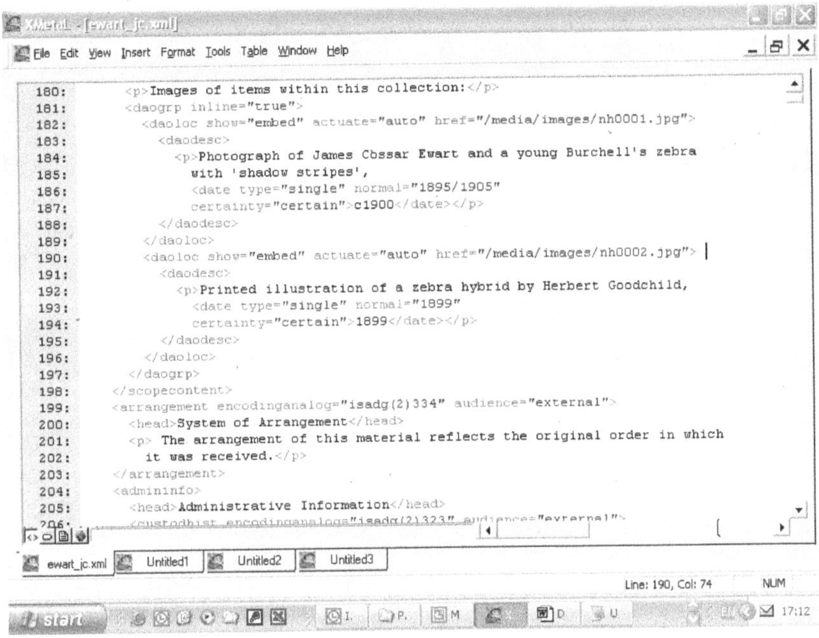

scope of the services differs from catering for many hundreds of contributors to three and from providing access to many thousands of separate finding aids to a few hundred. The depth of these finding aids also differs from single collection level descriptions to those that are detailed and multilevel. There are also significant differences in the workflow process of the services. The Archives Hub contributors either create finding aids in EAD themselves or make use of an online template, while the NAHSTE project creates finding aids in EAD centrally using an XML editor. Most of the A2A contributors also have little to do with EAD itself as creation is dealt with by mass retroconversion offshore. Some contributors store finding aid data as EAD, while others use proprietary archival management systems and interoperate with the service by means of import and export by EAD in XML. Finally, while a mixture of technologies (including XML and other data manipulation tools such as Perl) are used in the indexing, searching and presentation of the finding aids online to users, EAD plays a role in all three services.

FIGURE 14. NAHSTE: Images on the Internet

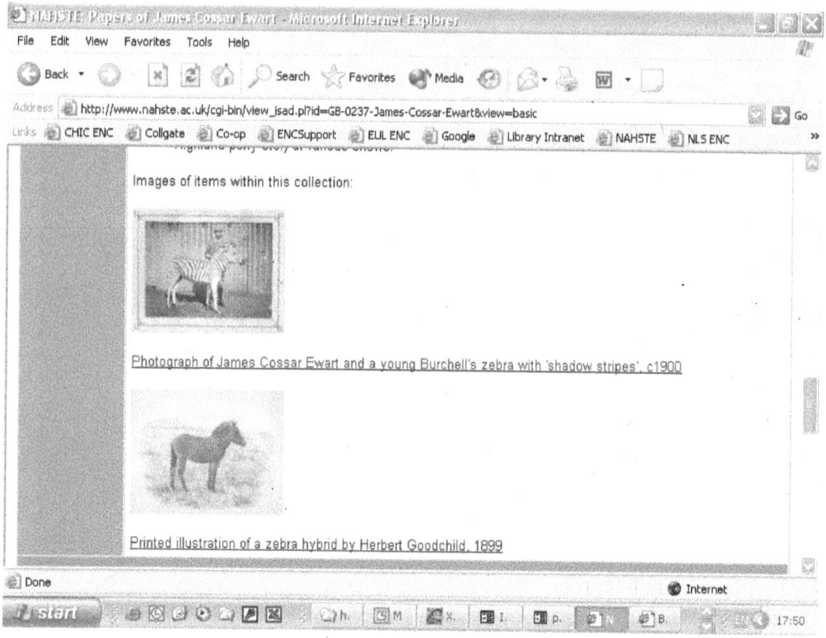

NOTES

1. Further information can be found at http://www.jisc.ac.uk.
2. Further information can be found at http://www.curl.ac.uk.
3. Further information can be found at http://www.mimas.ac.uk.
4. Guidelines for contributors to the Archives Hub can be found at http://www.archiveshub.ac.uk/arch/dcg.shtml.
5. International Council on Archives, *ISAD(G): General International Standard Archival Description*, 2nd edition (Ottawa, 2000) is available at http://www.ica.org/biblio/isad_g_2e.pdf.
6. The Archives Hub online template for EAD 1.0 can be found at http://www.archiveshub.ac.uk/template/new/eadform2.html.
7. The Archives Hub online template for EAD 2002 can be found at http://www.archiveshub.ac.uk/eadform2002.html.
8. Please see http://www.archiveshub.ac.uk/arch/spokes.shtml for more information about the 'Spokes' software.
9. A detailed discussion of the A2A Programme can be found in Sarah J. A. Flynn, Matthew Hillyard and Bill Stockting, "A2A: the development of a strand in the na-

tional archives network," *Journal of the Society of Archivists*. 22, No. 2 (2001), 177-191.

10. A copy of the template can be found as Appendix A of Bill Stockting, "Time to Settle Down? EAD Encoding Principles in the Access to Archives Programme (A2A) and the Research Libraries Group's Best Practice Guidelines," *Journal of Archival Organization* 2, No 3 (2004), 18-24.

11. RLG's EAD Best Practice Guidelines can be found at http://www.rlg.org/rlgead/eadguides.html.

12. A crosswalk of Dublin Core to EAD 1.0 can be found as Appendix B3 to the *Encoded Archival Description Application Guidelines* available at http://lcweb.loc.gov/ead/ag/aghome.html.

13. National Council on Archives (NCA), *Rules for the Construction of Personal, Place and Corporate Names*, which can be found online at http://www.hmc.gov.uk/nca/title.htm.

14. UNESCO, *UNESCO Thesaurus: a Structured List of the Descriptors for indexing and Retrieving Literature in the Fields of Education, Science, Social and Human Science, Culture, Communication and Information* (Paris, 1995). This thesaurus is now being used as the basis for the development of the United Kingdom Archival Thesaurus (UKAT), information about which can be found at http://www.ukat.org.uk/.

15. The UK code for repositories is that given by the online ARCHON directory available at http://www.archon.nationalarchives.gov.uk/archon/.

16. Further information about IXIASoft's TextML server as used in A2A can be found at http://www.ixiasoft.com/default.asp?xml=CUSTOMER-PUBLIC-RECORD-OFFICE.XML&result=1.

17. Available online at http://www.a2a.org.uk.

18. Archive category is a term noting the high-level functional provenance of an archive collection. Terms include *Charities* or *Schools* for example.

19. Available online at http://www.nahste.ac.uk/.

20. Full details of the work of the Research Support Libraries Programme can be found on their Web site at: http://www.rslp.ac.uk/.

21. S. Higgins, "Cataloguing Instructions for *ISAD(G)* Compliant Archival Descriptions Fully Tagged into EAD Using XMetal Software" (NAHSTE Project, unpublished internal manual, 2001).

22. *ISAAR(CPF): International Standard Archival Authority Record for Corporate Bodies, Persons, and Families*, Second edition, 2004. Available online at http://www.ica.org.

23. John Henry, *A Short History of Scientific and Technical Education in Edinburgh, Glasgow and Heriot-Watt Universities*, University of Edinburgh; MD Eddy, *John Walker*, University of Durham; David B. Wilson, *John Robison*, Iowa State University.

24. Available online at http://www.gashe.archives.gla.ac.uk/.

25. Full details of the work of the EDINA National Data Centre can be found on the Internet at http://edina.ac.uk/.

26. For further details see http://www.perl.org/.

27. *The EAD Cookbook*, available at http://www.iath.virginia.edu/ead/cookbookhelp.html offers advice and files for the implementation of EAD using a number of software of which XMetal is one.

28. Descriptions created for the Archives Hub Project can be searched over the Internet at http://www.archiveshub.ac.uk.

29. Full specifications by the World Wide Web Consortium for Cascading Style Sheets can be found at http://www.w3.org/Style/CSS/.

30. Available online at http://www.johnson-marshall.lib.ed.ac.uk/.

31. Available online at http://www.baillie.lib.ed.ac.uk.

32. Available online at http://encompass.endinfosys.com/.

EAD CONCLUSION

The Influence of American and European Practices on the Evolution of EAD

Kris Kiesling

SUMMARY. Widespread adoption of EAD in the United States and in Europe is attributable to a number of factors, including compatibility with *ISAD(G)*, availability of funding for data conversion, requirements of granting agencies, and the desire of archivists to use common standards. *[Article copies available for a fee from The Haworth Document Delivery Service: 1-800-HAWORTH. E-mail address: <docdelivery@haworthpress.com> Website: <http://www.HaworthPress.com> © 2005 by The Haworth Press, Inc. All rights reserved.]*

Kris Kiesling is Associate Director, Technical and Digital Services, Harry Ransom Humanities Research Center, University of Texas at Austin. She was part of the Bentley Team that transformed the Berkeley Finding Aid Project DTD into EAD and has chaired the Society of American Archivists EAD Working Group since its establishment in 1995. With Michael Fox, she has taught over fifty EAD workshops in the United States and abroad. She is a Fellow of the Society of American Archivists.

[Haworth co-indexing entry note]: "The Influence of American and European Practices on the Evolution of EAD." Kiesling, Kris. Co-published simultaneously in *Journal of Archival Organization* (The Haworth Information Press, an imprint of The Haworth Press, Inc.) Vol. 3, No. 2/3, 2005, pp. 207-215; and: *Encoding Across Frontiers: Proceedings of the European Conference on Encoded Archival Description and Context (EAD and EAC), Paris, France, 7-8 October 2004* (ed: Bill Stockting, and Fabienne Queyroux) The Haworth Information Press, an imprint of The Haworth Press, Inc., 2005, pp. 207-215. Single or multiple copies of this article are available for a fee from The Haworth Document Delivery Service [1-800-HAWORTH, 9:00 a.m. - 5:00 p.m. (EST). E-mail address: docdelivery@haworthpress.com].

Available online at http://www.haworthpress.com/web/JAO

doi:10.1300/J201v03n02_15

KEYWORDS. Archival description, EAD, Encoded Archival Description, standardization

I'd like to begin my paper with a quotation:

> "The MARC Archival and Manuscripts Control format has the potential to change the lives of archivists forever," wrote Steve Hensen at the beginning of his paper on the use of standards in the application of the AMC format. Twelve years later [it is now 18 years since Steve wrote that article] the same could easily be said of Encoded Archival Description [EAD], the next logical step in the evolution of archival descriptive standards and the answer to MARC for finding aids. Just as the MARC format was the mechanism that provided a consistent structure for archival catalog records and set archivists on a course toward acceptance of a host of bibliographic standards, so EAD will now be the impetus that leads us toward standardizing the structure and possibly the content of finding aids, and it may well unite the international archival community in the process.

I wrote this in an article that was published in the Summer 1997 issue of the *American Archivist*,[1] and I remember thinking at the time that, rather than being prescient or profound, I might in fact live to regret those words. What if EAD didn't gain acceptance in the United States, let alone in Europe and elsewhere? What if it was a total non-event? A complete flop? Apparently I needn't have worried, and certainly there are no regrets.

A few weeks ago at the International Congress on Archives in Vienna, Jan Dahlin referred to EAD as "the DTD for *ISAD(G)*," and Bill Stockting characterized EAD as being "the right tool at the right time" for archivists in the United Kingdom. In Vienna we also saw demonstrations of the very impressive implementations of EAD in Spain and Poland. Recently I Googled "Encoded Archival Description" and got a search result of 16,800 hits. A paltry sum by Google standards, but significant, I think, for an archival standard. My search result included the official Library of Congress EAD Web site; PDF files of articles, conference papers and PowerPoint presentations; faculty lectures and syllabi and student papers from schools of information and library science; information about institutional and consortial implementation projects from several countries; best practice guidelines; press releases announcing the availability of EADified finding aids; and a host of other documents. The EAD documentation has been translated into several languages–Spanish in 2000 with funding from the Council on Library and Information Resources and the Fundación Histórica Tavera, French in 2004 through the efforts of a very dedicated group of volunteers, and in spring 2005 it will be available in print and online in Chinese primarily through the efforts of two enterprising young archivists at the Academia Sinica in Taipei. In her paper in this edition, Angelika Menne-Haritz referred to the "globalized archival profession." I believe we have attained that united archival community.

As the last speaker on the topic of EAD at this conference, perhaps it is appropriate to take a moment to look back at EAD's history and development. It is now eleven years since the Berkeley Finding Aid Project (BFAP) began, nine years since the Bentley team transformed the BFAP DTD into EAD, eight years since the beta version of the DTD was released for a year of testing, six years since Version 1.0 was released, and already it has been two years since EAD 2002 was released. There have been two editions of the Tag Library.[2] Best practice guidelines for individual institutions and consortia abound. The EAD workshop originally offered by RLG beginning in 1996, known as FAST (Finding Aids SGML Training), and now sponsored by the Society of American Archivists (SAA), has trained approximately 1,300 archivists in the United States and elsewhere. The University of Virginia's Rare Book School has offered weeklong EAD courses fourteen times, reaching almost 200 more archivists. Consortial projects have developed their own training programs for participants. On the European side, The National Archives in the United Kingdom and archivists in France have carried out training programs for archivists in their respective countries, and we have heard at this conference about training programs elsewhere in Europe.

As someone who teaches EAD, I've noted a change in the nature of the trainees over the years and their purposes in learning EAD. Initially, many participants attended the workshops because their supervisors required them to do so, some because they were merely curious about this new encoding technique, and a few because they thought they might actually implement EAD. More recently archivists are seeking training because they need to create an EAD finding aid for a grant-funded project, because they are a new staff person at an institution that is already using EAD, or for professional development. Just a few months ago a young woman took the SAA workshop because she said she wanted a better job than the one she had, and thought knowledge of EAD would help her in that endeavor.

To what do we owe this widespread adoption of the data structure over which I needlessly fretted in 1997? While the first version of EAD was based on archival practice in the United States, it was also designed to be compatible with the first edition of the *General International Standard of Archival Description* (*ISAD(G)*), which had been published and adopted by the International Council on Archives (ICA) in 1992.[3] American archivists for the most part have ignored *ISAD(G)*, but manage nevertheless to create *ISAD(G)*-compliant finding aids. EAD development team member Sharon Thibodeau wore two hats–one reflecting her experience at the U.S. National Archives and Records Administration and the other reflecting her experience on ICA's Ad Hoc Commission on Descriptive Standards. And while in the back of our heads during that week in Ann Arbor the Bentley Team considered the potential of EAD acceptance abroad, the group was truly more concerned about whether archivists in the United States would consider EAD to be applicable to their work and a good match for their arrangement and description practices. Whether they would adopt a data structure that was more complicated to implement than simply marking up their finding aids in HTML was a significant question in our minds. We knew if we made the requirements of using EAD too stringent, it would be ignored. In a sense, we were walking a tightrope, trying to make EAD applicable to some very bad old finding aids while gently nudging archivists in the direction of a standard structure for their data.

For that reason, EAD was designed to be very flexible in its treatment of multilevel descriptions, with a minimum of required elements and attributes. That flexibility has turned out to be both a blessing and a curse. A blessing in that archivists can fold, spindle, and mutilate EAD in applying it to a variety of finding aid practices and it still emerges as EAD. A blessing also in that it could successfully be applied to a huge amount of legacy data. A curse in that the encoding flexibility can make it difficult to establish search and display protocols across finding aids within an institution, let alone across institutions. And perhaps a curse in that it encourages, but does not require, archivists to re-examine their descriptive practices and make finding aids more user-friendly. But EAD has proved itself to be as applicable to brief high-level descriptions as it is to very detailed item-level descriptions.

Despite its wide acceptance in the United States, EAD still has its critics and detractors (and perhaps this is true in Europe as well): those who see no point in standardizing their data, who argue that they don't have time to implement such a complex data structure or deal with the necessary technical infrastructure when they can provide quick access to their finding aids using HTML. No one would argue that implementing EAD is a trivial task, but it is much simpler now than it was in the mid-1990s when we were working with full SGML, plug-ins for browsers, and proprietary standards for stylesheets. Now there are tools in the "EAD Cookbook,"[4] templates and stylesheets that have been developed by institutions and consortia, and customized software available at very low cost that any archivist can tap into. All of the federal funding agencies in the United States, including the National Endowment for the Humanities, the National Historical Publications and Records Commission, and the Institute for Museum and Library Services, now require EAD for projects that intend to produce an online finding aid. This certainly encourages repositories that seek federal project funding to implement EAD, and even provides them with the financial resources to do so. In his paper in this edition Michael Webb mentions the availability of funding as an impetus for using EAD in the United Kingdom as well.

Although there is no set revision schedule for EAD, the Working Group determined in late 2000 that the DTD required some tweaking. The second edition of *ISAD(G)* had just been published by the ICA, XML had been approved by the World Wide Web Consortium (W3C), and enough institutions had experience with EAD to provide some informed feedback on the structure. Working from comments submitted by the archival community, most of them from European archivists, and most of which related to realignment with the new edition of *ISAD(G)*, the Working Group spent much of 2001 creating a slightly revised, less Anglo-centric DTD, which was published as EAD 2002. There is no question that its compliance with *ISAD(G)* and multilevel description was the key to the use of EAD in Europe and in other countries outside the United States.

What has EAD done for the archival community and, ultimately, for the people who use archives? First, it has forged some intriguing alliances. I used to tease my colleagues at Harvard University, saying that discussions about EAD were the first time the numerous repositories on that campus had ever talked to each other about anything. On further reflection, I realized that this was also the case at my own university. But these alliances have grown far beyond single campuses. The Philadelphia Area Consortium of Special Collections Libraries (PACSCL),[5] which began in 1985 as an informal cooperative of sixteen repositories and now comprises twenty-five institutions, includes special collections libraries from public and private universities, museums, historical societies, a foundation, and a branch of the National Archives, with holdings ranging from the theological, horticultural, medical, chemical, and philosophical, to the humanities, art and art history, literary, and historical. While the consortium was not formed around EAD implementation, the repositories have worked together on EAD, MARC, and digital imaging, all highly technical undertakings. The Access to Archives (A2A) Web site contains contributions from nearly 400 repositories in the United Kingdom.[6] These include the usual suspects, such the British Library, and various universities, but also such fascinating institutions as the Knitting and Crochet Guild, The Long Shop Steam Museum, the Shakespeare Birthplace Trust Records Office, and The Tolkien Society Archives. Some of the smaller repositories do not have a Web presence of their own and are using A2A as a way to make themselves more visible in the larger archival arena.

Second, EAD has encouraged the development of companion standards, such as the recently published *Describing Archives: A Content Standard* (*DACS*).[7] Based on *ISAD(G)* and the International Standard Archival Authority Record for Corporate Bodies, Persons and Families *(ISAAR(CPF))*,[8] *DACS* represents a milestone in the United States. For twenty years archivists used *Archives, Personal Papers, and Manuscripts* (*APPM*) as a content standard for catalog records, usually produced in the MARC format, but there was no related content standard for finding aids (for whatever reason, *ISAD(G)* was largely ignored in the U.S.). It was recognized ten years ago that *APPM* needed revision, but the emergence of EAD convinced the descriptive standards community that the creation of a content standard for finding aids was crucial. As a result, *DACS* supports the creation of standardized catalog records and finding aids. Although the rules are designed to be output neutral, that is, the rules can be used to create standardized descriptions of archival materials regardless of the system being used to present the description to users, each data element in *DACS* has examples encoded in EAD and MARC 21. A minimum or core record based on *DACS* has nine required elements, whereas *ISAD(G)* requires only six. The project that created *DACS* has also produced a revision of the Canadian *Rules for Archival Description* (*RAD*). Standardizing the content of finding aids by employing rules such as these will benefit the users of archives.

Third, EAD has encouraged archivists to standardize the appearance of their finding aids, particularly in an online environment. Many of the consortial EAD projects have created one or two stylesheets that govern online display of the finding aids in their databases, and the *EAD Cookbook* provides a wide selection of stylesheets that accommodate variations in the Description of Subordinate Components (<dsc>) portion of finding aids, but at the same time enforcing a similar look and feel. Even seemingly small changes, such as removing archival jargon from headings, enforcing an order on data elements, or adding an abstract to the high-level Descriptive Identification section (<did>) can have a significant impact on user understanding of finding aids and archival materials. We need constantly to remind ourselves that we have opened archival materials to inspection by the uninitiated in the cold world of cyberspace, removed from the warm and welcoming atmosphere of our reading rooms and the ministrations of our reference archivists.

Fourth, EAD has spawned related tools such as Encoded Archival Context (EAC) and Encoded Archival Guide (EAG). EAC is based on *ISAAR(CPF)* and will enable the standardization and sharing of archival authority information. Finding aids and authority records can be linked using EAD and EAC, permitting several fonds or records series to be linked to a single creator and for related creators to be more explicitly documented. The EAG DTD has been developed in Spain in support of the CENSO-GUIA project and supports the creation of guides to repositories. EAD has even spurred the development of computer software designed for archival description. A vendor in the United States attempted to develop a program specifically for creation of EAD files, but found that the market was too small to sustain the development effort. A more successful story emerges from Germany with the MidosaXML software. Data conversion vendors have also learned a bit about finding aids, as millions of pages of legacy data have been sent overseas for encoding. So while the world of archives was learning about and using technology, so too was the world of technology learning about the existence of archives. Michael Webb mentions this pairing of backgrounds and expertise in his paper in this edition, and Pierre-Yves Duchemin used the phrase "EAD engineer." With increasing frequency archivists and technical staff are speaking the same language.

Archivists have been creative in their approaches to EAD, frequently folding the standard into an existing workflow. Many repositories use EAD as a mechanism for creating, storing, and publishing their finding aids using a suite of software tools. Others continue to create their finding aids in Microsoft Word or other text editors for the purpose of producing a nicely formatted print version, and then copy and paste the text into a template in XML software to create the EAD for online purposes. Still others enter collection description information into a database and then map the data fields to EAD to publish the finding aids online. Some repositories export part of their EAD finding aids into MARC 21 records, making the information searchable in integrated library systems; others do the process in reverse, adding a container list to the information from the MARC record to create the finding aid. Whatever the mechanism, all end up with an EAD file in some form, making it possible to exchange data across institutional, regional, and national boundaries. This is already happening with the RLG's *Archival Resources* database, through which researchers may search across and browse finding aids from several countries.[9] It is truly remarkable that we have the ability to provide digital versions of our collection materials in conjunction with contextual information–the what, who, when, and why–to anyone who thinks to ask.

Will EAD be around for the foreseeable future? It seems likely. But even if it is replaced by a new technology sooner rather than later, EAD provides us with a solid basis for the next generation of tools. Archivists can map EAD elements to any data set or new system that happens along, and that is certainly something we could not have said eleven years ago. An EAD schema is being developed, which will enable interoperability with other encoding schemes such as Metadata Encoding and Transmission Standard (METS).[10] We have positioned ourselves very well to take advantage of whatever is before us.

In conclusion, I'd like to go back to my *American Archivist* article:

> . . . if EAD were to go away tomorrow, it would still have been worth the effort just to focus on the structure and content of finding aids. Perhaps the greatest and most enduring benefit of the entire EAD development process will have nothing to do with technology, but instead will be that we ultimately become convinced that there are common structural and intellectual elements in all types of archival finding aids and that a single data structure can support them. Perhaps all we needed was a catalyst that was more compelling than any we had yet encountered.[11]

Clearly we have found those common elements, and the catalyst was very compelling indeed.

NOTES

1. Kris Kiesling, "EAD as an Archival Descriptive Standard," *The American Archivist* 60 (Summer 1997): 345.

2. *Encoded Archival Description Tag Library Version 1.0* (Chicago: Society of American Archivists, 1998), and *Encoded Archival Description Tag Library Version 2002* (Chicago: Society of American Archivists, 2002).

3. International Council on Archives, *ISAD(G): General International Standard Archival Description*, 2nd edition (Ottawa, 2000) is available at http://www.ica.org/biblio/isad_g_2e.pdf.

4. The *EAD Cookbook* can be found online at http://www.iath.virginia.edu/ead/cookbookhelp.html.

5. Further information about the Philadelphia Area Consortium of Special Collections Libraries (PACSCL) can be found at http://www.pacscl.org/.

6. The Access to Archives (A2A) online database will be found at http://www.nationalarchives.gov.uk/a2a.

7. *Describing Archives: A Content Standard* (Chicago: Society of American Archivists, 2004).

8. International Council on Archives, *ISAAR(CPF): International Standard Archival Authority Record for Corporate Bodies, Persons and Families* (2004) is available at http://www.ica.org/biblio.php?pdocid=144.

9. Further information about RLG's Archival Resources database can be found at http://www.rlg.org/en/page.php?Page_ID=120.

10. For further information on Metadata Encoding and Transmission Standard (METS) see http://www.loc.gov/standards/mets/.

11. Kiesling, *The American Archivist*, 354.

Encoded Archival Context (EAC) and Archival Description: Rationale and Background

Richard V. Szary

SUMMARY. The use of contextual information about the creators and users of archival and manuscript resources has always been a critical method for discovering and providing access to them. Traditionally, this information has been unstructured and ephemeral, being part of the knowledge that experienced staff bring to reference queries. The development of Encoded Archival Context provides a methodology and structure for recording this information about the characteristics of creators and the circumstances of creation more explicitly and in ways that it can be used to support discovery of archival and manuscript sources.

Richard V. Szary is Carrie S. Beinecke Director of Manuscripts and Archives and University Archivist, Yale University Library, New Haven, CT (E-mail: Richard.Szary@yale.edu).

[Haworth co-indexing entry note]: "Encoded Archival Context (EAC) and Archival Description: Rationale and Background." Szary, Richard V. Co-published simultaneously in *Journal of Archival Organization* (The Haworth Information Press, an imprint of The Haworth Press, Inc.) Vol. 3, No. 2/3, 2005, pp. 217-227; and: *Encoding Across Frontiers: Proceedings of the European Conference on Encoded Archival Description and Context (EAD and EAC), Paris, France, 7-8 October 2004* (ed: Bill Stockting, and Fabienne Queyroux) The Haworth Information Press, an imprint of The Haworth Press, Inc., 2005, pp. 217-227. Single or multiple copies of this article are available for a fee from The Haworth Document Delivery Service [1-800-HAWORTH, 9:00 a.m. - 5:00 p.m. (EST). E-mail address: docdelivery@haworthpress.com].

Available online at http://www.haworthpress.com/web/JAO

doi:10.1300/J201v03n02_16

KEYWORDS. Archival description, contextual metadata, EAC, Encoded Archival Context, EAD, Encoded Archival Description

INTRODUCTION

Archival theory has long recognized that the context in which archives, manuscripts, and other primary source materials were created and used is a critical element in their faithful interpretation as evidence. They cannot be fully and accurately understood without understanding the environment and motivation that affected their creation and use. Bibliographic description, focusing primarily on the characteristics and content of the materials themselves, is simply insufficient. The evaluation of the authenticity of a primary source and its significance as evidence requires knowledge of the circumstances of its creation and existence, including an understanding of the roles, background, and environment in which its creator worked. This is essential and not auxiliary or supplemental knowledge. Competent historians and other researchers must arm themselves with this knowledge by extensive preparation in order to attempt a meaningful reading of documents and their placement in a web of evidence seeking to establish a hypothesis or explanation.

For many years, the gathering and use of this contextual information has been primarily a matter of research methodology, a part of the researcher's preparation for their encounter with the sources. In this arena, contextual information is individualized: selective and aimed at the focus of the researcher's area of investigation. Researchers review secondary sources, other primary materials, and contemporary documentation to construct a picture and sense of the environment in which the people and events that are the basis of their research lived. Portions of this background may be incorporated into the researcher's published writings, where it can be assimilated and critiqued by other researchers. Comprehensive assembly and dissemination of contextual information, as opposed to the selective use of it in focused research, is generally restricted to reference works, such as biographical dictionaries, encyclopedias, almanacs, registers, and similar products.

Contextual information is also a traditional and powerful retrieval tool for primary sources. While some discovery questions about primary sources address the characteristics of the materials themselves, one can expect that a significant number are stated in contextual terms. For example, what records reflect the activities of nineteenth-century

Australian women astronomers? This is actually a two-part query that requires one to first use contextual information–such as occupation, nationality, gender, or life dates–to identify the names of those astronomers fitting the criteria and then to search descriptions of archives and manuscripts by traditional author and subject headings. Richard Lytle and David Bearman were especially important in describing and drawing archivists' attention to the existence and value of what they called the provenance approach to archival retrieval in their articles in the early 1980s.[1] Since that time, there has been a growing recognition that the recording of contextual information in a standard and structured way so that it was readily available to support interpretive and access needs is an essential part of archival description.

Traditional archival bibliographic description often does contain contextual information. Unfortunately, it is generally found entombed in narrative passages where it is unavailable for effective searching in any kind of structured fashion. Even when it is specifically recorded in a structured fashion, it is often treated as a bibliographic subject heading–what the materials are about, rather than as contextual descriptors for the characteristics of its creator. Other information about the circumstances of creation, such as the functions or activities that generated the records, is similarly buried in narratives or occasionally recorded as a subject heading.

The development of Encoded Archival Context (EAC)[2] and the adoption of the *International Standard Archival Authority Record for Corporate Bodies, Persons, and Families* (*ISAAR (CPF)*)[3] have been the major ways in which this movement towards more explicit and structured recording of contextual information has been actualized into standards and structures. With the release of the beta version of the EAC Document Type Definition (DTD) in August 2004, the standard is now available for wide testing in the archival community.

CONTEXTUAL INFORMATION AS A COMPONENT OF A COMPREHENSIVE INFORMATION ARCHITECTURE FOR ARCHIVAL DESCRIPTION

This bibliographic approach to archival description has been strengthened in the United States by how systems and standards have evolved over the past 20 years. The development of the MARC format for Archival and Manuscript Control and the issuance of *Archives, Personal Papers and Manuscripts* (recently revised as *Describing Archives: A*

Content Standard)[4] have been key developments in establishing structural and content standards for archival description. Similar developments have occurred in other countries, and the international community adopted the *General International Standard Archival Description* (*ISAD(G)*) in 1994.[5] Many of these developments have been stimulated by attempts to use automation to support description and access and the resulting need for common practices and structures to make automated description and retrieval effective, whether in union catalogs, such as that maintained by the Research Libraries Group,[6] or local MARC-based library systems. The recent development of Encoded Archival Description (EAD)[7] as a standard, with the numerous implementations of it in working systems, has continued to stem from this bibliographic approach.

All of these standards have focused primarily on the bibliographic description of archival materials. Part of this may be attributed to the use of successful library models for description and retrieval systems and standards. Equally important, however, has been the lack of an explicit recognition in previous systems, mostly paper-based, of the interaction of bibliographic and contextual information. That interaction generally took place either as part of the researcher's preparation, as noted above; as part of their interaction with reference archivists, whose knowledge of their holdings incorporated much contextual knowledge; or through the review of an archival finding aid, which often included extensive narratives and chronological lists explaining the background of the creator of the records and other circumstances of creation. None of these avenues were described explicitly enough to allow them to be accommodated in the design of automated systems.

A notable exception to this trend has been Australian archival practice, which has explicitly recognized the value and need of distinguishing between bibliographic and contextual information. Separate but linked descriptions of records and their creators enable a much richer and robust information architecture for archival description.[8] It is worth noting the extensive and important contributions of our Australian colleagues to the recent discussion and development of contextual information in archives.

One of the early attempts at articulating the provenance approach and how it might be adopted looked at how the use of authority records in the library world offered some clues as to how to accomplish this.[9] While the standard format of library authority records, as embodied in MARC,[10] provides a number of fields for recording contextual descriptions for a particular entity, its primary purpose was very explicitly the control of name and subject headings so that they would be recorded and used consistently in bibliographic records. The addition of contextual information was aimed at providing catalogers with information that could guide their choice of the heading. Unfortunately, the adoption of "archival authority records" as a shorthand way of expressing the concept of archival contextual information has led to understandable, but regrettable, confusion about the inherent role of this information in archival description.

While the structure and methods for recording and using contextual information can serve as a mechanism for enforcing heading control in bibliographic records, this must not be seen as their primary purpose. Rather, the most important contribution of structured recording of contextual information is to support the model of separate but linked bibliographic and contextual descriptions. There are both pragmatic and philosophical reasons why this model is a better approach to archival description than one that relies exclusively on bibliographic structures and methods.

- A particular entity is often responsible for the creation of numerous bodies of records, each of which has its own bibliographic description. The incorporation of contextual information about the creator in each of these bibliographic descriptions requires a level of maintenance and synchronization across all records in which that information appears that is not present when the contextual information can be recorded in one place, updated there as needed, and then linked to multiple bibliographic records as appropriate.
- A shared standard for recording contextual information allows repositories to share these records and to avoid duplication of effort. Many record creators are represented in numerous repositories and a standard structure for recording a description of this information would make it possible for repositories to exchange this information and take advantage of the descriptive work done by others.
- The characteristics of individuals and organizations that are essential to supporting retrieval and interpretation of archival holdings cannot easily be accommodated in a bibliographic record structure. Many of the descriptors for these characteristics do not apply to the records themselves and it is misleading for them to be included in a bibliographic description. The Personal Information Questionnaire (PIQ) used by the Survivors of the Shoah Visual History Foundation as part of their descriptive system for Holocaust testimonies is a good example of how these characteristics

could be better handled.[11] Prior to recording their testimonies, witnesses are asked to complete a PIQ, which records extensive personal biographical background on the witness. This information includes details of birth, residence, activities and occupations, familial relationships, as well as information specifically related to their experience in the Holocaust. What is most interesting to this discussion is that this information may or may not be directly addressed in the testimony itself. A person born and raised in a particular town in Poland, for example, might not talk about their childhood in that town in their testimony. That information, however, is essential for certain types of queries that look at the fates of Jews from a particular locale. Putting that birthplace information in the bibliographic description of the testimony would be misleading because it would mistakenly imply that there is discussion of the town in the testimony. The separation of the bibliographic and contextual information handles this situation very neatly.

- Similarly, the complexity and evolution of bureaucratic entities and relationships can also be more effectively expressed in records that are structured for that type of relationship information. There are simply no provisions in a bibliographic record–nor should there be–to record the multiple changing relationships amongst record-creating entities. Defining record structures that explicitly and directly support contextual information is much more effective and efficient. Information about these relationships is particularly important since it is likely that documentation relevant to a particular query appears not only in the records of the agency that directly dealt with the issue at hand, but also in the records of superior, inferior, predecessor, successor, and other related agencies. Fonds or record groups try to address some of these relationships through *sous fonds* or subgroup arrangement schemes, but these mono-hierarchical structures are inadequate to reflect the multirelational links between entities that also change over time. Separating contextual information in the form of administrative histories and linking them to each other in all appropriate ways has a better chance of representing these relationships and allowing the researcher to discover additional avenues for exploration.
- Descriptions of record-creating entities are often created and maintained separately from any archival description system and provide a potential source for contextual information that does not need to be re-created by the repository. Biographical dictionaries, government locator systems, and similar files are especially com-

mon and useful in this regard. Having an information architecture for an archival description system that explicitly recognizes this contextual information and knows how to link it to bibliographic descriptions provides a potential search and discovery mechanism maintained externally to the repository.

- The *Online Historical Register of Yale University*, due to be released for public use in 2005, is an example of this type of reuse of existing information. Originally published as three volumes,[12] the *Register* contains brief biographical information on 23,000 individuals who have held appointments at Yale University from 1701 until 1982. The information recorded includes academic degrees that the person earned or was awarded and Yale appointment titles and dates along with the discipline, office, or other entity to which the appointment was made. Using this information, it is possible, for example, to discover which Yale professors held faculty appointments in anthropology and then search record descriptions by their personal names to find documentation on that discipline in places where records are only identified and described by personal name.

Archivists now recognize that a comprehensive and effective information architecture for archival description is more complex than was previously assumed. It includes not only the bibliographic description of the materials themselves but also the recording of an often complex web of relationships amongst records creators, functions, subjects, and the materials. This has always been an innate characteristic of archival description, but never fully articulated sufficiently to support the building of information systems to reflect and exploit it in a standard and effective manner. With the adoption of *ISAAR(CPF)* and the emergence of EAC, another aspect of the broader archival description universe is being recognized and incorporated into our description and access systems.

SOME COMMENTS ON THE DEVELOPMENT OF ISAAR(CPF) *AND EAC*

The development of EAC and *ISAAR(CPF)* has an interesting history that might have some implications for future standards development. When the ICA Ad Hoc Commission on Descriptive Standards circulated an early draft of *ISAD(G)* prior to its adoption in 1994, the Society of American Archivists' Committee on Archival Information Exchange response strongly suggested that the draft gave insufficient attention to the role of contextual information and that this needed to be strengthened. While the final version of *ISAD(G)* did give greater recognition to the possibility of separate but linked contextual descriptions, the Commission also charged a new working group in 1993 to address standards for such descriptions; the result was the first edition of *ISAAR(CPF)*, published in 1996.

Australian archivists continued to pursue their approach and implemented it in the retrieval system for the National Archives. The Research Libraries Group in the United States also began accepting "organizational history" records that provided a way of separately describing record-creating entities as pseudo-MARC records; this approach, however, provided no easy way to link these records to bibliographic descriptions.

With support from the Digital Library Federation, a meeting was held at Yale in December 1998 and included participants from Australia, Canada, the European Union Archival Network, Sweden, and the United Kingdom, as well as from the United States. This meeting took note of the scheduled revision of *ISAAR(CPF)* that was about to begin and expressed the need to link any work it would undertake with the ISAAR revision effort. An ad hoc working group was established and communication vehicles set up to keep participants informed about developments and foster collaboration. A number of preliminary projects were identified and individual members began investigating them. Most importantly, the group articulated a number of important assumptions that have guided work on contextual information since then, particularly the position of *ISAAR(CPF)* as a basis for further work, the expression of a structure in an XML-compliant document type definition, and the need for compatibility with EAD. The group also identified functions and activities as a separate area of investigation as another component of contextual information.

Based on this work agenda, the group invited Yale University to serve as the home for the international coordinating body and establish the necessary clearinghouse mechanisms for the project. Participants agreed to begin work on a number of the various projects outlined above with progress reports to be distributed through the mechanisms set up through Yale. The group also agreed to identify other archivists, repositories, or archival organizations that were either willing to collaborate on these projects or review their results, with the aim of encouraging an international, profession-wide dialogue on the issues.

Work proceeded informally following the 1998 meeting and a second meeting was held in Toronto, Canada, in March 2001 to determine how best to make further progress. The results of that meeting included a reaffirmation of the position of *ISAAR(CPF)* as the overall content standard for contextual information, the adoption of a set of principles,[13] preliminary work on identifying the major areas of a Document Type Definition, and the formation of a group to develop the DTD in all its technical glory and specificity. Not to be forgotten, in addition to his many other contributions, was Adrian Cunningham's suggestion of "Encoded Archival Context" as the name for the standard to provide both a way to suggest the broader principle embodied in the standard and to provide a parallel with EAD.

The result of this work was the development of the EAC DTD, which has just been released in its beta form for testing by repositories. The work on EAC has continued to be managed very informally by an ad hoc working group with the results being tested as they have emerged by interested projects and repositories. In the near future, this structure needs to become more formalized so that proper review and adoption of the standard can take place and a permanent maintenance agency established, as has been the case for other archival description standards.

In addition to the support that the development of EAC has given to implementation of a more robust information architecture, the process has also been instructive. The ad hoc nature of the project, with a set of self-identified and interested individuals, has not been as smooth or regular as it could have been for an undertaking of such significance. There has been a close connection with the members of the Committee on Descriptive Standards at ICA, with many of them serving on both the working group and the committee, but this has been a result of personal effort rather than organizational strategy. The process has also demonstrated the evolving nature of the standards developing process from one of national efforts that gradually became more widespread, to one in which international participation has been a component from the very beginning.

CONCLUSION

The work of fully integrating contextual information into archival description is just beginning. The continuing evolution of *ISAAR(CPF)* and its established position as a recognized and formally adopted archival description standard is of major significance. The next steps will involve the formal adoption of EAC and the establishment of a permanent home for it so that it can be maintained and revised. Finally, the largest outstanding question is the development of archival systems that fully integrate contextual information into discovery and interpretation. This requires not only the development of technological systems that can perform these tasks but the recognition that contextual information is a critical component of archival description and the application of the resources necessary to assemble and record it in effective ways.

AUTHOR NOTE

Richard V. Szary is currently Carrie S. Beinecke Director of Manuscripts and Archives and University Archivist at the Yale University Library. Prior to joining Yale in 1988, he was on the staff of the Smithsonian Institution for thirteen years in the institutional archives and in the Office of Information Resource Management. Szary received his BA degree in history from DePaul University and his MA degree in Asian studies from the University of Illinois.

NOTES

1. Richard H. Lytle, "Intellectual Access to Archives," *American Archivist* 43 (Winter and Spring 1980); Lytle and David A. Bearman, "The Power of the Principle of Provenance," *Archivaria* 21 (Winter 1985-1986).
2. Development work and papers on the Encoded Archival Context standard can be found at: http://www.iath.virginia.edu/eac/ and http://www.library.yale.edu/~rszary/context/.
3. International Council on Archives. *ISAAR (CPF): International Standard Archival Authority Record for Corporate Bodies, Persons, and Families*. Second edition (2004). Available at: http://www.ica.org/biblio.php?pdocid=144.
4. Society of American Archivists. *Describing Archives: A Content Standard.* (Chicago: Society of American Archivists, 2004).
5. International Council of Archives. *ISAD (G): General International Standard Archival Description.* Second edition (1999). Available at: http://www.ica.org/biblio.php?pdocid=1.
6. RLG's Archival Resources is a subscription database providing access to over 750,000 catalog records and nearly 48,000 finding aids for archival and manuscript materials. Information available at http://www.rlg.org/en/page.php?Page_ID=120.
7. Jackie M. Dooley, ed. *Encoded Archival Description: Context, Theory and Case Studies.* (Chicago: Society of American Archivists, 1998).
8. Peter J. Scott, "The Record Group Concept: A Case for Abandonment." *American Archivist* 29, no. 4 (1966).
9. David Bearman and Richard Szary, "Beyond Authorized Headings, Authorities as Reference Files in a Multi-disciplinary Setting." In "Authority Control Sympo-

sium." *Occasional Papers of the Art Libraries Society of North America, No. 6* (Tucson: Art Libraries Society of North America, 1987).

10. Library of Congress, Network Development and MARC Standards Office. *MARC 21 Concise Format for Authority Data*. The current edition (2003) is available at: http://www.loc.gov/marc/authority/ecadhome.html.

11. Further information on the Survivors of the Shoah Visual History Foundation and its access methodology can be found at http://www.library.yale.edu/mssa/vha/.

12. Yale University. *Historical Register of Yale University* (New Haven, Connecticut: Yale University, 1939-1969).

13. The statement of principles adopted at the Toronto meeting is available at: http://www.library.yale.edu/~rszary/context/Toronto%20Tenets.htm.

The French Translation of the EAC DTD: A Few Thoughts on Interoperability with Reference to Authority Data

Françoise Bourdon

SUMMARY. The translation into French of the Encoded Archival Context (EAC) DTD tag library has been in progress for a few months. It is being carried out by a group of experts gathered by AFNOR, the French national standards agency. The main goal of this group is to foster the interoperability of authority data between archives, libraries and museums, and the translation work provides an opportunity to think about the choices for standardization that underlie the EAC DTD, particularly in relation to *ISAAR(CPF)*. It is also an excellent way of gaining familiarity with the DTD and thereby answering the need of French information specialists to increase their competencies in the structuring of digital documents and data modeling. After explaining the standardization context in which the group is working, a few major themes in its thinking will be presented, in the hope of encouraging greater international cooperation in this field. *[Article copies available for a fee from The Haworth Document Delivery Service: 1-800-HAWORTH. E-mail address: <docdelivery@haworthpress.com> Website: <http://www.HaworthPress.com> © 2005 by The Haworth Press, Inc. All rights reserved.]*

Françoise Bourdon is affiliated with the Bibliothéque Nationale de France.

[Haworth co-indexing entry note]: "The French Translation of the EAC DTD: A Few Thoughts on Interoperability with Reference to Authority Data." Bourdon, Françoise. Co-published simultaneously in *Journal of Archival Organization* (The Haworth Information Press, an imprint of The Haworth Press, Inc.) Vol. 3, No. 2/3, 2005, pp. 229-242; and: *Encoding Across Frontiers: Proceedings of the European Conference on Encoded Archival Description and Context (EAD and EAC), Paris, France, 7-8 October 2004* (ed: Bill Stockting, and Fabienne Queyroux) The Haworth Information Press, an imprint of The Haworth Press, Inc., 2005, pp. 229-242. Single or multiple copies of this article are available for a fee from The Haworth Document Delivery Service [1-800-HAWORTH, 9:00 a.m. - 5:00 p.m. (EST). E-mail address: docdelivery@haworthpress.com].

Available online at http://www.haworthpress.com/web/JAO

doi:10.1300/J201v03n02_17

KEYWORDS. Agence Française de Normalisation, AFNOR, authority data, authority files, contextual metadata, EAC, Encoded Archival Context, interoperability, standardization

A CONTEXT OF STANDARDIZATION

The group of experts currently working on the French translation of the Encoded Archival Context (EAC) DTD is operating within the General Standards Committee "Information and Documentation" of the Agence Française de Normalisation (AFNOR, the French Organization for Standardization). This Committee, known as "AFNOR/CG46," is in fact the French mirror of the International Organization for Standardization Technical Committee 46 (ISO/TC46). More precisely, the group of experts reports to the National Committee 357 "Modelling, Production and Access to Documents" (AFNOR CG/46/CN357), which partly mirrors ISO/TC46/SC4 "Technical Interoperability" and ISO/TC46/SC9 "Identification and Description." The very name of CN357 demonstrates its priorities in the context of digital resources: data modelling, production of documents, and access to primary or secondary documents.

Five years ago, CN357 decided that it would keep maintaining, but stop developing, standards specific to the field of libraries and documentation. Indeed, in order to avoid marginalization, area-specific standards must no longer be elaborated but rather find a place in a larger standardization process. Adopting open and generic standards has become imperative. In the French context, AFNOR is the best possible venue for meetings of the three professional communities chiefly concerned (archives, libraries, and museums)–a much better venue than professional societies, for instance.

CN357 supervises nine Groups of Experts (GE), the various themes of which clearly show the environment in which the translation of EAC is taking place:

- a virtual group (working essentially via e-mail) contributes to the maintenance of the standard NF ISO 639-2: 1999, *Codes for the Representation of Names of Languages–Part 2: Alpha-3 Code*;
- a group contributes to the maintenance of the three parts of the standard NF ISO 3166, *Codes for the Representation of Names of Countries and their Subdivisions*;

- a group called "Modelling of information relative to cultural heritage" represents France in the work on the projected ISO/DIS 21127 standard "Reference Ontology for Interchange of Cultural Heritage Information";
- a group called "Evolution of Bibliographical Description of Published Resources" makes sure that the updates of ISBD decided upon by the Cataloguing Section of IFLA are taken into account in French cataloguing rules;
- a group working on "Metadata for Electronic Dissertations" has defined descriptive and administrative metadata for French dissertations which are deposited in electronic format; the group is now writing application guidelines for students and concerned administrative services;
- a group working on the French translation of the Text Encoding Initiative (TEI) DTD;
- a group called "Encoded Archival Description (EAD)," which has just finished translating the EAD 2002 tag library and is now working on application guidelines for French users;
- a group working on "Bibliographical Description of Modern Manuscripts," which is elaborating a French cataloguing standard, taking as a basis the existing guidelines in France (for instance the rules of the Manuscripts Department at the National Library) or abroad (mainly *Describing Archives: A Content Standard*);
- and finally the group called "Authority Data," which since its inception in June 2000 has focused on the standardization of authority data, and, more recently, on the translation of the EAC tag library.

The work on the EAC DTD is thus taking place in a standardization context focused not only on archives but also on manuscripts, on museum collections, on structured digital documents and on published materials traditionally kept in libraries. In the last five years, the group worked in two phases.

THE AUTHORITY DATA WORKING GROUP 2000-2003

During the first period, from June 2000 to June 2003, the goals were to conduct an interdisciplinary investigation on the processing and management of authority data, to put together a library of data elements common to the three professional communities, and to keep current with international work. The group was then composed of a very diverse panel of information specialists:

- librarians and documentalists from the Agence Bibliographique de l'Enseignement Supérieur, OCLC users' group, the Bibliothèque Nationale de France (BNF), the University Library of Nice, the École Nationale Supérieure des Sciences de l'Information et des Bibliothèques, the Fondation Nationale des Sciences Politiques, the Institut National des Techniques de la Documentation, and the Cité des Sciences et de l'Industrie;
- archivists from the Direction des Archives de France, and the Centre Historique des Archives Nationales (CHAN);
- managers of museum type databases from the Direction des Musées de France, the Department of Prints at the National Library, and the Bibliography of the History of Art;
- audiovisual material specialists from the Institut National de l'Audiovisuel, more precisely its Research department and the Inathèque (which collects all programmes broadcasted on the French television and radio);
- managers of rights on intellectual property at the Société des Auteurs et Compositeurs Dramatiques.

At this time, the group adopted a methodology that was both practical and theoretical. On the practical side, there were for instance presentations of their experiences by various group members. On the theoretical side, the group focused on training its members in data modelling and on keeping current with work conducted at an international level.

As a way of sharing acquired knowledge, the group has thus benefited from presentations on each of the fields represented by its members. The presentations were about authority files as management tools of library catalogues; lexicons and authority lists for museum and iconographic databases; established vocabularies at the Institut National de l'Audiovisuel; the role of authority data in archival description; subject authority data seen in the perspective of the principles of thesaurus development and in the perspective of indexing languages as facilitating tools for multilingual searching by subject; and the role of authority data in the management of rights on intellectual property.

As practical work, the group began establishing definitions common to all fields represented for the following authority data elements: corporate body, group, person, place, work, object, event, technique, material and medium. Each definition had examples, counter-examples, and a list of issues. For instance, corporate body was defined as: "An organization or group of persons or temporary function acting as a whole and identified by a name, a common action or the result of an action." Examples mention a program, a religious community, a government, etcetera. It is declared that a corporate body should not be confused with a temporary event such as a lecture, an exhibit, or a sports competition, et cetera. The risk of confusing a place, a building and a corporate body has been pointed out, examples of entities where such confusion may arise being 10 Downing Street, the Louvre Museum, or the Picasso Museum of Antibes which is located in the Chateau Grimaldi. How can authority data reflect these different "renditions" of the same entity?

The group also assessed current international projects, under the guidance of the group members whose institutions were involved in these projects. Among those were, for example, the *International Standard Archival Authority Record for Corporate Bodies, Persons, and Families* (*ISAAR (CPF)*), the Linking and Exploring Authority Files (LEAF) project, the conceptual data models of the International Federation of Library Associations (FRBR, Functional Requirements for Bibliographic Records and FRANAR, Functional Requirements And Numbering of Authority Records), the conceptual data model of the International Committee for Documentation within the International Museum Council (CRM, Conceptual Reference model, which has since become ISO/DIS 21117 "Ontology of reference for information exchange related to cultural heritage"), the Virtual International Authority File (VIAF) established between the Library of Congress and Die Deutsche Bibliothek, the INDECS and INTERPARTY projects that propose authority data models for identification of parties and management of rights on intellectual property for e-business.

At the end of this first phase of work, the working group, composed of individuals with diverse backgrounds, had acquired a common culture with regard to authority data. But progress in thinking was slowing down, and a certain level of absenteeism progressively appeared. It can readily be explained by the obligation for certain members to go back to activities more immediately "productive" (standardization work is often considered as a luxury!) and by a diminishing interest shown by those who had been expecting from the group answers that could be immediately used for their daily work. This as well as changes in the national and international context made the group all the more ready to revise its goals.

A NEW FOCUS FOR THE GROUP IN A CHANGING CONTEXT

At a national level, two events contributed to the realignment of the group's objectives with the needs of professionals working in the field. In 2001 the EAD DTD was chosen as the encoding standard for the digitization of the Catalogue Général des Manuscrits des Bibliothèques Publiques de France (CGM). A few months later, in 2002, the EAD DTD was selected as the cataloguing format for manuscripts at the BNF, in the context of the automation of the Special Collections departments. The elaboration of the specifications for the CGM conversion involved representatives from the National Library, public libraries, university libraries, and the Ministry of Culture and the Ministry of Education. The problem of access points to descriptive records arose when it became necessary to decide about the conversion of existing indexes. At the National Library, the problem of managing access points to the manuscripts and fonds described with EAD appeared very quickly, especially in the context of current cataloguing. Is the expertise acquired by the BNF in the area of authority data for access to published material usable in this new context? A new culture, the culture of EAD, was slowly spreading in French libraries.

At the international level, in February 2003, archivists and librarians met in Florence at an international conference on authority control.[1] A whole session was devoted to the procedures needed to create and manage multifield authority databases. *ISAAR(CPF)* and the EAC DTD were already holding pride of place. Finally in October 2003 the beta version of the EAC DTD, in English, was published on the Web.[2] This proved the deciding event that triggered the revision of the AFNOR group's objectives.

In June 2003, the Authority Data Working Group refocused its work on the interoperability of authority data between archives and libraries. It was between these two professional communities indeed that cooperation seemed to have the best chance of making rapid progress, especially as there was no longer a representative from the museum community in the group. It was decided to limit investigations to the two types of entities best controlled by archives and libraries: persons and corporate bodies. The practical part of the activities increased. The group commented on the draft of the second edition of *ISAAR(CPF)*, as part of the international review process, and it participated in the French translation of that standard, published in 2004. A detailed comparison of authority records established in EAC as XML and in MARC for the same entity has also been conducted. This work took place in the context of NOEMI

Project (NOtaires Et MInutes) at the CHAN. Authority records for Parisian notaries had been written by the CHAN; they were encoded in EAC as XML by the CHAN representative, in UNIMARC by the representative of ABES, and in integrated INTERMARC by the BNF representatives. Finally, in order to really understand the EAC DTD, it was decided to translate its tag library into French.

COMPARISON OF AUTHORITY RECORDS IN ARCHIVES AND LIBRARIES

The detailed reading of *ISAAR(CPF)* started passionate discussions between librarians and archivists. A sentence such as "Archival authority records are similar to library authority records in as much as both forms of authority record need to support the creation of standardized access points in descriptions"[3] sounds encouraging, since the records are described as "similar"; "similar," however, does not mean "identical." Where was the difference? The paragraph "Archival authority records, however, need to support a much wider set of requirements than is the case with library authority records. [. . .] As such, archival authority records go much further and usually will contain much more information than library authority records"[4] caused great turmoil within the group. Such a declaration suggests not only that information does not have the same granularity in authority records for persons and corporate bodies when these records are established by libraries or archives, but also that these records probably do not have the same function for archives and libraries. It was necessary, therefore, to identify these differences, in order to find out which ones are inherent to the specificities of each field and therefore "legitimate," and to eliminate all others.

Typology

A first difference springs from the very typology of the authority data records considered and it is not only a matter of terminological differences between archives and libraries. Archives limit themselves to creators, while libraries manage "persons" and "corporate bodies" way beyond their activities as creators. Such entities can have intellectual, artistic or commercial responsibilities regarding the material described in a bibliographic record; they can be also the subject of the said material. On the other hand, for a library a "family" is often a particular case of "persons," not necessarily an entity by itself. Libraries deal with many other types of entities in their authority files: geographical names, uniform titles, subjects, commercial and audiovisual brands, etcetera. It is thus necessary to think, from a standardizing viewpoint, about the typology of access points. To what extent are the needs of libraries and archives really different?

Functions

Regarding the functions of authority records, *ISAAR(CPF)* introduces them in the following order, going from the most important to the least important.[5] Authority records must serve to:

- Make the context understandable for users
- Give access to archival descriptions
- Identify the entity defined by the record
- Share authority records
- Control the form of the entity's name.

For archives the authority record is intended first and foremost to help users understand the production context of the material. For libraries, on the other hand, authority records are first and foremost a management tool for catalogers. Through the publication of authority files on microfiches and later on CD-ROM, other professionals have become interested in these files. Later, access to authority files via Web catalogues has allowed a larger audience to refer to them and to understand that they give context to bibliographic records and therefore to the described material.

In libraries, the functions of authority records are, going from the most important to the least important, are to:

- Give access to bibliographical descriptions
- Control the form of the entity's name
- Identify the entity defined by the record
- Share authority records
- Make the context understandable to users.

The most important function for the archives is the least important for libraries. This difference can affect the granularity of the content of the records, but not their structure itself, which fortunately remains centered on giving access to descriptions and identifying the entities.

Access Points

Regarding the normative arsenal put in place for access points to archival or bibliographical descriptions, notable differences exist between archival and library practices.

With *ISAAR(CPF)*, a standard that defines the functions and content of authority records, the archives community has done pioneering work. In libraries, if rules on form and structure of access points do exist, there are none on the content of the authority record itself. To this day the content is still defined by ad hoc MARC formats. The *Principles for Library Catalogs and Other Bibliographical Files* established by a conference of experts called by IFLA in 2003 actually recommend that processing of authority records be described in cataloguing codes.[6]

ISAAR(CPF) does not recommend any order for public display of the information contained in an authority record. Libraries, however, do have at their disposal a recommendation for the physical outlay of authority records: *Guidelines for Authority Records and References–GARR*.[7] Even the least logical minds will be surprised that there are recommendations on presentation of content while there are none on the content itself, but it is a fact. By the way, *ISAAR(CPF)* refers to *GARR* in section 2, *Related Standards*.

Both archives and libraries have rules and/or recommendations on the form and structure of access points. For libraries, there are for instance at the international level *Form and Structure of Corporate Headings*,[8] and at a national level, in France, NF Z 44-060 *Forme et Etructure des Vedettes de Collectivités-auteurs*.[9] For archives, *ISAAR(CPF)* refers in section 2, *Related Standards*, to the IFLA recommendation mentioned above; at a national level, there are for instance in the United Kingdom *Rules for the Construction of Personal, Place and Corporate Names*.[10]

Regarding the choice of access points to archival description, it appears that no recommendation exists, either at international or national level. For libraries, on the other hand, there is a chapter in AACR2, and at the national level there is Z 44-059: 1987–*Catalogage–Choix des Accès à la Description Bibliographique*, which gives rules for choosing personal names, corporate names and titles as access points.

Archivists and librarians have then cause for cooperation. It would be good also to take into account the needs of the museum community, for which no such normative efforts exist.

Relationships

Relationships between authority records are the same in archives and libraries: hierarchical relationship, chronological relationship or associative relationship. Even family relationships, that are rarely defined as such in libraries, would not cause any problems if there was a need to implement them.

In archives, however, the relationships between an authority record and its related archival description records are expressed in a very different way from the way an authority record is related to bibliographic records in libraries. Indeed *ISAAR(CPF)*[11] gives directions that are radically different from the ones used by libraries. *ISAAR(CPF)* recommends the inclusion of the following elements in the authority record: identifiers and headers of associated resources, nature of associated resources, nature of relationship and dates of associated resources or dates of relationships. Libraries have a totally opposite approach insofar as they try to create authority records completely independent from the bibliographic records (and therefore the catalogue) these records help to manage. No link to bibliographical descriptions is mentioned explicitly. Only with such a requirement can the sharing of authority records among several institutions be facilitated. For instance, it would be impossible to list in the authority record for Voltaire at the BNF the 700 links to related bibliographic records in the BN-OPALE PLUS catalogue.[12]

Figure 1 shows an example of a personal name authority record from the "Persons" authority file of the BNF.

The record does not include any explicit reference to the linked bibliographic records. One click on the button "See linked bibliographic records" will bring the screen illustrated in Figure 2.

The records are displayed in an abridged format. If record 11 is selected and called for full display, one gets the screen shown in Figure 3.

In the full record, André Masson appears as "secondary author" and his precise role regarding the described material is "illustrator" (which corresponds to the role attribute in a Personal Name (<persname>) EAD element). The heading of the authority record is displayed as a hypertext link that will bring the user back to the authority record.

In the integrated INTERMARC format, used by the BNF, the field code of a link between a personal name authority record and a bibliographical description expresses a level of responsibility. The same authority record can be linked to several bibliographic records by a field 100 (main author), 101 (main interpreter), 700 (secondary author), 701 (secondary interpreter), 703 (participant to a radio program), 720 (publisher), 721 (distributor), 722 (producer of audio material), 727 (manufacturer), et cetera. The role is indicated, for each field code, by a role

FIGURE 1. *Bibliothèque Nationale de France* (BNF): Personal Name Authority File

Masson, André (1896-1987) *forme savante à valeur internationale*

Nationalité : France
Langue : français
Sexe :
Responsabilité : Auteur
Naissance : 1896-01-04 -
Mort : 1987-10-28
La vedette peut être employée dans une vedette RAMEAU
La vedette ne peut s'employer qu'en tête de vedette
La vedette utilisée en zone 6XX n'admet pas de subdivision géographique

Peintre, graveur, illustrateur et décorateur de théâtre

Sources : André Masson et le théâtre , 1984
. - WW, France, 1988-1989. - Bénézit, 1976
. - BN Cat. gén.. - BN Cat. gén. suppl.

Notice n° : FRBNF11930229

FIGURE 2. *Bibliothèque Nationale de France* (BNF): Linked Bibliographic Records

No.	Record	Year
5	**[Exposition. Paris. Galerie Louise Leiris. 1970]** **André Masson : œuvres récentes, 1968-1970 : [exposition, Paris, Galerie Louise Leiris, 30 octobre-28 novembre 1970]. Lieux communs**	1970
6	**André Masson : textes de Jean-Louis Barrault, Georges Bataille, André Breton... [et al.]**	1940
7	**Masson, André (1896-1987)** [Correspondance] Les Années surréalistes : correspondance, 1916-1942	1990
8	**Bataille, Georges (1897-1962)** L'anus solaire	1931
9	**Aubray, Thérèse** Battements : poèmes	1933
10	**Moss, Armand** Baudelaire et Madame Sabatier	1975
11	**Moss, Armand** Baudelaire et madame Sabatier [Document électronique]	1995
12	**Neveux, Georges** La beauté du diable [Document électronique]	1995

FIGURE 3. *Bibliothèque Nationale de France* (BNF): Full Bibliographic Record

Type : texte imprimé, monographie

Auteur(s) : Moss, Armand
Titre(s) : Baudelaire et madame Sabatier [Document électronique] / Armand Moss ; avec un portr. de Baudelaire par André Masson
Type de ressource électronique : Données textuelles
Publication : 1995
Description matérielle : 236 p.- XIX p. de pl. : ill.
Reproduction : Num. BNF de l'éd. de Paris : A. G. Nizet, 1978. 24 cm
Autre(s) auteur(s) : Masson, André (1896-1987). Illustrateur
Sujet(s) : Baudelaire, Charles (1821-1867)

Notice n° : FRBNF37238607

code keyed in the subfield $4. Thus, in a 100 field, subfield $4 is used to define precisely the role of the secondary author regarding the described material: author of a foreword, illustrator, translator, et cetera. Reference lists of role codes are managed at an international level by the bodies that maintain the great international formats, UNIMARC or MARC21. It would be a real pity if that standardization work were ignored by archives in their work on role relationships undertaken under the wing of the International Council on Archives.

In libraries, the link between the authority record and the bibliographic record is explicit in the latter and implicit in the former. It does work both ways, however. On the other hand, *ISAAR(CPF)* recommends that the relationship be explicitly described in the authority record. Here is an example, taken from the standard.[13] The authority record created for "Department of state. Peace corps (03/03/1961-07/01/1971)" contains the mention of three associated resources, of which here are the first two:

First associated resource:

title & identifier: Photographs of Arts and Culture in Ghana (US DNA 558686)

type: Archival materials (series)

nature of the relationship: creator

dates of related resources and/or relationships: ca.1970 (approximate date of the record keeping system)

Second associated resource:

title & identifier: Remarks to Peace Corps Trainees (US DNA 193889)

type: Archival materials (file)

nature of the relationship: subject

dates of related resources and/or relationships: 1962/09/08 (creation date of the file)

Etc.

Following the directions offered by *ISAAR(CPF)* for managing links between the authority records and archival descriptions or archival resources, the links are explicitly mentioned in the authority record. What happens when the record is shared with other institutions? Will every one add their own links? Or will the links field be excluded from the sharing? The question needs further assessment.

CONCLUSION

There would be many other issues to investigate if one wanted to list exhaustively the similarities and differences in the management of authority data in libraries and archives. The goal of this paper, however, will be fulfilled if the reader comes to understand the shared interest in the active cooperation between these two types of institutions on standardization.

This then is a call to share our knowledge and experience and to address the differences in content and structure between our respective authority records, with the goal of reducing these differences. We should try to establish common reference tools, for the greater satisfaction of our common users, while preserving the specific identities of our respective fields. Our goal must be to work in a coherent way and to aim towards interoperability; but this does not necessarily mean that our practices must be strictly identical.

AUTHOR NOTE

Françoise Bourdon works for the Bibliothèque Nationale de France. She was responsible for the implementation of the personal names authority file, beginning in 1985. She is now Head of the Department of bibliographical cooperation at the Agence

Bibliographique Nationale and she chairs the working group that is writing institutional application guidelines for the EAD DTD. Since 2003, Françoise Bourdon has chaired the Standards Committee 357 "Modelling, Production and Access to Documents" within the Association Française de Normalisation (AFNOR). As a member of that Committee from 2000, she has chaired a group of experts geared towards the modeling of authority data and promoting French expertise in international projects: IFLA's Functional Requirements And Numbering of Authority Records (FRANAR), the European program LEAF, and the updating and revision by the International Council on Archives of *ISAAR(CPF)*. This group of experts is now in the process of translating in French the EAC DTD.

NOTES

1. See the proceedings of the International Conference on Authority Control at Florence online at http://www.sba.unifi.it/ac/en/home.htm.

2. Today, the version of EAC to be used is the version 3, released in August 2004. See http://xml.coverpages.org/EAC-Beta200408.htm or http://www.archivesdefrance.culture.gouv.fr/archivistique/index.htm.

3. International Council on Archives, *ISAAR (CPF). International Standard Archival Authorities Record for Corporate Bodies, Persons and Families*, 2nd edition, Paris, 2004 s. 1.8.

4. International Council on Archives, *ISAAR(CPF): International Standard Archival Authority Record for Corporate Bodies, Persons and Families* (2004), s. 1.9.

5. International Council on Archives, *ISAAR(CPF): International Standard Archival Authority Record for Corporate Bodies, Persons and Families* (2004), s. 1.10.

6. For further information on this decision see http://www.ddb.de/news/pdf/statement_french.pdf.

7. Guidelines for Authority Records and References, IFLA, 2001. Online at http://ifla.org/VII/s13/garr/garr.pdf.

8. *Form and Structure of Corporate Headings*, IFLA, 1980.

9. *Forme et Structure des Vedettes de Collectivités-auteurs*, AFNOR, 1996.

10. National Council on Archives (NCA), *Rules for the Construction of Personal, Place and Corporate names (1997)*, which can be found online at http://www.ncaonline.org.uk/materials/rulesfortheconstructionofpersonalplaceandcorporatenames.pdf.

11. International Council on Archives, *ISAAR(CPF): International Standard Archival Authority Record for Corporate Bodies, Persons and Families* (2004), 2004, s. 6.

12. See the BN-OPALE PLUS catalogue online at http://catalogue.bnf.fr.

13. International Council on Archives, *ISAAR(CPF): International Standard Archival Authority Record for Corporate Bodies, Persons and Families* (2004), 2004, s. 6.

What Are the Boundaries of Archival Context? The SIASFI Project and the Online Guide to the Florence State Archives, Italy

Stefano Vitali

SUMMARY. Creating archival descriptions in a digital environment and communicating across the Internet is not the same as traditional paper-based communication. As in other cultural domains, in archival description the medium influences the structure and content of information. The Siasfi Project and the Online Guide to the State Archives of Florence are good examples of these transformations. The article presents the main features of the Online Guide and discusses the theoretical and methodological assumptions underlying its conceptual model which are

---

Stefano Vitali works in the State Archives of Florence Viale Giovine Italia, 6, 50.100 Firenze, Italy (E-mail: s_vitali@archiviodistato.firenze.it). He is currently responsible for programs and projects of the application of Information Technology to the management and description of archives. From 2000 to 2004, he was the Chair of the Committee on Descriptive Standards of the International Council on Archives.

The appendix was prepared by Diana Spano, Centro di ricerche informatiche per i beni culturali Scuola Nomale Superiore di Pisa.

[Haworth co-indexing entry note]: "What Are the Boundaries of Archival Context? The SIASFI Project and the Online Guide to the Florence State Archives, Italy." Vitali, Stefano. Co-published simultaneously in *Journal of Archival Organization* (The Haworth Information Press, an imprint of The Haworth Press, Inc.) Vol. 3, No. 2/3, 2005, pp. 243-260; and: *Encoding Across Frontiers: Proceedings of the European Conference on Encoded Archival Description and Context (EAD and EAC), Paris, France, 7-8 October 2004* (ed: Bill Stockting, and Fabienne Queyroux) The Haworth Information Press, an imprint of The Haworth Press, Inc., 2005, pp. 243-260. Single or multiple copies of this article are available for a fee from The Haworth Document Delivery Service [1-800-HAWORTH, 9:00 a.m. - 5:00 p.m. (EST). E-mail address: docdelivery@haworthpress.com].

Available online at http://www.haworthpress.com/web/JAO

doi:10.1300/J201v03n02_18

rooted in the international descriptive standards, *ISAD(G)* and *ISAAR (CPF)*, as well as in a complex view of what archival context is.

KEYWORDS. Archival description, authority control, contextual metadata, EAC, Encoded Archival Context, EAD, Encoded Archival Description, standardization

INTRODUCTION

The SIASFI (Sistema Informativo dell'Archivio di Stato di Firenze) is a complex, flexible, modular information system designed to illustrate the history, structure and content of the Florence State Archives and to make its holdings accessible to the large and heterogeneous audience of Internet users. The system includes the following component parts:

- An Online Guide providing users with basic information on the fonds, sub-fonds and series held in the State Archives of Florence as well as their creators and other related entities;
- Online finding aids of archival fonds;
- Digitized reproductions of fonds and series such as the *Mediceo Avanti il Principato*, probably the most important archival source on the Renaissance in Florence;
- Special finding aids to guide searches on popular subjects (for example, the history of a building or property).

The primary purpose of this paper is to illustrate the central nucleus or core of the Florentine system, namely the Online Guide. The Online Guide is a tool designed to provide users with an initial outline of the fonds, sub-fonds and series of the Florentine Archives, enabling them to continue their investigations fruitfully in the online inventories and such digitized fonds as may exist, or to decide whether it is worth visiting the archives in person to consult the records at first hand.

The present Online Guide actually stems from a previous computerised archival description initiative launched during the 1990s by the

Italian Archives Administration (the Anagrafe Informatizzata degli Archivi Italiani). As a follow-up to this project, the Florence State Archives and the Research Centre for the Application of IT to the Cultural Heritage of Pisa University (Centro di Ricerche Informatiche per Beni Culturali della Scuola Normale Superiore di Pisa[1]) launched a project in 1998 to transfer the data gathered in the Florentine Archives for the national Anagrafe database into a new software environment. At the same time, the data model was to be revised to make it more compatible with the international descriptive standards, *ISAD(G)* and the *International Standard Archival Authority Records (Corporate Bodies, Persons, Families)* (*ISAAR(CPF)*).[2]

The first version of the Online Guide system was completed in 2000, using the relational DBMS Oracle on a Windows NT platform, and the second version, based entirely on Web technologies, including the data input client, was finalised in 2002. The Web interface accessible to users on the Internet has been available since January 2004.[3]

The data migrated from the Anagrafe database (some 18,000 records) is currently being revised, improved and completed to make it more consistent with the structure and the requirements of the new data model. Implementation of the Guide and the SIASFI as a whole has unfortunately been strongly affected by the scarcity of human and financial resources available in the budget of the Florence State Archives for such projects. We hope that these difficulties will soon be resolved and that the description of its holdings can be rapidly completed.

Before going on to illustrate the characteristics of the Online Guide below there follows an outline of some of the theoretical and methodological assumptions underlying its conceptual model and a justification of some of the technical decisions taken.

WHAT ARE THE BOUNDARIES OF ARCHIVAL CONTEXT?

As we know, context is crucial to any understanding and interpretation of records and archives. Archival description is simultaneously description in context and description of contexts. "Description in context" means that the descriptions of the individual archival entities must be placed within the archival context to which they belong. As the multilevel description rules of *ISAD(G)* clearly illustrate "the fonds forms the broadest level of description; the parts form subsequent levels, whose description is often only meaningful when seen in the context of the description of the whole of the fonds."[4] In archival description systems, there must be clear and explicit indication of the relations linking the individual archival entities (the parts) to one another and to the fonds (the whole) to which they belong. Individual archival entities must also be retrieved by the user within their context of belonging, as further stressed by the *Guidelines for the Preparation and Presentation of Finding Aids*.[5]

Archival description is, however, also "description of contexts," because archivists regard the context in which records are produced as an essential tool for orientation, understanding of structure and content, and interpretation of the records and information found.

Examination of the opinions expressed by archivists in various countries and especially of current descriptive practice reveals, however, that there is no full agreement on what precisely is to be understood as the "context of creation" of an archive, that is the set of elements prompting, affecting and influencing the creation of records and helping to endow them with meaning. There is, of course, full agreement on the fact that the key element in defining the context of creation is the creator's history (or biography), organisational structure, functions and activities. But is the relevant context only this or is there something more? And how is this supplementary set of situations, facts and circumstances marking the boundaries of the context to be determined? One only has to look at some of the arguments expressed in authoritative opinions or the descriptive criteria applied in various situations to soon realise just how problematic the definition of archival context really is.

We could begin with the best-known descriptive practice internationally that redefines the boundaries of the context of creation, namely the Australian series system, where a central role is played by entities of what could be described as "meta-context," such as functions. Proving more stable over time than the actual creators, these entities are in fact regarded by Australian archivists as perhaps also more significant than creators in characterising the nature of records.[6]

The definition of context also proves somewhat problematic in an area of great current interest, that is the analysis of the factors involved in the creation of electronic records and archives. The closing report of the first phase of the Interpares project maintains, for example, that the context of creation should not be regarded as an undifferentiated reality but organised into its various component parts (the administrative and legal context, the procedural context, the technological context, etc.), each of which is reflected in a particular way in the characteristics of digital records.[7] As regards Italian descriptive practices, we could recall the case of the *Guida Generale degli Archivi di Stato* published in the 1980s and 1990s, which places the archives created during the centuries prior to Italian Unification within the political or state contexts in which the creating bodies operated.

The boundaries of the concept of archival context are very blurred also in the international standards of description. For example, the second edition of *ISAAR(CPF)* includes the "general context" among the elements of information making up the authority records of creators ("To provide significant information on the general social, cultural, economic, political and/or historical context in which the corporate body, person or family operated, lived or was active").[8] Encoded Archival Context (EAC) also reflects a vision of context that is highly complex and rich in elements.

At the same time, I believe there is general agreement among archivists that records are sensitive not only to the context of creation but also to their "contexts" of custody, use and interpretation. The Florentine project itself provided a whole range of examples that bear out this view. I shall confine myself to recalling the case of the archives of the Florentine Republic, which would lose much of their meaning or could, more simply, lend themselves to misleading interpretations if considered with no reference to their strong relationship with the eighteenth- and nineteenth-century contexts of preservation and use in which they were radically reorganised and reshaped.[9]

These brief considerations appear to entail the conclusion that–above and beyond the consolidated disciplinary principles–the elements of context or contexts that contribute to the significance of archives and the individual records they contain can be multiple and that their relative importance is determined in each case by the nature and the history of the archives and records in question.

How and to what extent can or must this "expanded" view of archival context be reflected in archival descriptive systems? I believe that this question raises an issue of great contemporary relevance, one posed with particular force in the case of systems designed to describe a homogeneous set of archival information resources that, like those held in the Florence State Archives, have certainly been produced by a great many different creators over a very broad chronological span but nevertheless share other significant elements of context that seem to be essential in order to understand and interpret this set of information resources both as a whole and individually.

It was decided to take these problems into account in designing the structure of the Online Guide to the Florence State Archives. While the model of separate and linked descriptions of records and creators envisaged by *ISAD(G)* and *ISAAR(CPF)* was, therefore, fully accepted, it was decided not to limit the illustration of context exclusively to information on the history (or biography), structure, responsibilities and activities of the individual creators. The basic approach adopted was instead a broad vision of the contexts of creation, use and transmission of records, integrating into the descriptive system other elements and other entities with a bearing on those contexts.

This appeared particularly advisable precisely in consideration of the fact that the Online Guide is designed to be consulted in a Web environment where, above all, there is none of the mediation and integration of information that archivists carry out in face to face relations with users in reading rooms and where, moreover, the archival descriptions placed in circulation must be conceived as a component of a vaster world of information inside which data and knowledge should be susceptible to effective linkage and integration. An expanded vision of context is undoubtedly conducive to integration at least between information systems of similar and neighboring disciplinary sectors because it makes it possible to share or refer to materials that delineate the contexts common to the various information resources present in those systems. To take but one example, remember how fruitful the links with systems developed by museums, academic institutions and research bodies operating in the spheres of art history or history pure and simple have already proved (and will prove to an ever-increasing degree in the future).

An approach of this kind also helps to improve the potential of information retrieval in that the presence of a variety of descriptions of entities related to context opens up a larger number of navigation pathways inside the system. Searches by word are also strengthened due to the presence of authority control extended to the names of a great many entities and to the rich array of specific terms cited in the descriptions of the various "entities" present in the system.

The adoption of such a model in developing the Online Guide to the Florence State Archives has produced a highly structured system rich in connections between the different entities and links with external information resources. Thanks to the way in which information is stored, structured and linked in the Online Guide database, users can acquire knowledge and understanding of the fonds of the Florence State Archives as well as the historical context of their creation and the use of records in past centuries simply by browsing the database and following the network of connections between the various entities and between the descriptions in the database and the linked external information resources. The information structure and links are very often able to convey a more meaningful picture of the entities described than the descriptions themselves.

CHARACTERISTICS AND STRUCTURE OF THE ONLINE GUIDE

The Online Guide thus includes the description of numerous "entities," which are shown with their interrelations in Figure 1.

The description of the fonds, their structure and their creators constitutes the core of the system. Every archival entity (fonds, sub-fonds or series) is described and presented to the user in the classic hierarchical structure characteristic of archives. This structure is shown in a frame on the viewer's right while another on the left presents the description of the individual archival entity divided into five different areas as seen in Figure 2: Identity Area, Access Area, Description Area, Archival History Area and Control Description Area. The archival entities are linked to other entities, some of which constitute an equal number of possible points of access to their description. In addition to the obviously present description of their creator, they are linked to "documentary typology," that is typologies of recurring documentary sets, such as some typical record series, which are described once and linked to their instances to

FIGURE 1. Structure of the Online Guide

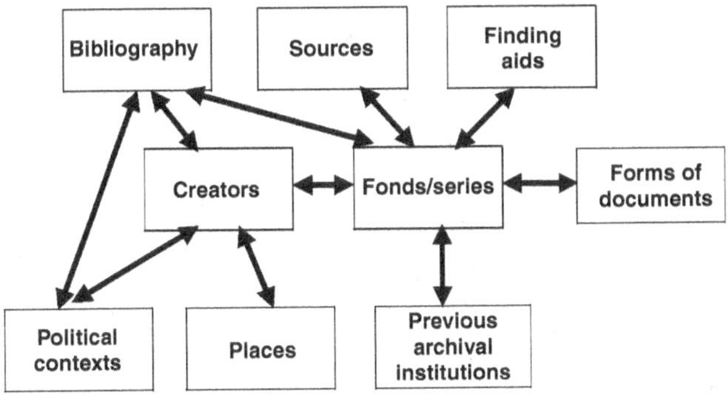

FIGURE 2. Fonds Description

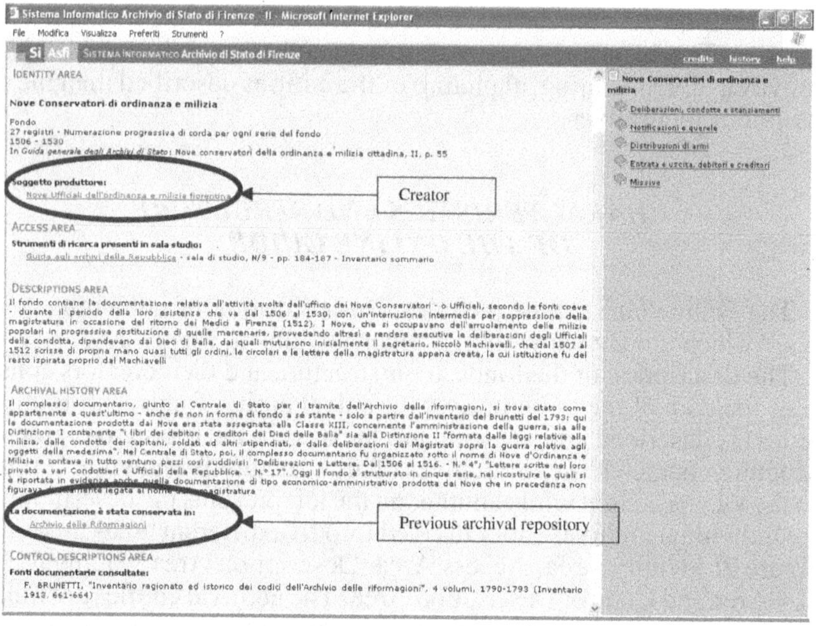

make it possible to retrieve descriptions of the same types of records held in different fonds as shown in Figure 3.

The descriptions of fonds and series are also related to the descriptions of their finding aids and directly linked to those available online. There are also direct links to related records held in other fonds of the Florentine Archives.

The description of the fonds offers direct access to digital reproductions of the same. While online availability is limited at present to the *Mediceo avanti il Principato* fonds, it is hoped that a considerable increase can be obtained in future with the Diplomatico fonds, a collection of parchment records of public institutions and ecclesiastical bodies. All those prior to 1400 have already been digitized for a total of approximately 85,500 units and 243,000 total images.

With a view to further clarification of the use of records and their custodial history over time, fonds and series are also linked to the descriptions of previous archival institutions and repositories where they were

FIGURE 3. Fonds Description

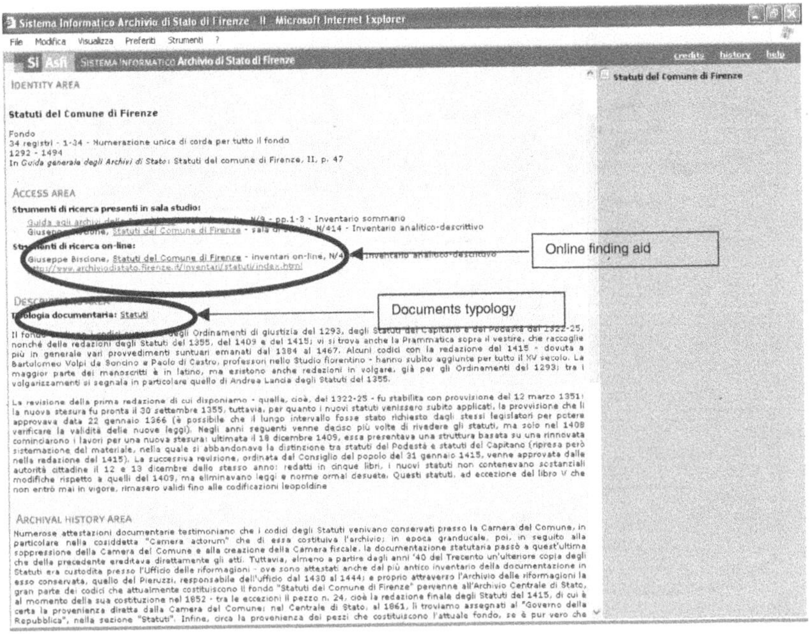

kept before the founding of the Florence State Archives. The descriptions of previous archival institutions are in turn linked to the fonds and/or series held in them, thus making it possible to obtain a broad view of the composition of these institutions over time. Links to the descriptions of the finding aids produced in them and the lists of material they subjected to disposal give a picture of the preservation strategies implemented by public authorities in the past as is again illustrated in Figure 2.

The descriptions of creators, as demonstrated in Figure 4, are divided into three areas (Identity Area, Description Area, and Control Description Area) and are again linked to a range of entities, primarily descriptions of the fonds and series produced and the localities and territorial spheres over which the creators exercised jurisdiction or in which they carried out their activities. The corporate bodies, persons and families can be linked to one another on the basis of general categories of relations (e.g., hierarchical or chronological) or of an associative relation-

FIGURE 4. Creators Description

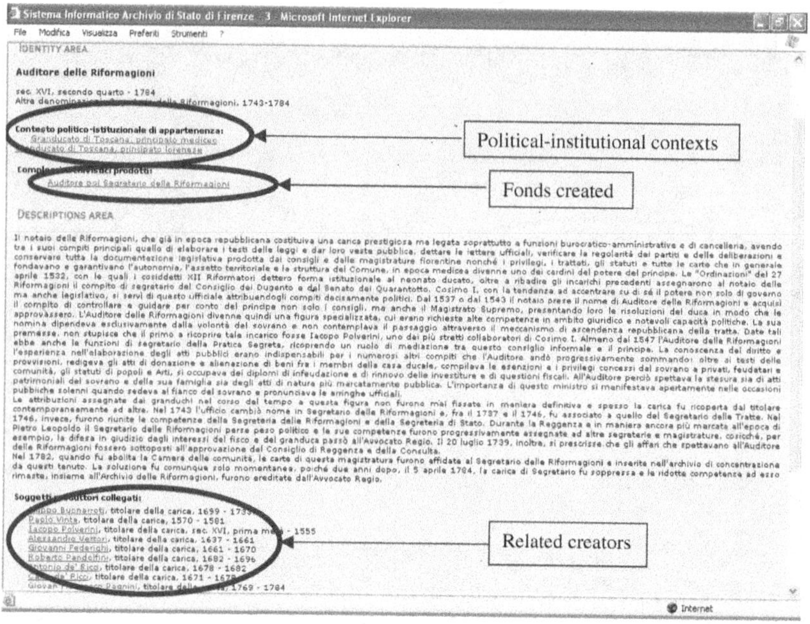

ship that is not defined a priori but whose nature can be specified in a special field. Users can follow the network of connections, both those happening at the same time (for example, administrative hierarchical relationships or the family or clientele relationships between persons and between persons and families) and those happening over time (for example, the ongoing transfer of functions from one institution to another). These connections and relationships often influence the arrangement of fonds as well as the presence, or indeed absence, of documents and records inside archival fonds, as the links to the respective fonds and series clearly show.

The creators (especially state institutions) are also linked to the descriptions of every period of Florentine, Tuscan or Italian constitutional history (the Florentine Republic, the Medici and Lorraine Grand Duchy, etc.) within which they operated. Each institution can be linked to more than one of these periods or "political-institutional contexts." The linkage between these broader "constitutional" contexts and the individual institutions is very useful to highlight the continuity of the administrative and bureaucratic structures on transition from one "constitutional" system to another, providing further context data that may prove significant both for search strategies on archival material and for evaluating the relevance and meaning of the archival documents to be consulted.

All the descriptions of the different entities include the bibliography and archival sources used in drafting them as well as the names of their respective authors and/or revisers and an explanatory note on the modifications, revisions and corrections carried out.

Seeking to expand contextual information about how the records were created, used and kept also means making the most of opportunities to achieve this by means of the information resources present on the Web related to the Florentine fonds and their creators, or the other entities included in the Online Guide. These resources can sometimes be published on the Web site of the Florence State Archives as the result of activities differing from traditional descriptive practices, for example, the drafting of articles, conference papers, etc. Alternatively, they can be suitably organised in reference files designed to provide interested users with further information on events, people, places and so on mentioned in the Online Guide. It was therefore decided to offer the user hyperlinks between the descriptions of the various entities and reputable and reliable Web sites containing information resources capable of adding valid elements of knowledge to the information already present in the Online Guide. The title of such resources is indicated together with a concise description and the date of writing. The description of the creator "Signori," the highest authority of the Florentine Republic, thus offers a link to the site of Brown University, in Providence, Rhode Island, which contains some interesting Web pages on electoral methods in medieval Florence.

Many of the entities described in the system also constitute access points to it (in addition to fonds, creators, political and institutional contexts, previous archival institutions, documentary typologies, and in future places/jurisdictions). Access to the database can therefore come about not only through the traditional free text search by word or specific queries in the different areas of the database, but also through special lists of the entities described, from which it is possible to follow the links between the same entities as shown in Figure 5.

An exploration can be launched, for example, by selecting a "political-institutional context" from the relevant list *(Repubblica fiorentina)*, going on from there to one of the institutions that operated in the historical phase selected, and then through the description of that institution (e.g., "Signori") to consult the fonds or archival series produced. In the

FIGURE 5. Navigation and Search Page: List of Creators (Corporate Bodies)

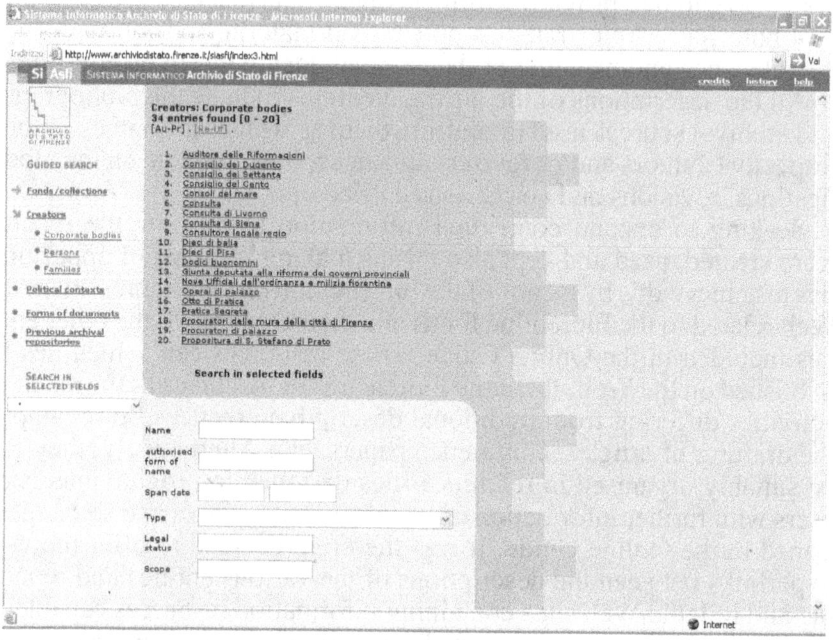

case of "Signori" there are three fonds: *Signori*, *Signori, Dieci di Balia, Otto di Pratica*, and *Signori e Collegi*.

Obviously, it is possible to directly access the fonds described. Alternatively, it is possible to navigate from "Documents typology" (*Tipologia documentaria*), selecting one (for example, *Statuti*), the description of which will provide a list of the fonds or series in which it is present. The selection of one of the items on the list of fonds and series takes the user to the associated description (for example, *Statuti del Comune di Firenze*), from which it is possible to obtain further information on the archival history of the fonds or series through the link to the "Previous archival repository" (*Precedenti istituzioni archivistiche*) (*Archivio delle Riformagioni* in this case). Alternatively, it will be possible to consult the online inventory published on the site of the Florentine Archives.

Search strategies can, therefore, also benefit from the expansion of the context of reference and its intelligent structuring. This, we believe, not only makes it possible for the user to pinpoint more effectively what they already know they are looking for–thanks to extension of authority control of the names of a greater number of different entities–but also enables the user to access new knowledge thanks to serendipitous discoveries that constitute the most fascinating aspect of using the Internet and search engines in the digital environment.

NOTES

1. For further information on the Centro di Ricerche Informatiche per Beni Culturali della Scuola Normale Superiore di Pisa see the web site at, http://www.cribecu.sns.it.

2. International Council on Archives, *ISAD (G). General International Standard Archival Description*, 2nd edition, Ottawa, 2000; International Council on Archives, *ISAAR (CPF). International Standard Archival Authorities Record for Corporate Bodies, Persons and Families*, 2nd edition, Paris, 2004. The two standards are available on the Web site of the International Council on Archives, http://www.ica.org.

3. The Online Guide is accessible on the Web site of the Archivio di Stato of Florence, http://www.archiviodistato.firenze.it/siasfi/.

4. International Council on Archives, *ISAD (G). General International Standard Archival Description*, 2nd edition, Ottawa, 2000, I8.

5. *Guidelines for the Preparation and Presentation of Finding Aids*, prepared by the Sub-committee on Finding Aids, 2001 available at http://www.icacds.org.uk/eng/findingaids.htm.

6. For an introduction to the Australian series system and to the role of functions in the description of archival context see C. Hurley, "The Australian ('series') system: an exposition" in The Records Continuum: Ian Maclean and the Australian Archives First Fifty Years, Sue McKemmish and Michael Piggott (eds), Ancora Press in association with Australian Archives, Canberra, 1994, 150-172 (also online at http://ourhistory.naa.gov.au/library/pdf/Records_Continuum_Hurley.pdf) and C. Hurley, "What, if anything, is a function?" Archives and Manuscripts 21, no 2 (November 1993), 208-220 (also online at http://www.sims.monash.edu.au/research/rcrg/publications/whatif.html).

7. See in particular the considerations put forward in presenting the results of the InterPARES (International Research in Permanent Authentic Records in Electronic Systems) project by H. MacNeil "Providing Grounds for Trust II: The Findings of the Authenticity Task Force of InterPARES," in *Archivaria* 54 (Autumn 2002), 33-34.

8. International Council on Archives, *ISAAR (CPF). International Standard Archival Authorities Record for Corporate Bodies, Persons and Families*, 2nd edition, Paris, 2004, section 5.2.8.

9. For the history of the archives of the Florentine Republic during the period of Pietro Leopold and at the time of the founding of the Central State Archives of Florence, see respectively S. Vitali, 'Conoscere per trasformare' and 'L'archivista e l'architetto: Bonaini, Guasti, Bongi e il problema dell'ordinamento degli Archivi di Stato toscani,' in *Salvatore Bongi nella cultura dell'Ottocento. Archivistica, storiografia, bibliologia, Atti del convegno nazionale, Lucca 31 gennaio-4 febbraio 2000*, ed. G. Tori, Rome, Ministero per i beni e le attività culturali, Direzione generale per gli archivi (2003), 519-564.

SELECTED BIBLIOGRAPHY

Bonelli, D. and S. Vitali, *Descrizioni archivistiche sul web: la guida online dell'Archivio di Stato di Firenze*. Last revision: December 2002, http://www.archiviodistato.firenze.it/materiali/siasfi.pdf.

"La guida online dell'Archivio di Stato di Firenze. Atti della presentazione." Edited by M. Taglioli and L. Valgimolgi in *Bollettino d'informazioni del Centro di Ricerche Informatiche per i Beni Culturali della Scuola Normale Superiore di Pisa*, XII (2002), 2, pp. 121-198 (also online: http://www.archiviodistato.firenze.it/atti/siasfi/index.html).

Vitali, S. "Authority Control of Creators and the Second Edition of ISAAR(CPF), International Standard Archival Authority Record for Corporate Bodies, Persons, and Families" in *Authority Control in Organizing and Accessing Information: Definition and International Experience*. Edited by A. G. Taylor and B. B. Tillett. New York, The Haworth Information Press, 2004 (also online: http://dois.mimas.ac.uk/DoIS/data/Papers/autautcon41.html).

APPENDIX A

SOME TECHNICAL FEATURES OF THE SYSTEM

System Architecture

The Online Guide is designed to manage archival information on the Florentine State Archives and to make the descriptions of its holdings accessible via a simple Web browser. The System consists of three different, and autonomous, component parts that are strictly connected, as illustrated in Figure 6:

- the Oracle database.
- the data input interface.
- the Web interface for data searching and retrieval.

It is important to note that this kind of architecture allows a complete separation between the data input logic and the data presentation logic. This feature provides the archivists with an interface for data input that doesn't affect the way in which the data will be presented to the general public. This way archivists do not have to worry that information will be provided to the final user (inserted in context) in a different way from the one they use to store it (as a single element).

The Data Input Subsystem

To access the data management interface the user must provide a user-id and password, as shown in Figure 7.

FIGURE 6. Florence State Archives Online Guide: System Architecture

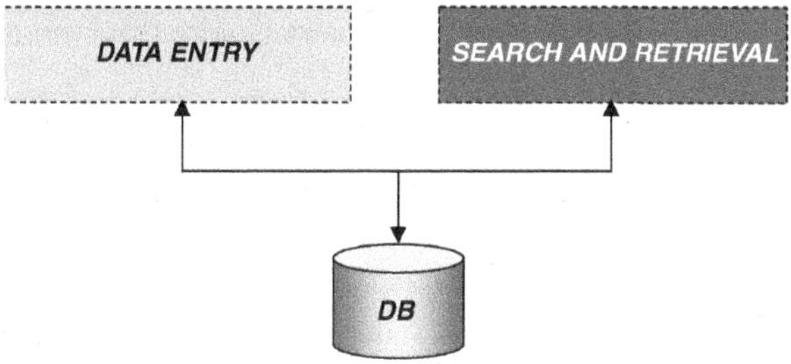

FIGURE 7. Florence State Archives Online Guide: Access to the Data Input Interface

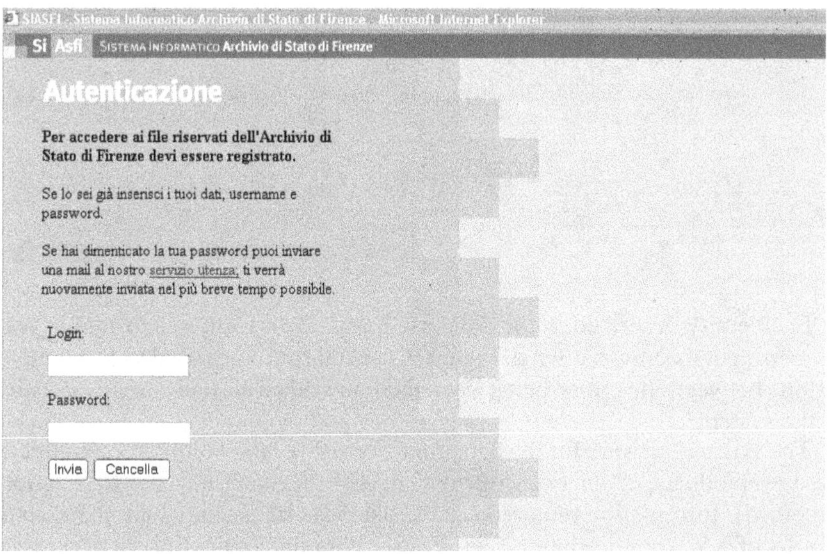

The user is allowed to perform only the operations (input, delete, modify, browse) that are granted for his or her specific profile. A "super user" (called "User Administrator") with special privileges, sets the user's permissions. After the authentication process, the user can access the data input (as shown in Figure 8) and modify page and choose the form to be filled in and the task (search/input) he or she would like to perform.

APPENDIX A (continued)

FIGURE 8. Florence State Archives Online Guide: Data Input Interface

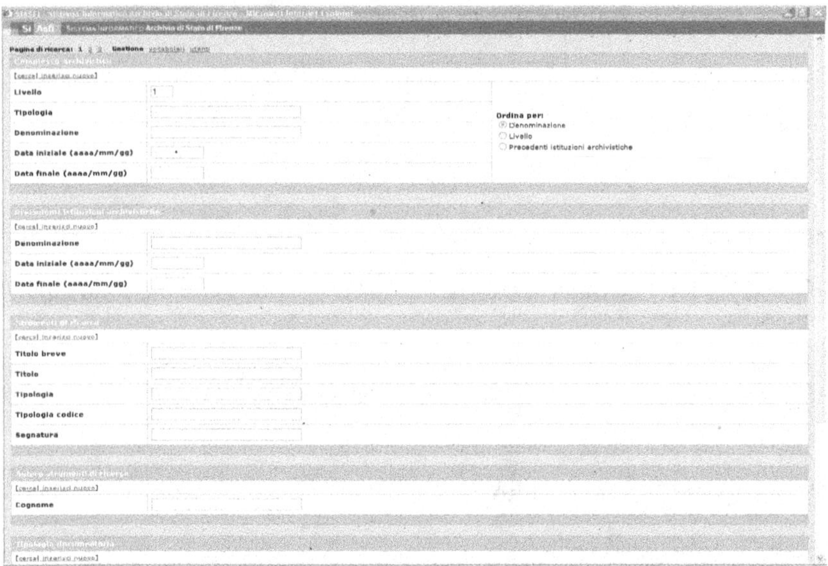

Each entity described in the database has its own form to be filled in with the pertinent data. As shown in Figure 9, special forms are used to generate relations between the entity being described and other entities already existing in the system.

The system software for the data input consists of a set of intercommunicating Java modules, which exchange data in XML format (database transactions excluded). Information required for the database transactions are maintained in a set of XML configuration files. These files contain the full database mapping. Information is rendered in HTML format, via an XSLT translation of the available XML data. The tools implemented offer the following advantages:

- Java makes it possible to build a platform-independent application, granting the maximum possible application portability;
- having the database configuration information stored in an XML file and not inside the Java source, makes it possible to perform configuration changes quite easily without modifying the source code;

- interaction with the system is realized via a common Web browser making the application virtually available to any PC connected to the Internet, without any further software;
- the extensive use of XML allows for high level application standardization and communication security;
- the use of HTML to publish the data makes it possible to easily generate customized layouts fitting the needs of end users.

Data Output Interface

The main characteristics of the Web interface and the different pathways, which can be used to enter the system, have been described above. The Web application interface is realized in a Linux operating system, using a CGI WEB interface built with Perl language. Once it was decided to use the Linux Open Source OS, there was the need to decide which would be the best language for implementing the Web interface. Perl was chosen because it is also an open source product and integrates well with a "NIX" environment. Perl, natively, allows for the integration of its scripts with various system tools

FIGURE 9. Florence State Archives Online Guide: Form for Inputting/Modifying the Description of a Creator (Corporate Body)

APPENDIX A (continued)

(like sed, awk, grep, mail, etc.) and process communication functionalities available in a "NIX" environment. The choice was also strengthened by the following considerations:

- Perl is meant to handle long text strings, like the ones commonly stored and retrieved from an archival database;
- it easily performs pattern matching and pattern substitution, which is often required in this sort of implementation;
- it easily performs operations on structured text files, like record sets, or non structured text files, which are the main data types handled in the system.

Taking into account such characteristics, the choice of Perl was almost a natural one.

EAC and the Development of National and European Gateways to Archives

Per-Gunnar Ottosson

SUMMARY. In the development of gateways to archives there are two different approaches, one focusing on the descriptions of the material and the other on the creators. Search and retrieval with precision and quality require controlled access points and name authority control. National registries of private archives have a long tradition in implementing the concept of archival authority records for corporate bodies, persons and families. With the development of the standards *ISAAR (CPF)* and EAC, a foundation is laid for developing this approach in the archival community, and for the provision of common access points to library and museum resources as well. The Linking and Exploring Authority Files (LEAF) project (2001-2004) was co-funded by the European Commission Information Society Technologies Programme and a

---

Per-Gunnar Ottosson is Senior Archivist at the National Archives of Sweden. At the National Archives, he previously held various positions, and participated in the development of the archival information systems (ARKIS I, ARKIS II). He is currently working on the development of the new National Archival Database (NAD), as well as on implementations of EAD and EAC. During the last three years, he has participated in the EU project LEAF (http://www.leaf-eu.org). He is also editing seventeenth-century diplomatic correspondence and developing tools for electronic publishing within the Oxenstierna project. The author is a member of the ICA Committee on Descriptive Standards and of the EAC Working Group (E-mail: per-gunnar.ottosson@riksarkivet.ra.se).

[Haworth co-indexing entry note]: "EAC and the Development of National and European Gateways to Archives." Ottosson, Per-Gunnar. Co-published simultaneously in *Journal of Archival Organization* (The Haworth Information Press, an imprint of The Haworth Press, Inc.) Vol. 3, No. 2/3, 2005, pp. 261-274; and: *Encoding Across Frontiers: Proceedings of the European Conference on Encoded Archival Description and Context (EAD and EAC), Paris, France, 7-8 October 2004* (ed: Bill Stockting, and Fabienne Queyroux) The Haworth Information Press, an imprint of The Haworth Press, Inc., 2005, pp. 261-274. Single or multiple copies of this article are available for a fee from The Haworth Document Delivery Service [1-800-HAWORTH, 9:00 a.m. - 5:00 p.m. (EST). E-mail address: docdelivery@haworthpress.com].

Available online at http://www.haworthpress.com/web/JAO

doi:10.1300/J201v03n02_19

consortium of fifteen partners, libraries, archives, documentation and research centers, in ten European countries. The major objective of the LEAF project was to provide shared access to authority information from various data providers, and thereby improve search and retrieval functionalities. LEAF adopted EAC as the format for both importing and storing authority records. The user interface allows for searching on names, dates, and free text. Registered users have also the right to add annotations to records, thereby helping cataloguers in improving their quality. In cases where data providers have open access catalogues, there are links to the original authority records and related resources. The LEAF project has provided a data model and technical solutions that can be implemented in both national and international gateways to archives.

KEYWORDS. Archival description, authority records, archival networks, Encoded Archival Context, EAC, Encoded Archival Description, EAD, LEAF, standardization

In the development of gateways to archives there are now two different approaches, one focusing on the descriptions of the archival material, and the other on the provenance or the context of the archival material. These two approaches are represented by the archival standards *General International Standard Archival Description* (*ISAD(G)*)[1] and *(International Standard Archival Authority Record for Corporate Bodies, Persons, and Families* (*ISAAR(CPF)*),[2] and their corresponding formats for data communication, Encoded Archival Description (EAD), and the now emerging Encoded Archival Context (EAC). There is also a third approach implying that archives should just add their unstructured data to the present Internet chaos. That alternative will not be elaborated here; it is predominant enough to speak for itself.

THE ARCHIVAL DESCRIPTION APPROACH

From MARC-AMC to EAD

The development of automated systems for search and retrieval of archival material started with the idea of adapting standard bibliographic cataloging processes. Archivists working in the environment of university libraries in the United States found it natural to develop the MARC format for library catalogues, which resulted in the development of the MARC format for archival and manuscript control: MARC-AMC. This format may contain the basic elements of archival description at one level of description with the name of the creator and other associated corporate bodies. The format has been much used for the creation of union catalogues of archives and manuscripts, such as the National Union Catalog of Manuscript Collections (NUCMC).[3] Very similar formats have also been used for national registries of private archives, such as the National Archival Database (NAD) in Sweden and also, for example, in Australia and New Zealand.[4]

The MARC-AMC format does not, however, allow for multilevel archival descriptions, so complete, detailed descriptions still had to be kept separately on paper or in other automated systems. This was the major reason that led American archivists to look for other solutions, a development that finally resulted in the SGML/XML format for archival descriptions, EAD. This format is now being used for developing a growing number of networks and union catalogues of archives not only in the United States but across Europe as well. The development and the success of EAD has now gone so far that it is difficult even for the specialist to get an overview of all such services available on the Internet. EAD has elements for the names of corporate bodies and persons with attributes allowing for links to authority files. There are also elements for narrative administrative histories and biographies, as well as elements for controlled access in terms of functions and geographic names. However, EAD does not provide full support for separate files of authority records and contextual information in accordance with *ISAAR(CPF)*.

MALVINE and EUAN

Two projects sponsored by the European Union have been exploring the possibilities of developing common gateways to European archives and manuscripts: MALVINE, an initiative of library manuscript departments, and EUAN, an archives project. Both these projects focused on the description of the material; MALVINE was dealing with item-level catalogue records in a bibliographical tradition, while EUAN had a top-down approach in accordance with *ISAD(G)*.

MALVINE started in 1998 as an EU-Project co-funded within the 4th Framework Program "Telematics for Libraries." It is now organized and maintained by the MALVINE Maintenance Agency, located at the Berlin State Library, and an independent consortium of libraries, archives and museums.[5]

The purpose of the project is to provide access to holdings of modern manuscripts and letters, kept and catalogued in European libraries, archives, and museums. It is aiming to form a network that is independent of the various local technical solutions and is accessible on the Internet. Although MALVINE searches across local systems, the researcher will have access to a system with the functionality and features of a union catalogue. The project has developed software that can handle catalogue data held in various local formats, using EAD as a communication format, and then presenting the data in a uniform style for the end user. The data providers will either have the special MALVINE software installed (MALVINE database, scripts, servlets and web pages) or a Z39.50 service searching the local catalogue. The MALVINE system operates a distributed search engine that queries the local databases. The interface allows for search in elements such as names and titles as well as free text.

Most of the contributors to MALVINE have provided catalogue data at item level without implementing the archival principles of multilevel description, which makes it very difficult for a user to get an overview of the holdings. By the end of the project it was clear to the participants in the project that effective search and retrieval of catalogue data is insufficient without the support of name authority control, which eventually led to the project initiative Linking and Exploring Authority Files (LEAF).

EUAN was a two-year project for the Info2000 initiative launched by DG XIII of the European Commission, responsible for telecommunications and the information market.[6] The partners were the National Archives of Scotland (coordinator), the National Archives of Sweden, the National Archives of Italy, the International Institute of Social History (Amsterdam), and the Scottish Archive Network Ltd (SCAN). In contrast to MALVINE, EUAN focused on top-level descriptions of archival materials in compliance with *ISAD(G)*. EUAN identified a common set of data elements as a means of searching archival holdings from many institutions, emphasizing also that the content of archival documents can only be fully understood when information about the context of their creation is also captured and presented to the user. A number of formats that might be used for exchange of data were explored, particularly MARC-AMC and EAD. EUAN proposed a data harvesting approach, in which high-level information from the catalogues of institutions would be uploaded to a central database and made available for users to search across. When a user had identified relevant material on the central database, the user would be directed to the Web site of the institution holding the materials to request access. The different traditions, languages, and standards for archival descriptions were problematic with this approach, and in the final report the project explicitly pointed out the approach of the then upcoming LEAF project as a model to explore.

THE ARCHIVAL CONTEXT APPROACH

The model presented in the first edition of *ISAD(G)*, and illustrated in Figure 1, presumes, even if it is not stated, implementation in a relational database with one module for the units of descriptions (fonds, series, files, and items) and one for the authority records.[7] These modules are linked together by means of a table for specifications on the actual relations between the authority records and the archival units in terms of being creators, authors, or subjects in the contents of records. Relations can also be established between the authorities in terms of predecessor/successor, parent/child, etc. This model was the starting point for the further development of standards for archival authority records, resulting in *ISAAR(CPF)* and EAC. This concept was also implemented early in archival information systems built in relational database environments, such as ARKIS I-II in Sweden, ASTA in Norway, and VAKKA in Finland.[8]

National Registries of Private Archives

In their development, *ISAAR(CPF)* and EAC have been very much influenced by the experiences and the needs of national registries of private archives. The national registers represent an approach that differs from archival descriptions. The starting point is not the material but the creators. In such registers it is the information on a particular person or organization that constitutes the record, whether it is a record in a card catalogue or in an automated system. Each record contains then references to one or several archives, and some brief notes on their contents, but the systems do not contain full archival descriptions.

The UK National Register of Archives (NRA) consists of records with authorized and other forms of names and brief descriptions of corporate bodies, persons and families, and has for that purpose elaborated

FIGURE 1. Relationship Between *ISAD(G)* and *ISAAR(CPF)*

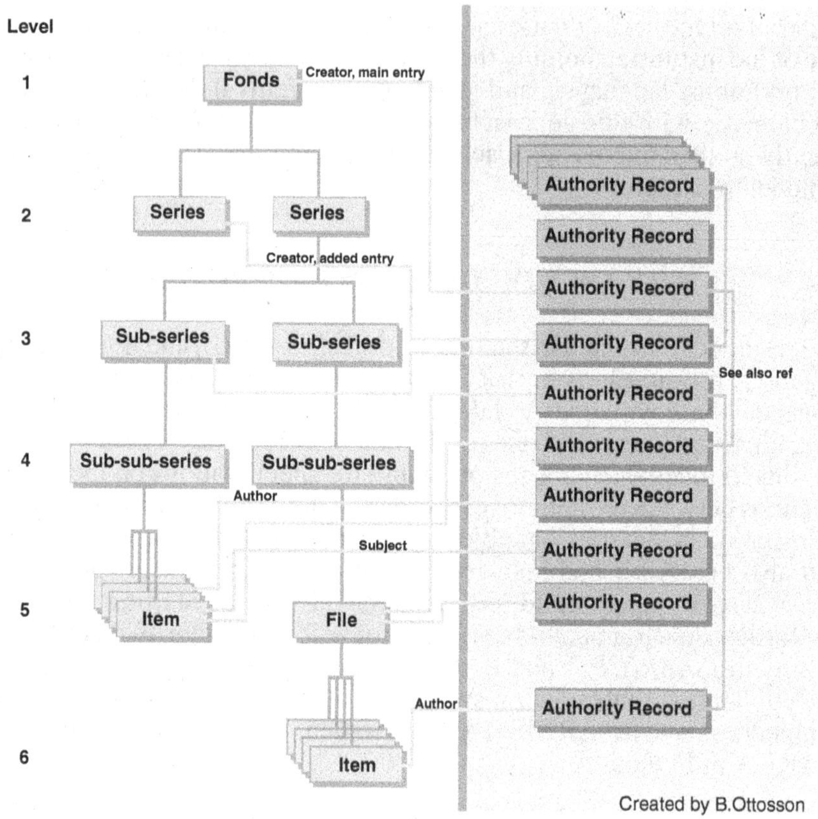

Adapted from H. Stibbe. *Archivaria* 34 (1992)

detailed guidelines.[9] It now intends to provide a national authority file for archival creators, and to provide links, whenever possible, to finding aids available online. The rapid growth of archival networks in the United Kingdom made up of archival descriptions based on *ISAD(G)*/ EAD has not diminished its importance; on the contrary, for users without detailed knowledge of British archives, the NRA is the only feasible starting point.

The archival information system of the Swedish national and regional archives (ARKIS II on MS SQL Server 2000) is based on a model with a separate authority file for corporate bodies and persons with relations to the archival units. The system is now being developed to support export and import of EAC records. The new NAD will primarily have the function of a national authority file of corporate bodies, persons, and families related to archives. These authority records will contain links to archival descriptions that may be stored either in the central system ARKIS II or in local Web pages or other archival networks. NAD will then be able to serve as a central data provider to a common European gateway for all archives and manuscript divisions in Sweden. The project is now developing the system for harvesting and processing information on creators from local and regional archives in Sweden. The data providers will be able to deliver records in EAC format or as text files to be converted by the NAD unit. Repositories with only a small number of archival collections will be able to enter basic information on their creators directly to NAD via a Web template. The records entered are then saved on the server as EAC files for processing. The harvested EAC records will be reviewed by the NAD unit before they are imported into the central system with the support of automated processes for control of duplicates and the consistency of data.

LEAF–Linking and Exploring Authority Files

Although authority files have been in use for a long time in libraries as means of supporting cataloguing, access to them has been limited and few attempts have been made to develop these into services for end users. The major objective of the LEAF project was to provide shared access to authority information from various data providers in order to improve the search and retrieval functionalities of a variety of applications. The system also had the purpose of supporting professionals in improving the quality of existing records. The LEAF project (2001-2004) was co-funded by the European Commission Information Society Technologies Programme and a consortium of fifteen partners–libraries, archives, documentation and research centers–in ten European countries, with the Berlin State Library as coordinator.[10]

The central system developed at Joanneum Research (Graz, Austria) is based on an Oracle Relational Database Management System (9i) in a Linux environment, and a range of PL/SQL stored procedures, as shown in Figure 2. The applications are developed in Java and XML technologies. A JRun application server is the Web server of the LEAF system Web site, and there is also a Cocoon XML publishing framework for controlling the flow between the various requested URIs and

FIGURE 2. Architecture of LEAF

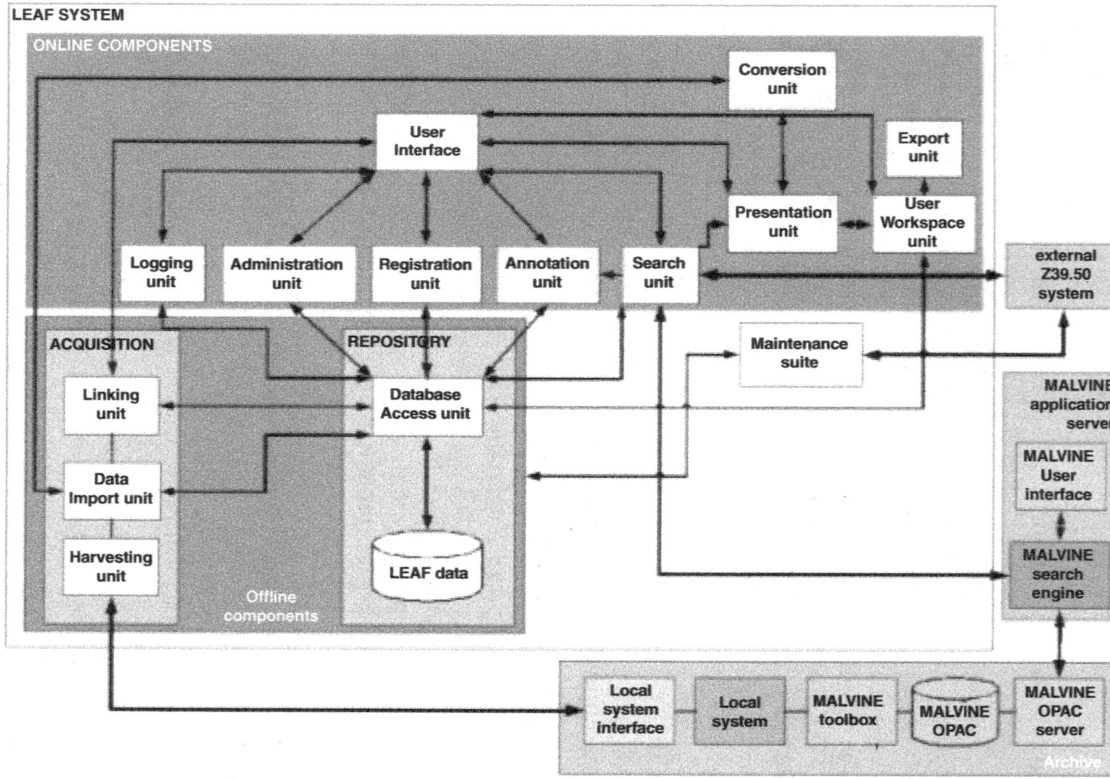

XSL transformations for output of the Web pages. The conversion module developed at Aksis (The Department of Culture, Language and Information Technology, University of Bergen, Norway) consists of scripts in Python, Perl and XSLT. To complete this comes a Web-based maintenance suite developed by Crossnet Systems for the administration of the system.[11] The data providers can use it to register their contact information and technical details about their local systems. Whenever such data is updated this maintenance suite will notify the LEAF system. There are also functions for controlling the connectivity of the local systems.

For transferring data to the central LEAF server, most data providers have used the FTP protocol, but the Open Archives Initiative (OAI) protocol for metadata harvesting via an HTTP interface has also been tried. The central LEAF system queries an OAI server at the provider's site to request a transfer of data to the central server. The Z39.50 protocol for search and retrieval is initiated by users querying the systems. Results from such searches are added to the overall result from the central system. External systems, such as MALVINE, can also query the LEAF system via an XML interface. The users of the external system, therefore, can utilize the authority records in LEAF both to improve search precision as well as broaden the search with other forms of names in the authority record.

For the present prototype of the system, twelve data providers had contributed test data in different export formats (EAC/XML, Unimarc, Marc21Auth, MAB, and local export formats). These data providers represent institutions at different levels of technical development, from small PC applications to advanced relational databases with updates of authority records from the German authority file PND (*Personennamen datei*). The selections of data were made especially for testing the linking processes of the system, and consist of a number of different records relating to the same persons.

The converted data is then processed by the LEAF system in order to group local records referring to the same entity in order to avoid redundancy and facilitate search and retrieval. There are only a few elements of a record that can be used for automated identifications in a multilingual environment: an ID reference to a national authority file, forms of name, and life dates. In the LEAF linking unit imported records are compared in accordance with the following rules:

1. ID of national/international authority file
2. Family Names equal AND First Names equal

3. Family Names equal AND Year of Birth equal AND First Names equal
4. Family Names equal AND Year of Birth equal AND Year of Death equal
5. Family Names equal AND Year of Birth equal AND First Names equal AND Year of Death equal

The first rule will always return a correct link while the others have different degrees of uncertainty. During the testing of the system the data providers were asked to make selections of records that-all other rules (2 to 5) can be tested and evaluated if necessary. The experience from the prototype is that these rules work well as long as the submitted records contain the minimum set of necessary data.

In a search scenario, a user searches on Voltaire's less well known pseudonym 'Vadé' in the simple search interface (as illustrated in Figure 3); the system finds not only the record containing the pseudonym, but also the other records grouped into the LEAF authority record, and

FIGURE 3. LEAF Prototype: Example Search for "Voltaire"

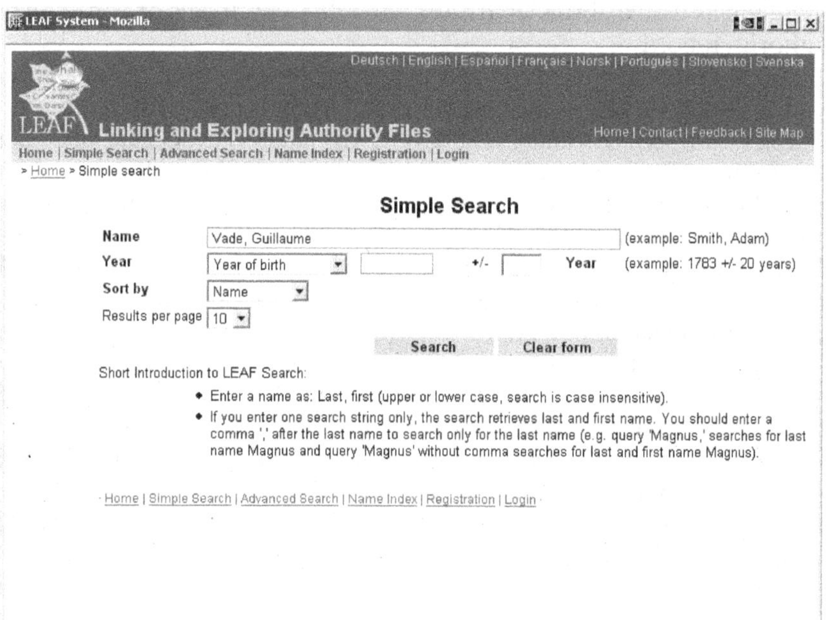

brings as a result one LEAF record composed of data from four data providers, as shown in Figure 4.

Turning to the 'Full view' as seen in Figure 5, all the data provided is accumulated into one record. Under the heading 'Local auth. record,' reference codes to local records are displayed. In one record it is in the form of a link to the local system available on the Web. In this case the user can directly get the information on holdings associated with Voltaire at the German Literary Archives.

The prototype also contains samples from the National Archives of Sweden in which the records contain links to online finding aids. Users can get also transformations on-the-fly of the retrieved records not only as EAC XML but also in Unimarc, Marc21, and MAB2 like formats.

Registered users of the LEAF system have the possibility of adding temporary annotations to the records, which suggest corrections or improvements. A researcher might know a birth date that was unknown to the cataloguer. Such annotations will automatically be sent to the data provider. Certain data or service providers can also add permanent an-

FIGURE 4. LEAF Prototype: Example Result for "Voltaire"

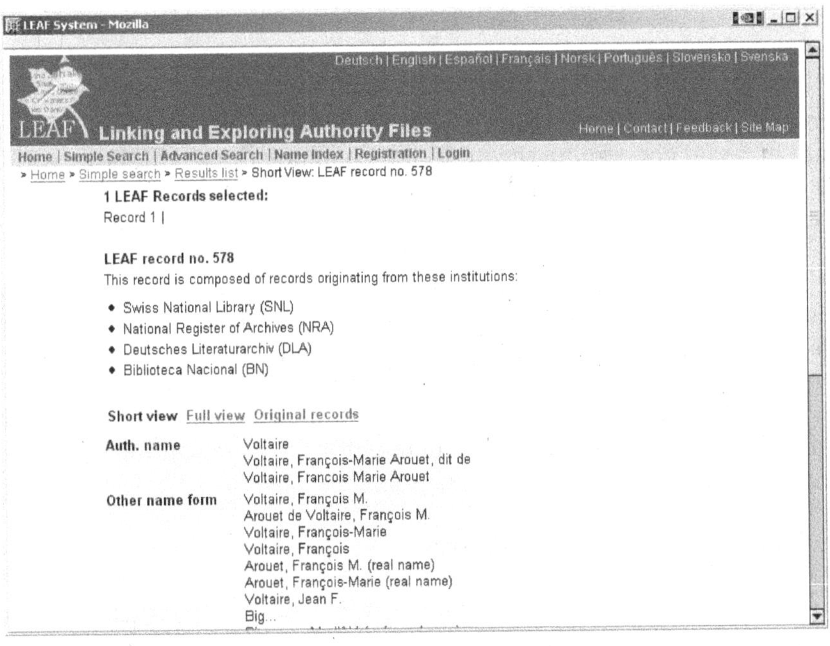

FIGURE 5. LEAF Prototype: Example Full View of Record

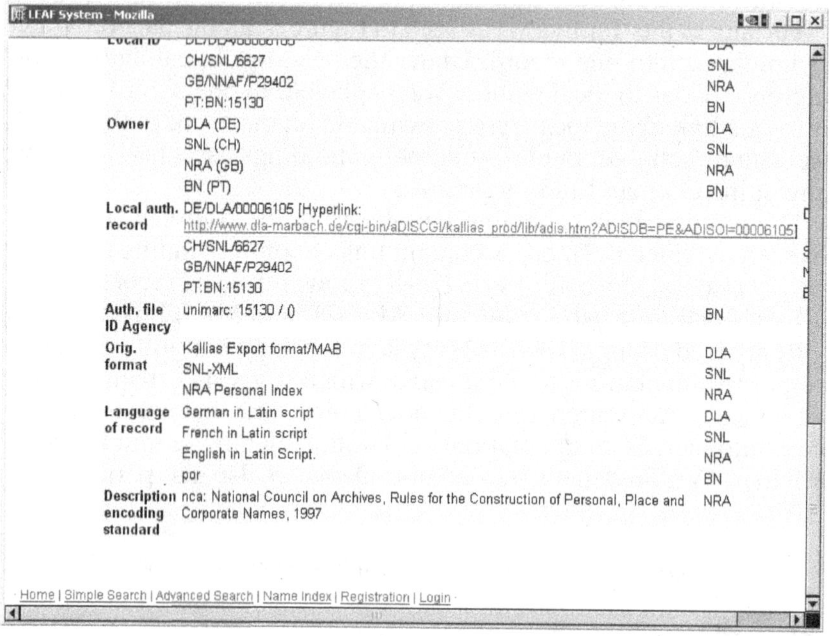

notations to the LEAF records with for example references to sources and material concerning the entity. Such annotations will, however, be reviewed by the maintenance agency. For users there will also be the possibility of making annotations for their own use in a workspace.

The LEAF system is now only a prototype, but it is advanced enough to be developed into a running service for search and retrieval of authority records for persons. In order to work for archives it must, however, also be supplemented with functions for handling records for corporate bodies. There are also results of functional and usability tests that need to be implemented. The Berlin State Library is intent on being the LEAF maintenance agency, but details for the organization of the service are not settled at time of writing.

A Gateway to European Archives

It is obviously difficult to establish a European infrastructure for coordinating and maintaining such services that will include archives as well as museums. National libraries and research libraries have a tradition of creating consortia for providing common services such as union catalogues. Recently the TEL project, i.e., The European Library, has been established.[12] The project results from collaboration between a number of European national libraries and has the purpose of providing a single access point to selected parts of their holdings. However, archives in Europe have no such traditions and also very limited budgets for maintaining such services. At present there is also no foreseeable financial support from the European Union. The problem with EU funding is that it only supports projects in development, rather than for applying and maintaining existing methods and technologies. For example, the European Commission activity called DigiCult (Digital Heritage and Cultural Content: Access to cultural heritage) has a mission to support *research* for the development of new technologies for accessing Europe's cultural resources and to build collaborative networks, 'thus making archives, museums and libraries accessible to everyone, everywhere and at any time,' but who will take the responsibility for maintaining such networks?[13]

While we are waiting for an answer to that question, we can nevertheless start the process by laying the foundation with data of high quality on local and national levels. That implies in practice that it should be a priority in our archival organizations to make sure that information about our holdings and their context is recorded in compliance with archival standards, so that it can be communicated and made available for our users. Establishing a Gateway to European Archives is no longer a matter of developing standards and technology; it is rather a matter of establishing an infrastructure to maintain the results achieved, and to provide data with the coverage and quality that the users have the right to expect. This is not something that can be solved by time-limited projects; it is a commitment for the future.

NOTES

1. *ISAD(G): General International Standard Archival Description*, Second edition, 1999. ISAAR(CPF): *International Standard Archival Authority Record for Corporate Bodies, Persons, and Families*, Second edition, 2004. http://www.ica.org.

2. *ISAAR(CPF): International Standard Archival Authority Record for Corporate Bodies, Persons, and Families*, Second edition, 2004. http://www.ica.org.

3. The National Union Catalog of Manuscript Collections is available online at http://lcweb.loc.gov/coll/nucmc/nucmc.html.

4. The National Archival Database (NAD) in Sweden was distributed on CD ROM. The Register of Australian Archives and Manuscripts (RAAM) is available online at http://www.nla.gov.au/raam/ and the New Zealand National Register of Archives and Manuscripts/Te Raarangi Puuranga, Tuhinga Ake o te Motu (NRAM) at http://www.nram.org.nz/.

5. MALVINE, Manuscripts and Letters via Integrated Networks in Europe, is available online at http://www.malvine.org.

6. EUAN, European Union Archive Network, Final Report, October 2002 can be found at http://www.euan.org/.

7. As well as ISAD(G) itself see also Hugo Stibbe, "Implementing the Concept of Fonds: Primary Access Point, Multilevel Description and Authority Control" *Archivaria* 34, (Summer 1992): 109-137.

8. For the Finnish database VAKKA see http://www.narc.fi/atengl.html.

9. The National Register of Archives is available online at http://www.nra.nationalarchives.gov.uk/nra/.

10. For further information on LEAF, Linking and Exploring Authority Files, see http://www.leaf-eu.org. See also Kaiser, Max, Hans-Jörg Lieder, Kurt Majcen and Heribert Vallant "New Ways of Sharing and Using Authority Information: The LEAF Project," *D-Lib Magazine*, 9 (2003), 11, online at http://www.dlib.org/dlib/november03/lieder/11lieder.html.

11. For further information see http://www.crxnet.com.

12. For further information on TEL, see http://www.europeanlibrary.org/.

13. For further information see http://www.cordis.lu/ist/directorate_e/digicult.

Index